Visual Basic .NET Database Programming For Dummies®

Cheat Sheet

Shortcut Keys in the VB .NET Editor

Command Name	Shortcut Keys	Behavior
Edit.Copy	Ctrl+C or Ctrl+Insert	Copies the currently selected item to the Clipboard
Edit.Cut	Ctrl+X or Shift+Delete	Removes the currently selected item but saves a copy in the Clipboard in case you want to paste it somewhere
Edit.GoToNextLocation	F8	Moves the cursor to the next item
Edit.GoToPreviousLocation	Shift+F8	Moves the cursor to the previous item
Edit.GoToReference	Shift+F12	Displays the reference of the selection in the code window
Edit.OpenFile	Ctrl+Shift+G	Displays the Open File dialog box
Edit.Paste	Ctrl+V or Shift+Insert	Pastes the contents of the Clipboard at the insertion point
Edit.Redo	Ctrl+Shift+Z or Ctrl+Y or Shift+Alt+Backspace	Restores a previously undone action
Edit.SelectionCancel	Esc	Cancels the current operation or closes a dialog box
Edit.Undo	Alt+Backspace or Ctrl+Z	Reverses the last editing action
File.Print	Ctrl+P	Displays the Print dialog box
File.SaveAll	Ctrl+Shift+S	Saves all documents in the current solution
File.SaveSelectedItems	Ctrl+S	Saves the currently active, or selected, items in the current project
Tools.GoToCommandLine	Ctrl+/	Places the caret (the blinking text-insertion cursor) in the Find/Command box on the Standard toolbar
View.NextTask	Ctrl+Shift+F12	Moves to the next task in the Task List window
View.ViewCode	F7	Displays the selected file (in Solution Explorer) in the code editor window
View.ViewDesigner	Shift+F7	Displays the selected file in the design (double-clicking the filename in Solution Explorer is easier)
View.WebNavigateBack	Alt+left arrow	Displays the previous page in the viewing hi...
View.WebNavigateForward	Alt+right arrow	Displ... histo...

D1361566

Visual Basic .NET Database Programming For Dummies®

Standardized Naming Conventions

Prefix	Corresponding Object	Example
acd	ActiveDoc	acdMainPage
cbo	ComboBox	cboDropper
chk	CheckBox	chkBoldface
cm	ADO command (database)	cmMyCommand
cmd	CommandButton	cmdExit
cmg	CommandGroup	cmgSelectOne
cn	Connection (database)	cnMyConnex
con	Container	cntframed
ctr	Control	ctrSeeThis
fld	Field (database)	fldTitles
frm	Form	frmColors
frs	FormSet	frsTypeIn
grc	Column (in grid)	grcQuantity
grd	Grid	grdGoods
grh	Header (in grid)	grhYearsResults
hpl	HyperLink	hplURL
lbl	Label	lblContents
lst	ListBox	lstNames
pag	Page	pagTurn
pgf	PageFrame	pgfRule
prj	ProjectHook	prjSuzerine
rb	RadioButton	rbBlueBackground
rs	Recordset (database)	rsTotalSales
sep	Separator	sepZone
spn	Spinner	spnWatch
tbl	Table (database)	tblTitles
tbr	ToolBar	tbrDropThis
tmr	Timer	tmrAnimation
txt	TextBox	txtAddress

For Dummies: Bestselling Book Series for Beginners

Visual Basic® .NET
Database Programming

FOR

DUMMIES®

Visual Basic® .NET
Database Programming

FOR

DUMMIES®

by Richard Mansfield

Hungry Minds™

Best-Selling Books • Digital Downloads • e-Books • Answer Networks • e-Newsletters • Branded Web Sites • e-Learning

New York, NY ◆ Cleveland, OH ◆ Indianapolis, IN

Visual Basic® .NET Database Programming For Dummies®

Published by
Hungry Minds, Inc.
909 Third Avenue
New York, NY 10022
www.hungryminds.com
www.dummies.com

Library of Congress Control Number: 2001093697

ISBN: 0-7645-0874-1

Printed in the United States of America

10 9 8 7 6 5 4 3 2 1

1O/QZ/RR/QR/IN

Distributed in the United States by Hungry Minds, Inc.

Distributed by CDG Books Canada Inc. for Canada; by Transworld Publishers Limited in the United Kingdom; by IDG Norge Books for Norway; by IDG Sweden Books for Sweden; by IDG Books Australia Publishing Corporation Pty. Ltd. for Australia and New Zealand; by TransQuest Publishers Pte Ltd. for Singapore, Malaysia, Thailand, Indonesia, and Hong Kong; by Gotop Information Inc. for Taiwan; by ICG Muse, Inc. for Japan; by Intersoft for South Africa; by Eyrolles for France; by International Thomson Publishing for Germany, Austria and Switzerland; by Distribuidora Cuspide for Argentina; by LR International for Brazil; by Galileo Libros for Chile; by Ediciones ZETA S.C.R. Ltda. for Peru; by WS Computer Publishing Corporation, Inc., for the Philippines; by Contemporanea de Ediciones for Venezuela; by Express Computer Distributors for the Caribbean and West Indies; by Micronesia Media Distributor, Inc. for Micronesia; by Chips Computadoras S.A. de C.V. for Mexico; by Editorial Norma de Panama S.A. for Panama; by American Bookshops for Finland.

For general information on Hungry Minds' products and services please contact our Customer Care Department within the U.S. at 800-762-2974, outside the U.S. at 317-572-3993 or fax 317-572-4002.

For sales inquiries and reseller information, including discounts, premium and bulk quantity sales, and foreign-language translations, please contact our Customer Care Department at 800-434-3422, fax 317-572-4002, or write to Hungry Minds, Inc., Attn: Customer Care Department, 10475 Crosspoint Boulevard, Indianapolis, IN 46256.

For information on licensing foreign or domestic rights, please contact our Sub-Rights Customer Care Department at 212-884-5000.

For information on using Hungry Minds' products and services in the classroom or for ordering examination copies, please contact our Educational Sales Department at 800-434-2086 or fax 317-572-4005.

For press review copies, author interviews, or other publicity information, please contact our Public Relations Department at 317-572-3168 or fax 317-572-4168.

For authorization to photocopy items for corporate, personal, or educational use, please contact Copyright Clearance Center, 222 Rosewood Drive, Danvers, MA 01923, or fax 978-750-4470.

Hungry Minds™ is a trademark of Hungry Minds, Inc.

About the Author

Richard Mansfield (High Point, NC) is an author and programmer whose recent titles include *Visual Basic .NET ASP.NET Programming* and *Visual Basic .NET Weekend Crash Course* (both published by Hungry Minds, Inc.). While he was the editor of *COMPUTE!* magazine during the 80s, he wrote hundreds of articles and two columns. From 1987 to 1991, Richard was editorial director and partner in Signal Research. He began writing books full-time in 1991, and has written 28 computer books. His books have been translated into 12 languages, and more than 600,000 copies have been sold worldwide.

Dedication

To my best friend, David Lee Roach

Author's Acknowledgments

First, I'm grateful that so many readers appreciated the previous version of this book. Your suggestions and kind comments were valuable. Project editor Susan Pink deserves credit for her patience and her thorough, thoughtful editing. In addition to combing through every line of the text and making a number of improvements on that level, she also offered a larger, more abstract analysis of this book. It's rare to find an editor who can see both the forest and the trees at the same time. Technical editor Allen Wyatt reviewed the entire manuscript and made important suggestions. Production Coordinator Regina Snyder ensured that this book moved smoothly through production. To all these, and the other good people at Hungry Minds who contributed to this book, my thanks for the enhancements they made to this book.

A book covering cutting-edge technology benefits significantly from expert suggestions. I have been fortunate, during the year that it took to write this book took, to have interacted with some of the best VB .NET programmers in the world. People on the Technical Beta, in newsgroups (both public and private), programmers at Microsoft, and friends such as Evangelos Petroutsos have all contributed ideas and improvements to this book.

Publisher's Acknowledgments

We're proud of this book; please send us your comments through our Hungry Minds Online Registration Form located at www.dummies.com.

Some of the people who helped bring this book to market include the following:

Acquisitions, Editorial, and Media Development

Project Editor: Susan Pink

Acquisitions Editor: Bob Woerner

Technical Editor: Allen Wyatt, Discovery Computing Inc.

Editorial Manager: Constance Carlisle

Permissions Editor: Laura Moss

Media Development Supervisor: Richard Graves

Editorial Assistant: Amanda Foxworth

Production

Project Coordinator: Regina Snyder

Layout and Graphics: Jill Piscitelli, Michael Sullivan, Julie Trippetti, Jeremey Unger

Proofreaders: Andy Hollandbeck, Marianne Santy, TECHBOOKS Production Services

Indexer: TECHBOOKS Production Services

Special Help

Ron Terry

General and Administrative

Hungry Minds Technology Publishing Group: Richard Swadley, Senior Vice President and Publisher; Mary Bednarek, Vice President and Publisher, Networking; Joseph Wikert, Vice President and Publisher, Web Development Group; Mary C. Corder, Editorial Director, Dummies Technology; Andy Cummings, Publishing Director, Dummies Technology; Barry Pruett, Publishing Director, Visual/Graphic Design

Hungry Minds Manufacturing: Ivor Parker, Vice President, Manufacturing

Hungry Minds Marketing: John Helmus, Assistant Vice President, Director of Marketing

Hungry Minds Production for Branded Press: Debbie Stailey, Production Director

Hungry Minds Sales: Michael Violano, Vice President, International Sales and Sub Rights

Contents at a Glance

Cartoons at a Glance

By Rich Tennant

page 311

"Give him air! Give him air! He'll be okay. He's just been exposed to some raw HTML code. It must have accidently flashed across his screen from the server."

page 177

page 235

"I started designing database software systems after seeing how easy it was to design office furniture."

page 9

page 95

"Our automated response policy to a large company wide data crash is to notify management, back up existing data and sell 90% of my shares in the company."

page 133

"Your database is beyond repair, but before I tell you our backup recommendation, let me ask you a question. How many index cards do you think will fit on the walls of your computer room?"

page 341

page 41

Cartoon Information:
Fax: 978-546-7747
E-Mail: richtennant@the5thwave.com
World Wide Web: www.the5thwave.com

Table of Contents

Introduction

··

Welcome to the world of database programming with Visual Basic .NET. Microsoft has put many of its best cutting-edge tools into this power-house package — and this book shows you how to use them.

For the past ten years, far more programmers have chosen Visual Basic than all other programming languages combined. Estimates of the number of active VB developers go as high as six million.

Visual Basic was the first — and I believe is still the best — rapid application development language. Nevertheless, some programmers complained that Visual Basic would not qualify as a "real" programming language until it had true inheritance, multithreading, and other features. Well, with VB .NET, Visual Basic's feature set is now equivalent to all other professional programming languages.

VB .NET is both powerful and diverse, enabling you to do almost anything with database programming. But, best of all, many of Visual Basic's features are designed to be easy to use. The tools include hundreds of efficiencies, step-through wizards, and shortcuts. For example, even if you have no experience adding a database to an application, you can do just that in about two minutes. (Seriously! See Chapter 1.)

Other tasks can't be accomplished as quickly. Otherwise, this book would be five pages long, and people wouldn't be paid so much money for database programming. Want to connect a Web page to a database? Want to design a new database? Those jobs do take longer (though in VB .NET, not much longer). Precisely how much longer depends on what you want the Web site to do or how complex your database is. But if you can click a mouse, write ordinary Visual Basic programming, and follow straightforward directions, you can do the job. This book shows you how to create effective Windows database applications and Web pages with database connections.

About This Book

My main job in *Visual Basic .NET Database Programming For Dummies* is to show you the best way to accomplish the various jobs that, collectively, contribute to successful database programming in VB .NET. If a task requires programming, I show you, step by step, how to write that programming. In other cases, I tell you when there's a simpler, better way to accomplish a job.

Otherwise, you could spend days hand-programming something that's already been built — something you can create by clicking a simple menu option, adding a prebuilt component, firing up a wizard, or using a template.

Because VB .NET is so huge, you can easily overlook the many shortcuts it contains. I've been on the betas for VB for about ten years and have been on the VB .NET technical beta for over a year now. I've also written several books on Visual Basic. All modesty aside, I do know Visual Basic well. But VB .NET is a whole new ball game — some call it an entirely new language. I can partly agree. VB .NET is big, and lots of it is new.

This book obviously can't cover every feature in VB .NET. Instead, as you try the many step-by-step examples in this book, you'll become familiar with the most useful features of Visual Basic database programming as well as many shortcuts and time-saving tricks — some of which can take years to discover on your own (believe me, some have taken me years to stumble upon).

I hope that all my work this past year will benefit you — showing you the many useful shortcuts and guiding you over the rough spots. I won't pull any punches: I confess it took me several days of wrestling with VB .NET to figure out how to get data successfully displayed in a grid. Now I can show you how to do it in a few minutes.

Also, unlike some other books about Visual Basic database programming (they must remain nameless), this book is written in plain, clear English. You can find sophisticated tasks made easy: The book is filled with step-by-step examples that you can follow, even if you've never written a line of database programming or designed anything.

Visual Basic .NET does require some brains and practice to master, but you can handle it. To make this book as valuable for you as possible without writing a six-volume life's work on all of Visual Basic's database-related features and functions, I geared this book toward familiarizing you with the most useful tools. You can use most of them to create either Windows or Web database applications. In VB, you often dozens of ways to accomplish a job, but there's always one way that's best: the sturdiest, most effective, and often, most efficiently programmed. It's those best ways that you explore throughout the book.

Whether you want to create stunning Web sites or impressive Windows applications, this book tells you how to get where you want to go with applications that use databases. It's estimated that more than 80 percent of VB programs written today involve databases, so if you haven't programmed with databases before, you're likely to find yourself working with them pretty soon. After all, computers are *data processing* machines. And the data they process mostly resides in databases.

Here are just a few of the goals that you can achieve with this book:

- ✔ Build professional-looking, effective database programs

- ✔ See how to move Windows applications to an intranet or the new Internet WebForms (and be smart enough to know when to use wizards to help)

- ✔ Make the transition from Microsoft's traditional ADO (ActiveX Data Objects) to the new ADO.NET technologies

- ✔ Understand how to best use the many database features built into VB .NET

- ✔ Kill bugs in Windows applications or Web pages

- ✔ Get the most out of VB .NET's new Server Explorer, Data Form Designer, DataSet controls and other great tools

- ✔ See how to use SQL, the database query language

Many people think that programming is hard and that database programming is even harder. It doesn't have to be. In fact, several common database jobs have already been written into VB, so you don't have to do the programming at all. If you're smart, you won't reinvent the wheel. Sometimes, all you need to know is where in VB to find the components, wizards, templates, and other prebuilt solutions. Then you can simply drop them into your application. And when you do want to program, Visual Basic .NET often makes the job both easy and enjoyable.

This book tells you whether a particular wheel has already been invented. It also shows you how to save time by using or modifying existing components to fit your needs instead of building new solutions from scratch. But if you're doing something totally original (congratulations!), this book gives you step-by-step recipes for creating database applications from the ground up.

Conventions Used in This Book

This book is filled with step-by-step lists that serve as recipes to help you cook up a finished product. Each step starts with a boldface sentence or two telling you what you should do. Directly after the bold step, you may see a sentence or two, not in boldface, telling you what happens as a result of the boldface action — a menu opens, a dialog box pops up, a wizard appears, you win the lottery, whatever.

I've tried to make the step-by-step examples as general as possible but at the same time make them specific, too. Sounds impossible, and it wasn't easy. The idea is to give you a specific example that you can follow while also giving you a series of steps that you can apply directly to your own projects.

In most of the examples, I use the pubs or Northwind sample databases that come with VB .NET. For instance, a ListBox is filled with particular records from pubs. Or you type some data, it's stored as a new record in pubs, and then you read the record back and see it on the screen. However, you can follow the same steps but substitute your own particular database connection for the pubs connection used in the examples.

Also note that a special symbol shows you how to navigate menus. For example, when you see "Choose File⇨New⇨Project," you should click the File menu and then click the New submenu, and finally click the Project option in the New submenu.

When I display programming code, you see it in a typeface that looks like this:

```
Dim pfont As Font
pfont = New Font("Times New Roman", 12)
```

And if I mention some programming within a regular paragraph of text, I use a special typeface, like this: `Dim pfont As Font`.

Every line of code that you see in this book is available for downloading from this book's Web site at `http://www.dummies.com/extras/VBNetDataProg/`. Take advantage of this handy electronic version of the code by downloading it from the Web site so you can then just copy and paste source code instead of typing it by hand. You'll save time and avoid pesky typos.

What You're Not to Read

The book is divided into eight parts, with several chapters in each part. But just because the book is organized doesn't mean you have to be. You don't have to read the book in sequence from Chapter 1 to the end, just as you don't have to read a cookbook in sequence.

If you want to design a user interface, go right to Chapter 7. You're not expected to know what's in Chapter 4 before you can get results in Chapter 7. Similarly, within each chapter, you can often scan the headings and jump right to the section covering the task that you want to accomplish. There is no need to read each chapter from start to finish. In a few cases, however, you do have to complete one chapter before tackling another. For instance, some chapters depend on your having followed a set of instructions in Chapter 3. I alert you in the text to these situations.

I've been careful to make all the examples as self-contained as possible. And each of them works, too — they've been thoroughly tested.

Foolish Assumptions

In writing this book, I had to make a few assumptions about you, dear reader. I assume that you know how to use Windows and have a general idea how to use Visual Basic's editor. However, you will find many tips and techniques involving new VB .NET editor features that I thought you might want to know.

I also assume that you have had some experience programming (that you know what a variable is, for instance). However, I don't assume that you know much about database programming. Perhaps most importantly, I assume that you don't want lots of extraneous details — you just want to complete your database programming job.

To use this book to the fullest, you need only one thing: a copy of VB .NET.

How This Book Is Organized

The overall goal of *Visual Basic .NET Database Programming For Dummies* is to provide an understandable reference for the Visual Basic programmer. This book will be accessible to developers and programmers with little or no database programming experience. The following sections give you a brief description of each of the book's eight main parts.

Part 1: The Basics of Databases

This part of the book demonstrates the elements of databases and database management. You are introduced to the main features of Visual Basic .NET's generous suite of database programming tools. You see how to use some of Visual Basic's specialized tools to make almost any database-related job easier.

Part II: Making a Connection

Part II covers the tools and techniques necessary to connect a component, Web page, or Windows application to a database. You find out about the VB DataSet Command Wizard and see how to make various types of connections between a data store and your programming.

Part III: Contacting the User

Part III explores how to bind to a data source so that you can display data to users (such as bosses who ask for reports). When the time comes to display data in organized, helpful reports, Visual Basic .NET offers you good assistance, such as the DataGrid control. You also see how to construct a sturdy and intuitive user interface for the front end of your database application.

Part IV: Building a Database

Sometimes, you have to start from the ground up, and this part demonstrates how to design and build a DataSet (VB .NET's new minidatabase) from scratch. You find out how to manage DataSets and also experiment with various approaches to indexing and data validation.

Part V: The Internet Connection

Part V covers the various ways to use databases with a Web site, including how to migrate existing traditional Windows (WinForm) applications, transforming them into WebForm-based applications. You also find out how to work with the new ASP.NET technology to build intelligence into your Web site programs.

Part VI: Hands-On Programming

Part VI is all about programming — writing and testing source code. You see how to use tried-and-true database programming strategies. You discover how to make the important transition from the older ADO to the newer ADO.NET tools. You focus on the various alternative database techniques that Microsoft offers to see what's best for each particular programming job. Finally, Chapter 17 zeros in on the most common database programming errors, showing you how to trap them and what to do to correct the critters when you do trap them.

Part VII: Working with Queries

Part VII demonstrates the many ways you can retrieve sets of records from databases using SQL, the standard database query language. You see how to employ VB's useful Query Designer tool to design and test new queries and stored procedures. You also find out more about creating joins, relationships between data from different tables.

Part VIII: The Part of Tens

Part VIII includes a chapter that describes ten outstanding programming techniques and tips that I believe you will want to study. You'll find out about working with the Windows Clipboard; randomizing; accessing the Registry; and seven other essential topics.

Chapter 21 covers such subjects as the best Web sites for staying current with VB .NET and database-programming issues; how to customize the Visual Basic IDE (Integrated Development Environment) by writing your own macros and keyboard shortcuts; which technical conferences you might want to attend; and how to download the latest VB .NET upgrades and free add-ons.

Icons Used in This Book

Notice the eye-catching little icons in the margins of this book? They're next to certain paragraphs to emphasize that special information appears. Here are the icons and their meanings:

The Tip icon points you to shortcuts and insights that save you time and trouble.

I use the Technical Stuff icon to highlight nerdy technical discussions that you can skip if you want to.

A Warning icon aims to steer you away from dangerous situations.

Where to Go from Here

Where you turn next depends on what you need. If you want the lowdown on Visual Basic's database-related tools, as well as some important database terms and concepts, turn to Part I. If you're looking for the answer to a specific problem, check the index or the table of contents and then turn directly to the appropriate section.

Part I
The Basics of
Databases

The 5th Wave — By Rich Tennant

"I STARTED DESIGNING DATABASE SOFTWARE SYSTEMS AFTER SEEING HOW EASY IT WAS TO DESIGN OFFICE FURNITURE."

In this part . . .

*U*nderstanding — and doing — database programming doesn't have to be a tough job. If you've tried
before and were baffled or you're trying for the first time,
you've chosen the right language (Visual Basic .NET) and
the right book (this one).

Have you been confused by blizzards of acronyms (ADO,
RDO, ADO.NET, UDA, SQL, ODBC, OLE, BAM-BAM)? Been
turned off by books that make most everything hard to
understand? Been to bewildering classes in school? Part I
wafts you gently into the world of database programming
and ensures that you have a good, solid understanding of
what databases are, how they work, and what you can do
with them.

In Visual Basic .NET, Microsoft has assembled tools that
are highly effective and, in most cases, easy to understand
and use. I tell you which tools are not useful and should
be avoided. I also demonstrate how to use the majority,
which are useful.

So, turn on your favorite music, get something to drink,
fire up Visual Basic .NET, and start having some fun. (The
big secret that programmers try to keep from bosses is
that creating computer programs with Visual Basic *can* be
lots of fun.)

Chapter 1

The Big Picture

. . . .

In This Chapter

▶ Understanding servers and clients

▶ Making databases scalable with ADO.NET

▶ Finding out about connection, adapter, and DataSet objects

▶ Connecting a VB .NET application to a database

. . . .

Experts estimate that 80 percent of all computer programming involves databases. Fortunately, VB .NET has many tools to help you create, revise, manage, and otherwise deal with databases efficiently. This book shows you how easy it is to use those tools.

Nevertheless, in spite of VB .NET's many RAD (Rapid Application Development) tools, a programmer also has to *program*, to write source code by hand — without the assistance of wizards, prewritten code, built-in components, add-ins, and the many other helpful features that VB .NET offers. When you find yourself wondering how to solve a database-related task in VB .NET, you're likely to find example source code in this book that will show you how to do the job.

In this chapter, I explain the meaning of the current buzzwords in database programming: the client-server relationship, n-tier applications, distributed programming, and scalability. However, this chapter does not attempt to describe all the terms and concepts of database programming. Chapter 2 attempts that. So if you come across a word or two or a concept that's unclear in this chapter and can't wait for a definition, take a look at Chapter 2 or this book's index for additional explanation and examples.

At the end of this chapter is a short example that shows you how to connect a VB .NET application to a server database in seven quick steps. This example should prove to you beyond any doubt that you made a wise choice when deciding to use Visual Basic to do your database programming.

Servers and Their Clients

VB .NET is designed to build client-server database applications. You can certainly use VB .NET tools to create a database that resides only in your local computer. But this is The Age of the Internet. Confining yourself to your private little hard drive is . . . well . . . old fashioned at best.

A client-server database application creates a one-to-many relationship: one database that resides on a server computer and can be accessed through your VB .NET database application from many client computers on a network or indeed on the Internet.

You can test this client-server communication by simulating it in your personal computer. No actual network or server is needed. In Chapter 3, you see how to install Microsoft's SQL Server and use it as a virtual server for testing your VB .NET database applications.

In a client-server application, the VB .NET client-side database application does most of the work. Specifically, the client application

✔ Establishes communication between the client and server machines

✔ Defines the connection to the database

✔ Specifies what particular type of data it wants to see

✔ Displays the data to the user

✔ Optionally permits the user to modify the data

✔ Optionally validates the data (checks it for errors)

✔ Optionally does other data processing, such as totaling monthly expenses

✔ Returns the data to the server asking for permission to update the database with any changes the client made

And what, you ask, does the *server* do? Well, it holds the database (which might be very large and require lots of storage space). The server also has the job of accessing the data from the database and sending it to the clients. Finally, a server might have the responsibility of performing validation checks of its own on the data clients submit to it.

Dividing a database application between a pair of client and server computers is known as a *two-tier application*. It is also common to find *three-tier applications*: a user computer (running the part of the application that displays a visible user-interface, data entry forms, and such), a second computer holding the business *logic* (determining what data is needed from the database and how to contact the database), and a third computer holding the database itself (along with programming that answers requests for data and handles updates to the database). The idea of breaking an application into separate parts and spreading those parts among different machines on a network is known as *distributed computing*. Some database programs — called *n-tier* applications — are divided among even more than three machines!

Now that you've seen the relationship between client and server, you no doubt fear that the onus is on you. You're the one who will be writing the client application that does all the jobs necessary to manage data. I don't know about you, but I've never liked having onuses on me.

You're in luck. You chose VB .NET as your programming language. Fortunately, VB .NET comes with a set of components and wizards that do most of the work for you. Visual Basic was the first Rapid Application Development language — and I think it's still the best. And after you've worked a bit with VB, you'll understand just how rapidly you can get from idea to application with the world's most popular computer language. Because VB .NET comes with so many built-in, prewritten solutions to common programming problems, you can sometimes create sophisticated behaviors just by dragging and dropping controls onto a VB .NET form (see the example at the end of this chapter). By taking full advantage of VB .NET's features, you, the database programmer, can pass the onus to VB .NET.

ADO.NET: It's about Scalability

You find out about ADO.NET throughout this book. ADO.NET is the database technology built into VB .NET. Chapter 15 provides you with a brief tour of alternative technologies as well as an explanation of ADO.NET's place in the world of database management. In this chapter, you get a preview of what is probably the main reason to use ADO.NET: It makes database management highly scalable.

Briefly, the problem is large local area networks and the Internet. For most of the history of personal computing, your database application could establish a connection to a database and *keep that connection open* until the user was finished reading or modifying the data.

This approach works okay if you have a few people, perhaps ten or so, who need a connection with the database at the same time. But hundreds or possibly thousands of people on the Internet cannot be simultaneously looking through your catalog of Irish Flannel Sweaters. They simply cannot all be connected at once! This problem is referred to as *scalability*.

Can your application handle five clients and then grow gracefully to five thousand? Or will it — like Microsoft's Access database system and others — grind to a halt and smolder as soon as more than ten connections are open?

A few people can sit close together on a couch and read the same book at the same time. It can work if they like each other and all have splendid hygienic habits. But you can see that this cluster-read idea cannot be expanded much. Ten people would find it difficult; more than ten would find it impossible no matter how often they wash themselves.

So the solution to this problem is a "library" model, albeit a library that can make as many copies of a popular book as are requested. Each person who wants one can check out his or her own copy and return it later.

In ADO.NET, you use *disconnected DataSets,* which are copies of data from the database. Here's what happens: A brief connection to the server's database is made while a DataSet is "checked out." Then the connection is broken. The DataSet is sent to the requesting client application. The client can keep the DataSet as long as necessary and manipulate the data as much as desired. When the client is finished and if the client wants to update the database, a new (and brief) connection is established with the server database. The DataSet is submitted to the server, which decides whether to merge the changes into the database.

Using this library model, your database system is quite scalable. The server database has been uncoupled from sustained connections to clients.

ADO, VB 6's database technology and the predecessor of ADO.NET, did feature a recordset, which could be disconnected from a database. But the ADO.NET DataSet, which replaces the recordset, is more capable and more robust. In fact, a DataSet is practically a database itself in many ways, just smaller and more portable. The recordset was a far more limited object.

The Big Three: Connection, Adapter, and DataSet Objects

VB .NET's Toolbox contains three controls that can work together to simplify creating a data application. These controls are the DataSet, the Connection object, and the DataAdapter object.

The *DataSet* is like a mini-database that sits in your local computer until you have finished with it. It is detached from the primary database. Throughout this book, I have much more to say about the DataSet object, and you put it through its paces in many examples.

The *Connection object* is uncomplicated. It merely holds a ConnectionString property that usually looks like this:

```
myConnection.ConnectionString =
        "Provider=SQLOLEDB.1;Integrated
        Security=SSPI;Persist Security Info=False;Initial
        Catalog=pubs;Data Source=DELL"
```

The `Catalog` name, however, might be Northwind or whatever database you want to connect to from VB .NET. `Data Source` is the name of your computer. (You see how to figure out that name in Chapter 3.) My computer's name is *DELL*. While testing your VB .NET applications, you specify the name of your computer as the `Data Source` because your own computer poses as a remote server. When you are ready to deploy your application in a real-world situation, the `Data Source` is a path (or Internet address) to a remote server that holds a database.

The Connection object's other property of interest specifies how many seconds the Connection object should spend attempting to connect to a database before giving up and generating an error message. The default is 15 seconds; you can set it to any value between 10 and 30 seconds for a *WinForm* (Windows style application) and somewhat longer for a *WebForm* (Internet-style application). Here's how you can add this property to ConnectionString:

```
myConnection.ConnectionString = "user
        id=sa;password=ra24X;initial
        catalog=northwind;data source=DELL;Connect
        Timeout=30"
```

As you can see by comparing the two ConnectionStrings you've looked at in this section, you can specify security for a connection between a client application and a server database in different ways (`Integrated`, `password`, `user id`, `Persist Security Info`).

Even though the Connection object is fairly simple, it does have a lot of possible parameters. Fortunately, VB .NET happily helps you define new connections using a wizard (more on that next).

The *DataAdapter object* is the workhorse of the DataSet support controls. Adding a DataAdapter control to a VB .NET form launches the Data Adapter Configuration Wizard. This wizard steps you through the process of creating a connection to a database and defining a query (such as "send me the names of customers in Boston"). It also writes lots of source code for you. When the wizard closes, you can use the DataAdapter to create a DataSet object. In fact, the only source code you have to write is this:

```
SqlDataAdapter1.Fill(DataSetName, "tablename")
```

Your DataSet will be loaded with the data you requested in your query. But I'm getting ahead of myself.

Two primary database types are accessed in VB .NET: OLE and SQL. OLE is the older technology and is the one you use with Access-style databases and others. SQL works with SQL Server and is the one I focus on in this book. To service these two types of databases, VB .NET includes two sets of connector controls and two sets of adapter controls: the OleDbDataAdapter and OleDbConnection controls and the SqlDataAdapter and SqlConnection controls. VB. NET has two separate Command controls as well.

Getting Results in Seven Easy Steps

In this section, you see how quickly you can connect to a server database with VB .NET's tools. No human hands will write any programming! Yet, in seven quick steps, you'll watch as a big table of data travels from its server database and is displayed in a client grid before your very eyes. You'll be slap speechless! Seven quick steps! Seven!

Don't try to imitate this next example at home, folks. You get to do hands-on programming soon enough in Chapter 2. And throughout this book, you work with the powerful DataAdapter control I'm illustrating here. But you're not quite ready to manage such a powerful tool. For now, just sit back and watch me work it.

I end this chapter by showing you how much VB .NET can do to help you with your database programming. You see VB .NET make a connection, define a query, access the data, and preview the DataSet it created:

1. **After starting a new VB .NET Windows-style project, I open Server Explorer, as shown in Figure 1-1.**

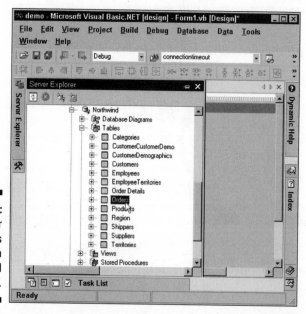

Figure 1-1:
Server
Explorer is
new in
Visual
Studio .NET.

You can do *lots* of things with Server Explorer, including adding, editing, and deleting tables and columns. You can even *create* a database! Later in this book, you see how.

2. **I drag a table (named Orders) and drop it onto the VB .NET form, as shown in Figure 1-2.**

   This table is from the Northwind database, one of the databases in Server Explorer. As soon as the Orders table is dropped onto my form, a Connection control and DataAdapter control are added to my project. They are placed in the tray below my form.

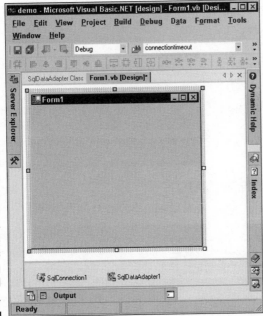

Figure 1-2: Adding tables from an SQL database is as easy as dragging and dropping.

3. **To create a DataSet that contains the Orders table, I right-click the SqlDataAdapter1 icon in the tray and choose Generate Dataset, as shown in Figure 1-3.**

   The Generate Dataset dialog box appears.

4. **My only job is to give this new DataSet a name.**

   I call it Maxie, as shown in Figure 1-4.

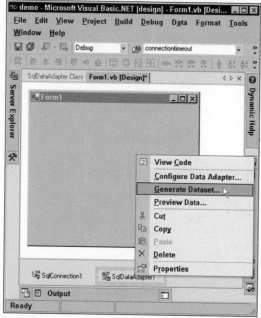

Figure 1-3:
A DataAdapter can generate as many DataSets as you want.

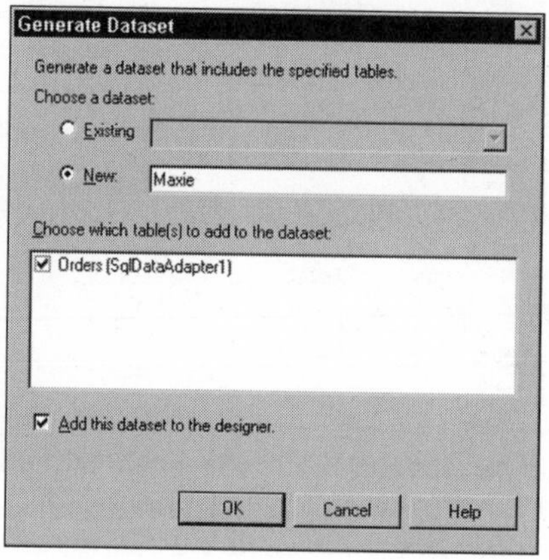

Figure 1-4:
Use this dialog box to name a new DataSet (or modify an existing one).

5. **I click OK, and my new DataSet appears in the tray, as you can see in Figure 1-5.**

   My new DataSet was created for me courtesy of the DataAdapter control.

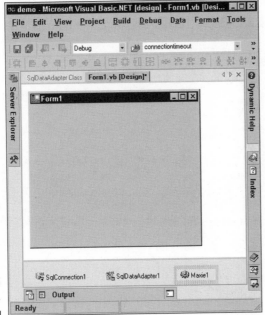

Figure 1-5:
There's
Maxie1
sitting
proudly in
the tray.

6. **I right-click the SqlDataAdapter1 icon again but this time choose Preview Data.**

   The Data Adapter Preview utility opens,

7. **I click the Fill DataSet button.**

   All the data in the Orders table rolls into view, as you can see in Figure 1-6. That didn't take long, did it?

You discover much more about DataSets in the coming chapters. I believe that you'll soon consider the VB .NET DataSet your friend.

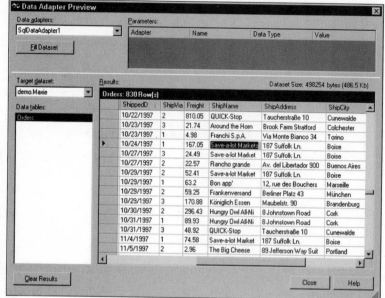

Figure 1-6:
The Orders
table is
extracted
from the
server and
sent to the
DataSet.

Chapter 2

Databases 101: How Databases Work

A *database* is a collection of information organized in some fashion and stored in a computer. If you have an address book, it's almost a database. All it needs to get formal recognition as a proper database is for you to copy its information into a computer and save it — in some orderly way — in a file.

But consider what happens when you take the names, addresses, and phone numbers of all your friends and relatives and copy that data into the computer. Just randomly typing data isn't going to result in an organized store of information. You must first define a database structure, perhaps a structure similar to that in your address book.

This chapter introduces you to the components of a database. You also find out the meaning of various database terms, including row (record), column (field), index, and DataSet.

Understanding Rows, Columns, Tables, and All the Rest

There are various types of databases, but this book concentrates on what is by far the most popular: the relational database. A *relational database* has three primary qualities:

- ✔ **Data is stored in tables (which are subdivided into columns or, as they used to be called, fields).** For example, your personal address book could be a table with columns such as LastName, FirstName, Street, City, State, ZipCode, and PhoneNumber. The columns are the categories into which the data will be subdivided.

- ✔ **You can join tables (in a *relationship*) so that you can later extract data from more than one table at a time.** For example, suppose you have a table you've named *Gift* that contains a PhoneNumber column (as a unique identifier of each person in your database) along with the price of the gift you received last Christmas from the person identified with that column. You could join the PhoneNumber column in the Gift table with the PhoneNumber column in an AddressBook table. Then you can get information from both tables at once. (Both of these tables must include that same PhoneNumber column for this *joining* to work.) The term *relational database* derives from these relationships you can create by joining tables.

- ✔ **You can query tables, getting back DataSets (subsets of a table or tables).** One example of a DataSet is a query (or request) for a list that includes the FirstName and GiftPrice columns of each record.

Read on.

Rows are filled with information

Suppose that on each page of your personal address book, you always write information about only one person. That way, you don't get confused; each page describes a single individual. In database terms, each page, after it has some information filled in, is a *row* (what used to be called a *record*).

As shown in Figure 2-1, the top line on each page in the address book is labeled Name, the next several lines are labeled Address, and the last line is labeled Phone. In database terms, these labels are called *columns*. You can see where the term *column* comes from. Reading down a column tells you the same category of information about all the different entries in the table.

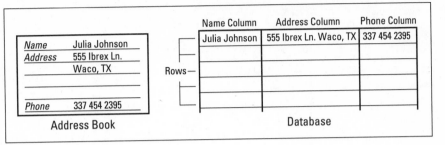

Figure 2-1:
A single page in an address book is equivalent to a single record in a database.

Columns are labels

Each column has its own name, or label, such as TotalSales. A row contains the information that fills the column, such as $156. Rows do not have label names but do have row numbers.

Each row usually contains several columns. In the address book example, each row has three columns: Name, Address, and Phone. Here's an example of a single row in this database:

```
Julia Johnson      555 Ibrex Ln., Waco, TX     337 454-2395
```

Recall that Microsoft is now using the term *column* to mean what used to be called a database's *field*. Likewise, they are now using the term *row* for what used to be called a *record*. This seemingly endless shifting of terminology sure keeps us on our toes, doesn't it? The terms *column* and *row* have been used in database terminology historically. Some companies, such as IBM, prefer to use *column* and *row*. And that usage is perhaps superior because it can help you see the meaning visually: A column is read vertically; a row is read horizontally.

One way to think of the relationship between rows and columns is to think of a baseball scoreboard. Across the top are two labels: Home and Visitor. These are the columns, and they describe the columns of data below them. The rows contain the data, such as 2 under the Home label and 4 under Visitor, as you can see in Figure 2-2.

Depending on what type of database you're accessing, if a column's name is two words, such as Personality Drawbacks, you might need to enclose it in brackets or single quotes: [Personality Drawbacks] or 'Personality Drawbacks'. Some database access forbids two words (the use of spaces). See the following tip.

Columns

HOME   VISITOR

Row | 2 | 4 |

3   2

TIP

If you're having trouble with a two-word column name when programming, try enclosing it in brackets or single quotes.

Although Microsoft Access-style databases permit spaces in column names, most relational databases do not permit spaces. If the database does not permit you to use spaces, you must resort to using an underscore character to separate words (such as Personality_Drawbacks) or slamming the two words together (such as PersonalityDrawbacks).

Tables are made up of columns

Back to the address book example. Suppose that you decided to create a database, and at first all you had in it was the information from your address book. This small, simple database has only one table, which you name Addresses. (Tables are relatively large-scale collections of data, but a database can be even larger; it can contain multiple tables.) You define the contents of a database when you create it, so you determine how many tables it has.

You've already marked the birthdays of all your friends and relatives on your calendar, and now you decide to put this data into a second table in your database. You name the table Gifts and define five columns for it: Name, Birthday, [Favorite Color], [Shoe Size], and Comments.

Notice that both your Addresses table and your Gifts table have a Name column in common. These two Name columns contain *the same data* in both tables. This common column enables you to *join* the tables. You can then *query* (ask for information from) both these tables at once. You can use a query such as, "What is Marie's address and birthday?" Her address information is held only in the Addresses table, and her birthday is listed in the Gifts table. But because both tables contain *Marie* in a Name column that is identical in both tables, they can provide their respective additional information about Marie: her address from the Addresses table and her birthday from the Gifts table. The *result* of this query (the information you get back) is made available in what's called a DataSet.

Why use multiple tables?

Why have two tables: Addresses and Gifts? Why not just put all the data into one big table? Bulging, single-table databases are less flexible and less efficient than multiple, smaller tables — both when used by average people and when manipulated by a programmer. You separate data into tables, and then separate it further into columns, for the same reason that most people use labeled folders in their filing cabinets. It's easier to store, retrieve, and manage the contents of an organized filing cabinet than a big pile of unsorted papers.

Here's another somewhat more technical description of why multiple tables are useful. You typically divide information into multiple tables if there is something other than a one-to-one relationship between rows in the tables. For instance, if the Gifts table was more generic (it didn't apply only to birthdays), there would be multiple Gift table rows for each Address table row. In that case, Marie could have a Gift row for her birthday, another row for her anniversary, and yet another for her graduation. With a one-to-many relationship like this, using multiple tables makes more sense and is more efficient than trying to cram all that information into a single table.

If the database is small, however, its organization doesn't matter much. You don't have to worry about dividing your little address book database into several tables because it doesn't have that many entries. You're not that popular, are you? But if you're designing a multiuser database with 250,000 rows, every little efficiency matters. By creating several tables, you can improve the organization of the database, write programming for it more easily, and generally make retrieving rows faster. Why? Primarily because putting everything into one big database can result in dreadful redundancies.

To understand how and why to use several tables rather than one big one, consider a database that lists 100 book publishers and 8,000 books. The database is divided into four tables: Authors, Publishers, TitleAuthor, and Titles. If all this information were stored in a single table, serious redundancy would result. Why? Do you want to repeat the publishers' names, addresses, and phone numbers many times for each of the 8,000 books? Or would you rather have a separate table for Publishers, listing each publisher's name, address, and phone number only once, plus a single PublishersName column in the Titles table? The second solution makes much more sense.

When you look up a title in the Titles table, the publisher's name is part of each title's row (so you do have to provide the publisher's name 8,000 times). But if you want the publisher's address, phone number, and other details, no problem — the Publisher's table and the Titles table both contain a PublishersName column. That way, you can get the other details about a publisher by matching the PublishersName column in the two tables. You store each publisher's address and phone number only once because you have separate tables. What's more, if you need to change the publisher's phone number later because they move to new offices, you have to change it in only one location in the entire database.

Tangled relationships: Using unique data to tie tables together

When you specify a relationship between tables while designing a database, you're saying: I might need additional information about this fellow, and if I do, it can be found in this other table using a column that is identical in both tables — the *primary key*.

Suppose that you have several tables in a database, and all have a column named ID. In each of these tables, John Jones has an ID number of 242522. The database might have several people named John Jones, so that's not going to provide you with a unique key to a unique row (record) about a particular Mr. Jones. To find out more about a specific Mr. Jones, I look up the ID number in the second table. (I explain the reasons for storing information about the same guy in separate tables in the preceding section. And you can find a discussion of using keys with multiple tables in Chapter 18.)

A *key* is a table column that ensures that each record in that table is unique. Sometimes called the *primary key*, a key column prevents confusion. You can't use the FirstName column as a key because you might have several Bobs in your organization. You can't use the LastName column because there could be more than one person named, for example, Smith. You can't use the home phone number column because your office might suffer from raging nepotism and all four of the boss's wretched offspring work for Daddy. Because these slackers also still live at home, they all share the same phone number. What's a poor database designer to do? Well, don't sit there wringing your hands and moaning. Choose a column that *must be unique* for your key. A Social Security number column, for example, makes a good key column. Or, as you see next in this chapter, you can generate a series of unique ID numbers in a table automatically.

Let the database do it for you: AutoNumber columns

You can let the database generate a unique ID number for each row. These serial numbers start with 1 when you add the first row and go up by 1 for each new row entered into the database. (Some database programmers insist that every table should have a column with a unique serial number so that you can ensure that every row will be unique.)

Such database-generated serial numbers are put into an AutoNumber column. The AutoNumber column acts as a unique key, but its main function is to permit tables to be linked. How? When designing the database, you specify that the AutoNumber column be included in more than one table as a way of joining tables.

An AutoNumber column isn't just any ordinary old index, though. (I describe ordinary indexes in the next section.) Unique keys like this are called *primary index keys*. They differ from other indexed (sorted) columns because the *primary key column will never contain repeating data*. For example, an ordinary index (sorted column) might well have ten rows with a LastName column containing the same last name *Jones*. Recall that a LastName column can't be made a primary index and used to create relationships between tables.

Why not just make a list?

Why go to all the trouble to define tables and then divide those tables into columns? Why subdivide a database into neat little boxes? Why not just jot down the information sort of randomly, the way you would in a loose-leaf notebook or on a paper napkin?

Organizing data makes manipulating it far easier, particularly if you have large amounts of data. If your company has 12,000 customers and one of them questions his or her last bill, you don't want to have to search through a loose-leaf notebook, page by page, to find this customer's rows. You want to see an organized, alphabetical list of customer names in a list box. You can then quickly locate and double-click the name to display the rows. Alternatively, you could type the name in a text box to locate the customer. Either interface is far more useful than a drawer full of scribbled napkins.

Indexes — a Key to Success

Information in a relational database is not automatically stored alphabetically (or by numeric order, if the column is numeric). In a Name column, *Anderware* can follow *Zimbare*. Or maybe not. It doesn't matter.

The point is, you can't expect rows to be in any particular order. When someone adds a row to a database, it's put at the end of a table. No attempt is made to place it in some particular position. When a row is deleted, who cares? A relational database has a real la-ti-dah attitude about alphabetization. When designing a database, however, you can specify some of its columns as indexes.

Imagine nonalphabetic yellow pages

If you want to search for a particular row in a column that's not indexed, the database software must search every row until it finds the right one. How would you like it if the Yellow Pages in the phone book were not alphabetized? You'd be turning pages all night, looking for a plumber, hoping to stumble on the right page. And what started as an overflowing bathtub would become a real problem for your downstairs neighbor.

An index in a relational database is the one exception to the blithe, uncaring order I've just described. An indexed column solves the problem of finding a particular row in the jumble of data. The database software can quickly locate a specific row if a column is indexed. So, when you're designing a database, you need to decide which columns should be indexed. (Unindexed data can be searched; it just takes longer.)

Here's the general rule: You should index any columns that are likely to be searched. In the example address book database, you are far more likely to search some columns than others. You'd probably search the Name and Birthday columns, but would not likely search the [Favorite Color], [Shoe Size], or Comments column.

So, for this database, you might specify that the Name and Birthday columns should be indexed and that the others should be left unindexed. But what happens if you later buy some size 8 blue shoes on sale and want to search the database to see whether any of your friends or relatives wear that size and likes blue? No problemo: The database can still conduct searches on unindexed columns; it just takes longer to find the information you need.

The database software automatically creates and maintains the indexes you specify. You need do nothing more than specify which columns should be indexed.

Hey, let's index every column!

Some of you are probably thinking, "Why not index all the columns? That would be super efficient." Wrong. When publishers create an index for a book, they don't index all the words in the book, do they? They include the words likely to be searched for, not words such as *the* or *twelve*. An index of all the words would suffer from several drawbacks. In particular, it would be bigger than the book, and most of the index would be of little use to anyone. A quick scan of the book itself would be faster than slogging through a massively bloated, highly repetitive, index.

You don't index every column in a table for a similar reason: Too much of a good thing is a bad thing. Efficiencies start to degrade, storage space gets tight, multiuser traffic jams can occur, and other bugaboos arise. Each index always slows down updates to a database, at least a little.

Building Your First DataSet

But enough theory. Time to get your hands out of your pockets and build a little DataSet. In the process, you'll discover the exact meaning of column, row, table, key and DataSet. After you know what these terms mean, you'll understand several major concepts underlying VB .NET database management.

A DataSet can contain all the basic elements of a database. So by creating a DataSet, you'll be discovering the structure of a database at the same time. The fundamental differences between a DataSet and a database are that a database generally resides on a hard drive in one or more files and is usually larger. A DataSet usually holds a subset of the data in a full database.

A DataSet can be stored on a hard drive, but it can also simply be pulled out of an existing database — and therefore reside merely in the computer's memory while someone manipulates or views it. Then, if changes are made, the DataSet can be merged back into the database from which it was extracted.

Creating a DataSet object

In the following example, you create a DataSet object and then find out how to add rows to it and how to read those rows. You can create and manipulate DataSets using VB .NET data controls and .NET Server Explorer in many ways. However, to get off to a good start, you use the simplest approach of all: dropping a DataSet control from the Toolbox onto a form. Follow these steps:

1. **Start VB .NET and then choose File⇨New⇨Project.**

   The New Project dialog box appears.

2. **In the Name column, type** AddressBook.

3. **Double-click the Windows Application icon.**

   The dialog box closes and you see an empty form.

4. **Arrange VB .NET IDE (Integrated Design Environment) so that it looks similar to the one in Figure 2-3.**

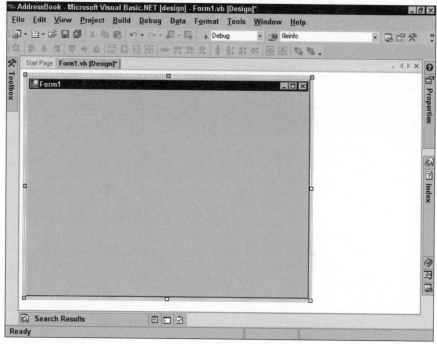

Figure 2-3:
A typical
arrangement
of the VB
.NET IDE,
with the
design
window
ready for
you to add
controls.

My preference is to leave the Toolbox set to Auto-hide. That way, it stays out of my way when I want to use the code window but can be quickly summoned by clicking the Toolbox tab on the left side of the code window, as shown in Figure 2-3. To auto-hide the Toolbox, right-click its title bar and choose Auto-hide. In fact, if you want the cleanest work environment, you might want to set to auto-hide several other common windows, including Solution Explorer, Help Index and Search, Output, Task List, Command, and Properties, as shown in Figure 2-3. To pop one of these windows back into view, just pause your mouse pointer on it.

5. **Open the Toolbox (press Ctrl+Alt+X or click its tab).**

6. **Click the Data tab in the Toolbox.**

   You see a set of database-related controls.

7. **Double-click the DataSet icon in the Toolbox.**

   The Add Dataset dialog box appears, as shown in Figure 2-4.

8. **Choose the Untyped Dataset option.**

   You have no DataSet in this project yet, so you can't use the Typed Dataset option.

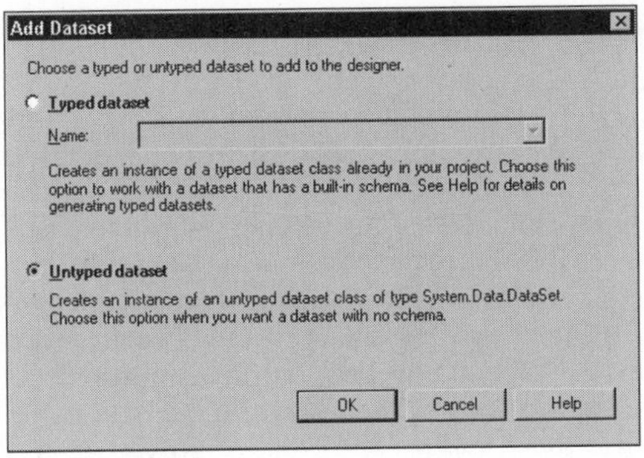

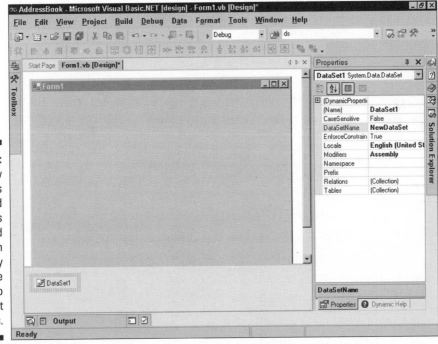

Figure 2-4:
Use this
wizard to
add a
DataSet to a
project.

9. Click OK.

The dialog box closes and a new DataSet object icon appears in the tray below your form, as you can see in Figure 2-5. The tray is where VB .NET puts controls that are never made visible to the user, such as a Timer.

Figure 2-5:
Your new
DataSet has
been added
to this
project and
appears in
the tray
below the
form to
which it
belongs.

Adding a table to a DataSet

Now it's time to define the structure, or *schema,* of your new DataSet. In other words, it's time to add a table to it. Inside that table, you'll define two columns: one for the last name of each person in your address book, and the second for the first name. You'll define the last names column as a special column called a *key* by requiring that each piece of data added to this column be *unique.* (For example, you can't have two people with last name of *Smith.*) Sure, this wouldn't be a sensible requirement in a real-world address book database because you're likely to know people with duplicate last names. But relax, friend. You're merely looking at a simple example here to better understand how to manipulate the structure of a DataSet. To keep things simple, you'll make the LastName column your key.

1. **Click the DataSet1 icon in the tray, and then press F4.**

   The Properties window is displayed, showing the properties of DataSet1.

2. **In the Properties window, change the Name property (not the DataSetName property) of DataSet1 to** dsAddresses.

   The DataSet icon in the tray changes to display its new name. (Behind the scenes, VB .NET also changes the name in the source code that it writes automatically when you add a control to a form. You look at that code in a moment.) You use the Name property in your programming to refer to this DataSet.

3. **In the Properties window, click the Tables property and then click the ellipsis (the three dots).**

   The Tables Collection Editor appears, as shown in Figure 2-6.

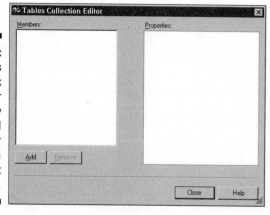

Figure 2-6:
Use this
dialog box
to create or
modify
tables and
their
columns in a
DataSet
control.

4. In the Tables Collection Editor, click the Add button.

The Table's properties are displayed, as shown in Figure 2-7.

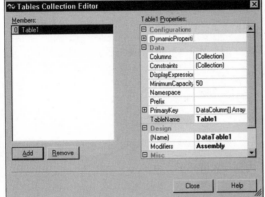

Figure 2-7:
Here's where you can define tables and their properties.

5. Change the Name property (not the TableName property) to Friends.

VB .NET again changes the source code behind the scenes. Here are a few of the lines of code that reflect this new table name and the new DataSet name you specified in Step 2:

```
Friend WithEvents dsAddresses As System.Data.DataSet
Friend WithEvents Friends As System.Data.DataTable
```

Notice that this code declares (announces) a new DataSet named dsAddresses and a new DataTable named Friends. (The Friend command is similar to the Dim command, but when you use Friend to declare a variable, it can be accessed from anywhere in your project. Variables declared with Dim can be accessed only in the form where they're declared.)

6. In the Properties list of the Tables Collection Editor, click Columns and then click the ellipsis.

The Columns Collection Editor appears.

7. In the Columns Collection Editor, click the Add button.

You can now define a new column and its properties, as shown in Figure 2-8. Note that the DataType property for all columns defaults to the string (text) type. This is the data type you want for the LastName and FirstName columns.

8. Change the Name property (not the ColumnName property) to LastName.

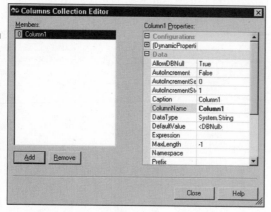

Figure 2-8:
Use this
dialog box
to add
columns to
a table and
edit the
properties
of those
columns.

9. **Click the Unique property.**

   It changes from False to True. Now the DataSet will refuse to permit two
   rows to contain identical data in the LastName column.

10. **Click the Add button.**

    Column2 is now created.

11. **Change this column's Name property to** FirstName.

12. **Click the close button twice.**

    The Columns Collection Editor and the Tables Collection Editor close.

Viewing a DataSet's Code

While you've been sitting on your fancy perch using dialog boxes and controls to create a DataSet, VB .NET has been busy in the code window doing all
the grunt work to write the programming. Here's what you'll see if you open
the code window by double-clicking Form1 in the design window. You must
also click the + symbol next to Region to reveal code that VB .NET doesn't
think you need to bother your pretty head about:

```
Region " Windows Form Designer generated code "

    Public Sub New()
        MyBase.New()

        'This call is required by the Windows Form Designer.
        InitializeComponent()

        'Add any initialization after the
            InitializeComponent() call
```

```
End Sub

'Form overrides dispose to clean up the component list.
Protected Overloads Overrides Sub Dispose(ByVal disposing
        As Boolean)
    If disposing Then
        If Not (components Is Nothing) Then
            components.Dispose()
        End If
    End If
    MyBase.Dispose(disposing)
End Sub
Friend WithEvents dsAddresses As System.Data.DataSet
Friend WithEvents Friends As System.Data.DataTable
Friend WithEvents LastName As System.Data.DataColumn
Friend WithEvents FirstName As System.Data.DataColumn

'Required by the Windows Form Designer
Private components As System.ComponentModel.Container

'NOTE: The following procedure is required by the Windows
        Form Designer
'It can be modified using the Windows Form Designer.
'Do not modify it using the code editor.
<System.Diagnostics.DebuggerStepThrough()> Private Sub
        InitializeComponent()
    Me.dsAddresses = New System.Data.DataSet()
    Me.Friends = New System.Data.DataTable()
    Me.LastName = New System.Data.DataColumn()
    Me.FirstName = New System.Data.DataColumn()
    CType(Me.dsAddresses,
        System.ComponentModel.ISupportInitialize).BeginIni
        t()
    CType(Me.Friends,
        System.ComponentModel.ISupportInitialize).BeginIni
        t()
    '
    'dsAddresses
    '
    Me.dsAddresses.DataSetName = "NewDataSet"
    Me.dsAddresses.Locale = New
        System.Globalization.CultureInfo("en-US")
    Me.dsAddresses.Tables.AddRange(New
        System.Data.DataTable() {Me.Friends})
    '
    'Friends
    '
    Me.Friends.Columns.AddRange(New
        System.Data.DataColumn() {Me.LastName,
        Me.FirstName})
    Me.Friends.Constraints.AddRange(New
        System.Data.Constraint() {New
```

```
System.Data.UniqueConstraint("Constraint1", New String()
        {"Column1"}, False)})
     Me.Friends.TableName = "DataTable1"
     '
     'LastName
     '
     Me.LastName.ColumnName = "Column1"
     '
     'FirstName
     '
     Me.FirstName.ColumnName = "Column2"
     '
     'Form1
     '
     Me.AutoScaleBaseSize = New System.Drawing.Size(5, 13)
     Me.ClientSize = New System.Drawing.Size(480, 357)
     Me.Name = "Form1"
     Me.Text = "Form1"
     CType(Me.dsAddresses,
         System.ComponentModel.ISupportInitialize).EndInit(
         )
     CType(Me.Friends,
         System.ComponentModel.ISupportInitialize).EndInit(
         )

   End Sub

#End Region
```

The following sections describe some of this code. There are lessons here that you'll want to remember when you need to do some programming of your own because no wizard or dialog box is there to generate it for you automatically. Remember that .NET is a major adjustment for all of us. VB .NET is not a new version of Visual Basic — it's a new language, and understanding it will take some time.

Verbosity

Me refers to the form, Form1 in this case. So Me specifies the form that various objects belong to. In traditional VB, you would write

```
Form1.Text1.Text = "Hi."
```

or the shortened version:

```
Text1 = "Hi"
```

You used to be able to assume Form1 and not name it because the TextBox was located on Form1. Also, each control had a default property that you could also assume — Text was the TextBox's default property. *Neither* of these assumptions or defaults are permitted in VB .NET. As you'll discover, VB .NET requires more verbose code than you're accustomed to.

In VB .NET, you must specify Me as the container (the form) for a control, specify the full name TextBox1, and include the Text property, like this:

```
Me.TextBox1.Text = "Hi."
```

Overloads, overrides, yadda yadda

The OOP technique called *inheritance* is controversial. Programmers disagree as to whether it helps prevent programming errors or contributes to them. It's almost a religious argument. The very technique that I recommend (copying and pasting code) is cited as a problem by C++ programmers. In their view, you don't want to copy and paste because if you have to make changes, you must make them to all copied-and-pasted versions. If you simply make an object, you have to modify only the base class, and the changes propagate through all the inherited classes. In other words, I see errors in using polymorphism; they see errors in not using polymorphism — thus the argument. (By the way, these same arguments are used by those who favor or condemn the use of *constants* in computer programming. Oddly, not too many programmers create constants for use in their programs, though people who write computer *languages* such as VB .NET use lots of constants, which they now prefer to call *enumerations* or, when they're feeling radical, *enums*.) One final point: The acronym *OOP* (which stands for Object-Oriented Programming) is now out of favor among OOP proponents. They feel that because of its association with the word *oops*, it is best now to simply use the acronym *OO*, pronounced "oh-oh."

Notice this bizarre Sub declaration:

```
Protected Overloads Overrides Sub Dispose(ByVal disposing As
        Boolean)
```

The Overloads command means that two or more functions named Dispose are available, but VB .NET knows which one to use based on the fact that their arguments are different. This version of Dispose uses disposing As Boolean for its argument, and the other version of Dispose uses a different variable type or a different number of arguments. I find this a confusing way to program. Having two identically named procedures active at the same time is conducive to errors. Enough words are available to provide procedures with unique names, so I think you should avoid overloading.

The `Overrides` command has to do with inheritance. VB .NET now has the capability to use "full" inheritance, which has evidently been the longtime wish of some VB programmers. Why, I'm not sure. Inheritance is a way of reusing existing source code. The problem is that when you inherit existing code, you might modify it a little (this is called polymorphism). Then, no one knows which of two or more versions of the original class is being used or should be used in a particular context. Lots of errors are generated this way, and lots of effort is wasted trying to figure out ever more complex ways of reducing those errors.

If you want to reuse some code from a previous project, my advice is to just copy it using Notepad or some other text utility and then paste it into your new project. Problem solved. If you want to get fancy, you can compile reusable code into libraries. (They're called *assemblies* in VB .NET, presumably to distinguish them from the now-disgraced DLLs of the past, which caused so many "which version is it?" problems.) Then attach those libraries to your VB .NET project (right-click References in VB .NET's Solution Explorer window and choose Add Reference). Lest you assume that I've thrown the baby out with the bathwater, I don't want to leave you with the impression that I feel OOP is a worthless set of techniques. Particularly for people who must program together in groups, the idea of encapsulation can be useful if not carried to extremes. Nevertheless, always remember this old joke when you are tempted to take OO and inheritance too seriously: Before, C++ programmers had to code all their bugs by hand; now they inherit them.

Behind the scenes of a region

Essentially, the code that you see when you click the + symbol next to a Region in the code window is housekeeping. In previous versions of VB, you would not have seen the code that specified, for example, the Name and Text (title bar caption) properties of your form. However, VB .NET lets you view and, if you really want to live dangerously, modify housekeeping code, such as this:

```
Me.Name = "Form1"
Me.Text = "Form1"
```

You're better off using the Properties window in design mode to make changes to the properties of forms and controls. And you're better off using the Toolbox to add controls to your form.

But some will ignore this advice and prefer to do the hard way in source code what they could do the easy way with the Toolbox. If you're one of those people, here's what you type to create a new TextBox. Up where all the Friends are listed, type this:

```
Friend WithEvents TextBox1 As System.Windows.Forms.TextBox
```

That line declares a new object variable named TextBox1.

Then down lower in the source code, just below the Me.dsAddresses line, add the part in boldface, which brings the object into existence:

```
Me.dsAddresses = New System.Data.DataSet()
Me.TextBox1 = New System.Windows.Forms.TextBox()
```

Finally, specify the minimum number of essential properties, down lower where the dsAddresses DataSet and Form1 properties are listed:

```
Me.TextBox1.Location = New System.Drawing.Point(208, 104)
Me.TextBox1.Name = "TextBox1"
Me.TextBox1.Size = New System.Drawing.Size(176, 20)
Me.TextBox1.TabIndex = 0
Me.TextBox1.Text = "TextBox1"
```

However, be warned. You aren't really supposed to modify most of the code in the Region areas. As VB .NET says with a comment in the code itself:

```
'NOTE: The following procedure is required by the Windows
        Form Designer
    'It can be modified using the Windows Form Designer.
    'Do not modify it using the code editor.
```

So, you've been warned. You are allowed to insert initialization (startup housekeeping) code here in Sub New:

```
Public Sub New()
        MyBase.New()

        'This call is required by the Windows Form Designer.
        InitializeComponent()

        'Add any initialization after the
            InitializeComponent() call

End Sub
```

Following the InitializeComponent command, you can insert your own initialization code. However, most VB programmers prefer to use the Form_Load event for initialization code instead.

To see how to connect to an existing database and then extract some of its data into a DataSet, see Chapter 3. You can also find out what the word *verbose* really means when you take a tour of the XML that underlies every DataSet.

Part II
Making a Connection

In this part . . .

*1*n Visual Basic .NET, Microsoft has assembled tools that offer you many, many shortcuts, including prebuilt components, templates, designers, and wizards. Using these tools, you can often get a jump-start on a job — for example, you may be able to customize a wizard's dialog pages rather than begin your project from ground zero. Some wizards write hundreds of lines of code — lines that *you* don't have to write.

Part II demonstrates all the useful tools and techniques you need to establish a connection between a database and components, Web pages, or traditional Windows applications. You see how to use some of the VB data controls, and you find out how to work with the powerful DataSet Command Wizard.

Chapter 3

Getting Connected with Data Controls

*V*B .NET is based on XML, a way of saving information that is in some ways quite simple (it's just plain text, readable in Windows Notepad or any text editor or word processor). I have more to say about XML in other chapters, but for now, just realize that XML is similar to HTML (the language used to describe how Web pages should look and behave).

Also, as you'll see in this chapter, XML is what programmers call verbose. Too true; XML takes many lines to define what you could probably describe in a much shorter list. But XML does have its virtues as a way of storing and transmitting information. A primary reason XML is used so much these days is that it *is* plain text. It doesn't endanger anyone's computer because viruses cannot (as yet anyway) sneak into your computer's hard drive in a plain text file. In addition, firewalls, which examine incoming information and decide whether to let that information get into a network or an individual computer, are trained to let XML and HTML pass through.

This chapter's example illustrates how to use some VB .NET controls to connect to a database and build a DataSet. You also see the XML that VB .NET creates when it prepares to send a DataSet to another computer or store the DataSet on a hard drive.

Generating DataSets the Easy Way

Connecting an application to a database may seem formidable, but if you use the tools available in Visual Basic .NET, it's a snap. More precisely, it's a drag and drop.

You drop a data-related control onto a form from the Toolbox. You add a few other controls to make the connection and generate a DataSet. You answer a few questions: the name of the database, the table of data that you want to use, and the particular information (all authors' last names, for example) that you want to fill the DataSet with. Then you use the Properties window to attach the data-related control to your DataSet. To do all this you need to write only one line of programming! Promise.

For many applications, prebuilt components such as the data-related controls work just fine and are all you need to get a database application up and running quickly. In this chapter, you explore how to get VB .NET to display data to the user from a database.

As is usual with VB .NET, there are many paths to reach a given goal. Because data access can be tested and explored somewhat more efficiently in the Windows style of programming in VB .NET (the results are displayed faster in the editor and some of the testing is simpler), I begin by illustrating some data-access techniques using WinForms (traditional Windows) examples. VB .NET programming is divided into roughly two styles of programming: traditional Windows programming that VB has specialized in for the past ten years and the newer Internet-style programming that places different requirements on both the programmer and the language itself. VB .NET therefore includes two different fundamental programming "containers." The classic Windows *form*, now known as the WinForm, and the new Internet-style document, known as the WebForm.

The differences between programming for WinForms and WebForms (server-side controls and server-side VB .NET) are generally trivial. You see just how trivial in the examples in Part V. If you aren't sure what *server-side* means or how database programming can be used in Internet applications, be patient. If you're not the patent type, flip to Part V satisfy your raging curiosity right away.

In any event, this chapter focuses on one way to get information from a data store in VB .NET: using the SqlDataAdapter control with the SqlConnection control.

Here's a bit more explanation about the word *store*. VB .NET uses technologies that permit you to manipulate, receive, and transmit DataSets (packages of data) in various ways. So rather than dealing solely with databases, as in the past, VB .NET can work with data in less traditional forms, such as data in HTML-like (Internet page) files called XML files or even plain TXT files.

Although most examples in this book deal with a sample databases called pubs and Northwind, be aware that you can build a DataSet from many different types of data sources (or *stores*).

Need an industrial-strength database connection? As is so often the case in life — with shoes, furniture, hamburgers, and many other items — making something by hand can sometimes get you the best results. If you're constructing a specialized or heavy-duty database application, you may need to hand-tailor the project. In those situations, there's no substitute for line-by-line programming. Part VI covers this approach in depth. So, if the techniques I describe in this chapter aren't robust enough to handle a job you're working on, take a look at Part VI. You'll know that they're not robust enough if you can't figure out a way to accomplish your job using only VB .NET's wizards and other built-in database components.

Nonetheless, some coding jobs are simply too tedious for anyone to attempt. You're likely to go nuts long before you get all the typos and other errors worked out of a DataSet of any significant size after it has been translated into XML files. Fortunately, you can save a DataSet such that all the tedious VB-to-XML translation is performed for you. (I explain these DataSet `WriteXML` and `WriteXMLSchema` translators in Chapters 8 and 9.)

So, before you can actually get DataSets out of the sample databases — and also test Internet-style (WebForm) programs — you have a few housekeeping chores to do. The following sections ensure that the examples in this book can work for *you* (even though they've been well-tested and certainly work for *me*).

Connecting to a Database

SQL Server is Microsoft's heavy-duty database technology, and it works with .NET to offer scalable (expandable) solutions to problems presented when a business tries to manage such things as inventory, order processing, and other database-related tasks on the Internet.

Connecting to SQL Server

If you haven't installed SQL Server 2000, install it now from your Windows CD or download it from the Microsoft Web site (it's 324 MB, so Microsoft also offers an option on the same Web page for getting SQL Server by mail):

```
http://www.microsoft.com/sql/evaluation/trial/2000/download.
        asp
```

Understanding scalability

Writing programs for the Internet is different in many ways than traditional Windows programming. For one, your application must be *scalable*, that is, it must be able to expand its capabilities rapidly if necessary. This has several implications (using more than a single server, for instance). Traffic might increase to the point where you can't manage that traffic using only a single computer. You have to scale up to a server "farm." All the computers in such a farm must work together to provide services; this means an application must be able to communicate with more than one computer at a time. That's one aspect of what is meant by *distributed computing*.

But as a programmer, you want your applications to be able to handle sudden surges of users visiting your Web site. This means you must write your programming that manages this site in a way that doesn't slow things to a crawl if, say, 500 people try to interact with your programming simultaneously. That's one reason for the detached DataSet: When the user is interacting with an order-entry form in the user's browser, that user is not putting any burden on your server. By detaching a DataSet and then sending it to the user to fill in (as a form), your server can turn to other users and serve them. Only after the form is filled in and the user has clicked the Submit button does your application on the server have to interact by accepting the transmitted DataSet, reattaching to the database, storing the results, and perhaps sending a thank-you message. Data detached into DataSets is sometimes called a loosely coupled system. (In traditional Windows programming, the connection between the user and the database would be maintained until the user finished filling in the data on the form.)

If you've downloaded SQL Server, you must run the SQLEVAL.EXE program to extract the files and place them in a folder. Then go to that folder and run SETUP.BAT to install the software itself.

Why use Internet Information Services and virtual directories?

If you expect to use the capabilities of VB .NET over the Internet or even a local network, after you've installed SQL Server 2000, you must then create a connection to IIS (Internet Information Server) and also build some virtual directories. The reason for taking these steps is that when you work with ASP.NET (Internet-based .NET applications, as opposed to traditional Windows-based applications), you want some sample database connections available from a server (on the Internet or just on a corporate network). However, you'll actually use a *local* (in your hard drive) host that *pretends* to be a remote server connected to your local copy of Internet Explorer (IE). This local host communicates with the IE (the client) just like a real Web site server communicates with IE when you surf the Internet. But all interaction between the local host and IE takes place in your computer. It's a simulation, allowing you to write and test VB .NET WebForm applications in a context that mimics the Internet (or corporate network) connection between a client browser and an IIS server located perhaps half the world away.

You don't perform any WebForm Internet VB .NET programming in this chapter. (That's left for Chapter 6 where you try your first Internet programming experiments with VB .NET.) But as long as you're installing SQL Server and otherwise setting up your computer to work smoothly with VB .NET, you might as well get the virtual directories up and running too.

To create a few virtual directories, follow these steps:

1. **Choose Start➪Programs➪Microsoft SQL Server➪Configure SQL XML Support in IIS.**

   The IIS Virtual Directory Management for SQL Server dialog box appears.

2. **In the left pane, right-click Default Web Site.**

   If you see a message telling you that there was an error connecting to your computer, you're probably logged on as someone other than the original user (identity) who installed SQL Server 2000. When working with VB .NET, you should be logged on as the person who originally installed VB .NET and SQL Server 2000. The solution is to log off Windows 2000 and then log back on using the original identity, or reinstall VB .NET using your current identity. Also ensure that you have Administrator privileges as well. If you don't know what *administrator privileges* mean, ask your administrator. Or press F1 in the Windows desktop, and then use the Index feature of Windows Help.

3. **From the context menu, choose New➪Virtual Directory.**

   The New Virtual Directory Properties dialog box appears.

4. **In the General tab, type the name** pubs.

   You can access this new virtual directory later by using the following address:

   ```
   http://computername/pubs
   ```

   Replace *computername* with your computer's name, as displayed next to a computer icon in the IIS Virtual Directory Management for SQL Server dialog box. You need to use your computer's name later, so remember it or jot it down.

5. **Click the Browse button next to the Local Path box and locate** C:\Inetpub\Wwwroot\VirtualRoot. **(If you're using a different drive, replace** C **with that drive's letter.)**

   Note that if you're connecting to a physical directory on a separate computer, the Browse button isn't available. You must type the remote computer's VirtualRoot path.

6. **Click the Security tab, and then choose Use Windows Integrated Authentication.**

7. **Click the Data Source tab.**

8. **In the list of available databases, select pubs (see Figure 3-1).**

If no databases are listed, SQL Server isn't turned on or isn't actively running. (After SQL Server is installed, it turns itself on by default whenever you power up your computer.) Look in your Windows tray (which also holds your clock and Volume icon) and you should see an MSSQL Server icon. Right-click it and choose MSSQLServer — Start. Now you'll be able to click the ... button on the Data Source tab of the New Virtual Directory Properties dialog box to locate either SQL Server (which is the name of your computer) or the word (local). Then you can click the arrow icon in the same Data Source tab to drop down the list of available databases and locate pubs.

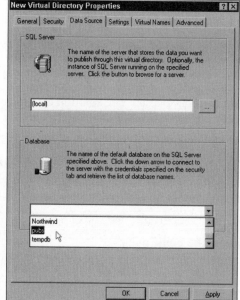

Figure 3-1:
Here's where you specify which database you want to connect to.

9. **Click OK to close the dialog box.**

If you see a message that says this virtual directory already exists, that's fine. You (or someone posing as you) has already made this connection.

You'll also want to have a connection to the Northwind database, another sample database. So repeat Steps 4 through 9 to create that new connection, but in Step 4 type **North** instead of pubs. And in Step 8, locate the Northwind database rather than the pubs database.

Using SqlDataAdapter

Finally! You can now get back to business. Specifically, in this section you see how to use VB .NET's data-related controls to access a data store and let the user work with the data.

Connecting to a database is fine, but you also want to get all or some of that data out of the database. And often you want to show that data to the user. In some cases, you'll let the user only read the information, not change it, such as when you display a product catalog. In other cases, you'll go so far as to let the user edit the database.

Most Visual Basic controls can be used to display data. Such controls are called data-aware, or data-bound, controls. You could use a Label or PictureBox for read-only data and a TextBox for data that the user can edit. You'd be surprised how many VB .NET controls can be bound to a data store. Any control that has a DataBindings property is data-aware. (The DataBindings property is the first property in the Properties window.)

In earlier versions of VB, only a handful of controls could bind to data. In VB .NET the only controls that *don't* bind to data are those (such as the Timer) that go on the tray below the form when you drop them from the Toolbox.

Your goal now is to connect a Visual Basic form to a database. The following examples illustrate the various steps you take to give a user access to a database, using VB .NET.

The first step in getting data to the user (at least in the following example) is to add an SqlDataAdapter control and an SqlConnection control to your project. A similar pair of controls work with OLEDB databases, but you focus on SQL Server, a popular and robust database technology well supported by Microsoft. The SqlDataAdapter control is Data Central — your main tool when dealing with ADO.NET data through controls rather than hand programming. With the SqlDataAdapter control, you can configure, generate, and preview the contents of a DataSet.

But enough promises, roll up your sleeves and begin:

1. **Start a new project in VB .NET (choose File⇨New⇨Project).**

   The New Project dialog box appears.

2. **Name this project** Connecting.

3. **Double-click the Windows Application icon.**

4. **In the VB .NET Toolbox, click the Data tab.**

5. **Double-click the SqlDataAdapter control, as shown in Figure 3-2.**

   The Data Adapter Configuration Wizard appears.

Figure 3-2:
You can
begin
creating a
connection
between
your
VB .NET
application
and a
database
with this
control.

6. **Click Next.**

7. **Click the New Connection button.**

   The DataLink Properties dialog box appears.

8. **On the Provider tab, choose Microsoft OLE DB Provider for SQL Server and then click Next.**

9. **On the Connection tab of the DataLink Properties dialog box, do the following:**

   a. **In item 1, select the your computer's name in the drop-down list titled Select or Enter a Server Name.**

   If you don't know the name of your computer, right-click My Computer (in Windows Explorer) and choose Properties. Then click the Network Identification tab in the System Properties dialog box. You'll see *Full computer name* followed by, guess what, your computer's name.

   b. **In item 2, choose Use Windows NT Integrated Security.**

   c. **In item 3, Select the Database on the Server, click the down-arrow icon and choose Northwind.**

   Northwind is now the database attached to the connection you're creating.

10. **Click the Test Connection button to reassure yourself that you're now connected to the sample SQL database named pubs.**

11. **Click OK to close the DataLink Properties dialog box, and then click Next in the DataSetCommand Configuration Wizard.**

12. **Choose Use SQL Statement and then click Next.**

13. **Click the Query Builder button.**

    This opens the useful Query Builder utility, as shown in Figure 3-3.

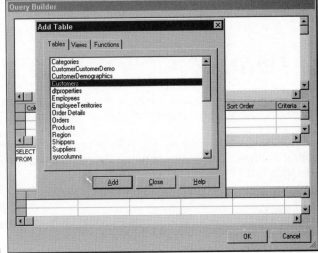

Figure 3-3:
Use the
Query
Builder to
construct
SQL queries
the easy
way.

SQL, Structured Query Language, is the most popular way to ask for a set of data from a data source such as a database. SQL is a fairly straightforward, English-like query language that allows you to request a DataSet comprised of, for example, all authors who live in New Jersey or New York. Questions (well, *queries*, if you want to be formal about it) like this are easily constructed in SQL. You spend a good bit of time working with SQL in Chapters 18 and 19.

14. **In the Add Table dialog box, double-click Customers.**

    That table is added to your query.

15. **Click Close.**

    The Add Table dialog box closes.

16. **In the top pane of Query Builder, choose CompanyName and ContactName.**

    Those columns are added to your query.

17. **Click OK, then Next, and then Finish.**

    Two icons are displayed under your main document window: SqlAdapter1 and SqlConnection1.

A number of VB .NET controls, such as the Timer and SqlConnection1, provide features but are never seen by the user when the program runs. Unlike a TextBox, which the user can interact with and view, a database connection control such as SqlDataAdapter1 isn't something the user directly interacts with. So, rather than put icons for these "invisible" controls on the design window's form, they are shown to the programmer in a separate window, or *tray,* below the design form window.

Seeing Your DataSet

The data controls have properties (actually, some of the properties pop up as wizards) that you might want to experiment with. For example:

1. **Click the SqlDataAdapter1 icon, and then press F4 to display the Properties window. At the bottom of the Properties window, click the Preview Data link.**

   Alternatively, you can right-click the SqlDataAdapter1 icon and choose Preview data.

   The Data Preview dialog box appears.

2. **Click the Fill DataSet button.**

   You see the two columns you selected for your query, plus the ID column (which is the *key column* and is always displayed).

3. **Click Close.**

Creating an SQL Query

Now you'll take a quick look at working with Query Builder. This tool makes it easy for you to create SQL queries. An SQL query specifies the data you want to extract from a database and put in a DataSet.

To build an SQL query, follow these steps:

1. **In the tray below the form, click the SqlDataAdapter1 icon to select it, and then press F4 to display the Properties window. At the bottom of the Properties window, click the Configure Data Adapter link.**

   Alternatively, you can right-click the SqlDataAdapter1 icon in the tray and then choose Configure Data Adapter.

2. **Click Next three times.**

   The SQL Generation page in the Data Adapter Configuration Wizard appears.

3. **Select the existing query, which is SELECT CompanyName, ContactName, CustomerID FROM Customers, and then press the Del key to delete the query.**

   This is the query you created in the preceding section.

4. **Click the Query Builder button.**

   Instead of working with the Customers table, you'll create a query that gets data from the Employees table.

5. **In the Add Table dialog box, click the Employees table and then click the Add button.**

   The Employees table is added to Query Builder.

6. **Click the Close button.**

   The Add Table dialog box closes.

7. **In the top pane of Query Builder, click LastName and FirstName.**

   Query Builder creates this SQL statement for you:

   ```
   SELECT      LastName, FirstName
   FROM        Employees
   ```

8. **Click OK to close Query Builder, and then click Finish to close the Wizard.**

To see the data that your SQL statement generates, follow these steps:

1. **Right-click the SqlDataAdapter1 icon and choose Preview data.**

   The Data Preview window appears.

2. **Click the Fill DataSet button.**

   You see the DataSet generated by the SQL statement you built.

3. **Close the Data Preview window.**

Creating a DataSet

Now it's time to generate a usable DataSet object and put it into your form's source code:

1. **Click the SqlDataAdapter1 icon, and then press F4 to display the Properties window. In that window, click the Generate DataSet link.**

   (Alternatively, you can right-click SqlDataAdapter1 and choose Generate DataSet.)

2. **Type** dsEmployees **as the name for your new DataSet class.**

   It's good practice to add *ds* (for DataSet) to the start of any DataSet name.

3. **Click the Add This DataSet to the Designer check box, and then click OK.**

   (Notice that VB .NET sometimes uses the term *designer* to refer to the design window or to the code window. Don't ask.) The new DataSet is added; you can tell by the new icon labeled dsEmployees1 in the tray.

4. **Double-click the title bar of Form1 to view the source code.**

5. **Click the + next to Windows Form Designer generated code.**

   You can see that quite a bit of source code has been added to your application — more than 170 lines. VB .NET has been a busy beaver creating the necessary programming to define your new DataSet class.

Binding Controls to a DataSet

Now it's time to make this new DataSet visible to the user. Big fun for us!

In general, *binding* means attaching a control to a DataSet or some other source of data. More specifically, *binding* causes a property (such as the Text property) to change the data it displays when the user moves to a different row in a DataSet. Binding keeps the data (or other property) synchronized between what the user sees and where the program is currently located in the data source.

For example, binding can keep a group of TextBoxes synchronized so that when the user clicks a button to move to the next row, all these TextBoxes display the new row's data automatically. Put another way, bound controls are governed by an object called `BindingContext`, which sits in the background and keeps track of which row is the "current" (visible, for example) row in a DataSet.

To bind controls to a particular column in a DataSet, you use the DataBindings property. Big surprise there.

To bind a TextBox's Text property to the DataSet you created in the preceding section, follow these steps:

1. **In the main window, click the Form1.vb [Design] tab.**

   The visual elements of the form are displayed.

2. **In the Toolbox, click the Windows Forms tab.**

   Using the Toolbox, you'll add three TextBoxes to Form1.

3. Click TextBox1, and then press F4.

TextBox1 is selected and its properties are displayed in the Properties window.

4. Click the + symbol next to the DataBindings collection.

If you click the Advanced button, you'll see that you can bind virtually all properties (as well as multiple properties). Here, however, you bind to just the Text property.

5. Under the DataBindings collection, click Text, and then click the down arrow next to Text.

A list appears, permitting you to specify the binding for the Text property.

6. In the drop-down list next to the Text property, click as many + icons as necessary to locate the data source's FirstName column.

7. Double-click FirstName (the word *FirstName,* not the icon).

The FirstName column is listed as the Text property in the DataBindings collection for TextBox1.

8. Repeat Steps 3 through 7 to assign LastName to TextBox2 and EmployeeID to TextBox3.

You have now bound your TextBoxes to the DataSet.

When you set a DataBindings property, VB .NET inserts code like the following in the `InitializeControl` section of your form's source code. (You can find the Bindings property definition in the code window right along with source code for the TextBoxes' other properties, such as Location and Size.)

```
Me.TextBox1.DataBindings.Add(New
        System.Windows.Forms.Binding("Text",
        Me.dsEmployees1, "Employees.FirstName"))
```

By the way, VB .NET refers to the currently active form or object as Me. If you want to change, say, the BackColor property of a form in code, you do this:

```
Me.BackColor = NewColor
```

Now, let's see the data from dsEmployees1 in the TextBoxes. Go to the code window, and type the following in the `Form_Load` event:

```
Private Sub Form1_Load(ByVal sender As System.Object, ByVal e
        As System.EventArgs) Handles MyBase.Load
        SqlDataAdapter1.Fill(dsEmployees1, "Employees")
End Sub
```

I promised that you'd have to type only one line of code to extract data from a database, generate a new DataSet, bind controls to that DataSet, and display the results. Promise kept.

The `Fill` method of an SqlDataAdapter object generates the DataSet's contents (fills the rows with information). The DataSet's structure — the table(s) and columns — is already defined in the SqlDataAdapter object and also in the DataSet object. The `Fill` method needs to know two arguments: `Fill(NameofDataSet, NameofTable)`, as illustrated in the example code.

Press F5. If all goes well, you see the first row of data displayed in the three TextBoxes, as shown in Figure 3-4.

Figure 3-4:
Congratulations!
Here's your
DataSet,
loaded and
visible.

Notice in Figure 3-4 that by default VB .NET selects the first TextBox's contents, assuming I guess that the user might want to start typing and replace the text. To get rid of that selection, add this to the `Form_Load` event:

```
TextBox1.SelectionLength = 0
```

Viewing a DataSet's Properties

To see or modify the properties of a DataSet, click its icon in the design window. (In the example, click the dsEmployees1 icon.) Then press F4 to display the Properties window. You'll immediately see some of the DataSet's properties (other properties are hidden from view until you click the DataSet Properties link at the bottom of the Properties window). In the main Properties window, note the difference between the Name property you use in code to identify the DataSet object — in this example, dsEmployees1 — versus the DataSetName property, which is the name of the cache — in this example, dsEmployees. (A *cache* is a location in RAM or on a hard drive where information is stored temporarily.) Unfortunately, as you'll see later in this book, sometimes you have to use *both* of these "name" properties in your code when referring to a DataSet. It's too bad that this type of confusing redundancy continues in computer languages.

Now notice the two links at the bottom of the Properties window: View Schema and DataSet Properties. Click View Schema (or right-click the DataSet's icon and choose View Schema). You'll see a diagram of your DataSet's structure. It shows columns (called *rows* in traditional database lingo and *elements* in the new XML lingo).You can see also the data types of each column and a key symbol next to any key (index) column, as shown in Figure 3-5.

Now it's time to see the underlying XML code (remember that DataSets are stored and transmitted over networks or the Internet in XML format). Click the XML tab at the bottom of the design window to see the XML code, as shown in Figure 3-6.

Now click the Form1.vb [Design] tab and then click the dsEmployees1 icon again. Click the DataSet Properties link at the bottom of the Properties window. You can see a variety of additional properties of this DataSet, as shown in Figure 3-7. Sometimes you can modify the tables or columns and their properties in this dialog box. In this case, however, the properties are all dimmed (gray), which means you can look but can't touch. This DataSet doesn't permit you to mess with its structure.

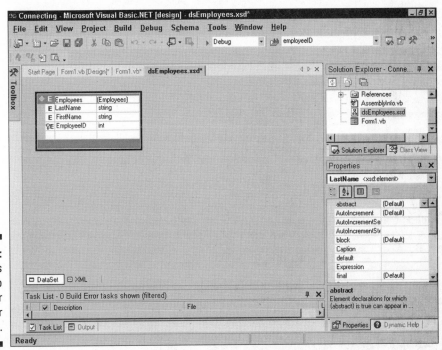

Figure 3-5: Use this feature to view your DataSet or its XML.

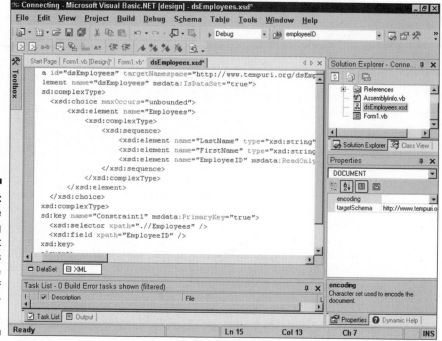

Figure 3-6:
The
underlying
XML that
describes
the
structure of
your
DataSet.

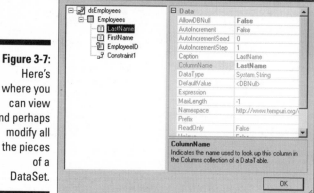

Figure 3-7:
Here's
where you
can view
and perhaps
modify all
the pieces
of a
DataSet.

Now that you have your feet wet and have explored how to connect to a database, specify a query, create a DataSet, and then bind a control to that DataSet, you're ready to move on to such topics as the new .NET DataForm Wizard and how to use a DataSet in an Internet-style application, or WebForm, rather than in this chapter's traditional WinForm.

One Final Trick

Some of you might be saying, "How would I ask VB .NET to display different rows in the three TextBoxes in the example?"

It's easy. Add a Button to your form, and type this in the Button's `Click` event:

```
Private Sub Button1_Click(ByVal sender As System.Object,
        ByVal e As System.EventArgs) Handles Button1.Click
    Me.BindingContext(DsProducts1, "products").Position()
        += 1
End Sub
```

Press F5, then repeatedly click the button to move up through the records. You come back to the `BindingContext` object in greater detail in Chapter 7. Curious about that +=? It's a new operator in VB .NET. It means the same as the boldface code in the following classic VB code:

```
Me.BindingContext(DsProducts1, "products").Position() =
        Me.BindingContext(DsProducts1,
        "products").Position() + 1
```

I'm sure you can see why having to repeat VB .NET's *looooong* object references to raise a property by 1 is, well, dreary. So you can avoid that second object reference by merely using `+= 1`.

Chapter 4

Exploring the Data Form Wizard and Other Assistants

● ●

In This Chapter

▶ Using the Data Form Wizard to create a DataGrid interface

▶ Modifying DataSets

▶ Using the Data Form Wizard to create a single-row interface

▶ Taking a look at some interesting code

▶ Working with stored procedures

▶ Employing the Enterprise Manager

▶ Understanding Server Explorer

● ●

*F*ew things in this life make a VB .NET database programmer's heart gladder than finding out about new productivity tools to make coding easier. This chapter focuses on several such wizards and utilities. When you know how to use the Data Form Wizard, Enterprise Manager, and Server Explorer, creating databases and connecting to existing databases is a snap.

Using the Data Form Wizard

In VB .NET, you can display data to the user in several ways. One of the best is to use the Data Form Wizard to add a *grid,* or alternative view, of a DataSet. You begin this chapter by seeing how to use this most excellent wizard.

I'm assuming that you've already followed the instructions in Chapter 3 to create an SQL Server connection to the pubs sample database. Such a connection lives outside your VB .NET projects, so the connection still exists even if you start a new VB .NET project.

To see what the Data Form Wizard can do for you, follow these steps:

1. **Choose File⇨New Project to create a new project in VB .NET.**

   The New Project dialog box appears.

2. **Name your new project** datWiz.

3. **Double-click the Windows Application icon.**

   VB .NET builds the default components of a WinForm project.

4. **Choose Project⇨Add New Item, and then double-click the Data Form Wizard icon.**

   The Wizard is displayed.

5. **Click Next.**

   You are asked which DataSet you want to use.

6. **Type** dsAuthors **as the name of your new DataSet, and then** click Next.

   You're asked to choose a connection to a database.

7. **Click the down-arrow button and select the *computername*.pubs.dbo connection.**

   Your computer's name will be listed as the first part of the pubs.dbo name.

8. **Click Next.**

   You're shown the tables in this database, as shown in Figure 4-1.

9. **Double-click the Authors table.**

   This table moves from the left pane to the Selected Item(s) pane on the right side.

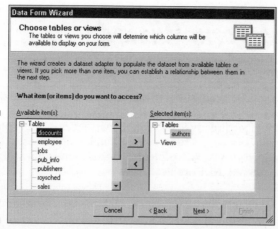

Figure 4-1:
Select
which
tables you
want to
access.

10. Click Next.

You can now specify which columns you want to display in the DataForm grid.

11. Leave all columns selected (the default) in the Authors table, and then click Next.

You're now asked which of the two types of Data Form Wizard displays you want to use, as shown in Figure 4-2.

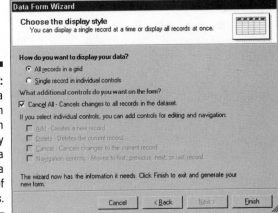

Figure 4-2: The Data Form Wizard can display either a grid or a series of TextBoxes.

12. Leave the All Records in a Grid option checked.

You'll now display multiple rows when this grid is displayed to a user.

13. Click Finish.

The Data Form Wizard closes.

You now see the DataForm, complete with a DataGrid control that already has all the column names from the Authors table filled in, as shown in Figure 4-3.

Locate the dsAuthors.XSD file in Solution Explorer. An additional file (currently hidden) also supports your DataSet. To see it, click the fourth icon on top of Solution Explorer to show all files. (The icon looks like a collection of files and folders.) By default, Solution Explorer hides some files. To see them, click the name of your project (the line in boldface in Solution Explorer) to reveal the icons in the Solution Explorer toolbar. Then click the Show All Files icon. Now click the + symbols in Solution Explorer to reveal the hidden files. Then click the + symbol next to dsAuthors.XSD, and there it is: dsAuthors.VB. Right-click dsAuthors.VB and choose View Code. You see a hair-raising chunk of 354 lines of code *you* didn't write: classes within classes, imported namespaces, overridden functions, and members without end. It's best to close this window and not tamper with it. VB .NET does lots of things for you behind the scenes. In cases like this, the less you know, the better. That's my advice.

Figure 4-3:
After a
DataSet
object has
been
created, a
DataGrid
bound to
that DataSet
displays
column
names (the
DataSet's
basic
structure).

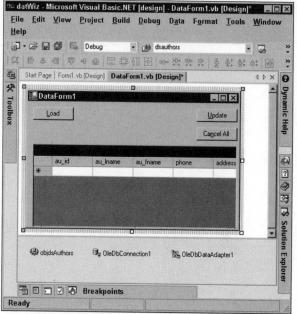

Before you press F5 to see the DataForm in action, you must make VB .NET display it. By default, Form1 is now the Startup object. This means only Form1 is automatically displayed when the project executes.

Displaying an alternate form

To display the DataForm, you can write some code for the Form1_Load event, like this:

```
Private Sub Form1_Load(ByVal sender As System.Object, ByVal e
        As System.EventArgs) Handles MyBase.Load

        Dim df As New DataForm1()
        df.Show()

End Sub
```

Setting the Startup object

Or, more in line with your wishes for this project, you can simply make DataForm1 the default Startup object. Follow these steps:

1. **Open the Solution Explorer window (press Ctrl+R).**

2. **Right-click datWiz (the name of this project) and choose Properties.**

   The dialog box shown in Figure 4-4 appears.

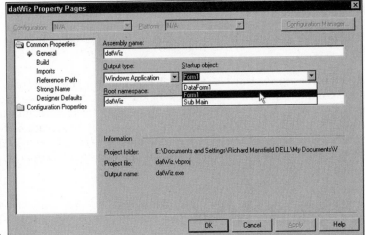

Figure 4-4:
Make the
DataForm
the startup
object here.

3. **Change the startup object to DataForm1, and then click OK.**

4. **Press F5, and then Click the Load button when the DataForm is displayed, as shown in Figure 4-5.**

Figure 4-5:
The
DataForm,
with its
DataGrid
filled with
your
DataSet.

If you're experimenting while learning VB .NET, it's sometimes useful to start with a blank slate — an empty form that has no leftover source code from a previous experiment. In this book, I tell you to start a new VB .NET project. However, you can save time by simply choosing Project⇨Add Windows Form (or other item), and then making that new form the Startup object. Then, when you press F5, the new form is displayed. Note that if you are working on an Internet-style VB .NET project (a WebForm), you can right-click the WebForm's name in Solution Explorer and set that form as the Startup object directly in the context menu — no need to open the dialog box shown in Figure 4-4.

As you can see in the tray below your design window, the Data Form Wizard added your dsAuthors DataSet automatically. However, the Wizard renamed it objdsAuthors from your original name, dsAuthors, for reasons only a wizard knows. Technically, dsAuthors is the *class* name, and objdsAuthors or dsAuthors1 or some other slightly modified name is the *object* that has been instantiated (brought into existence) from that class during program execution.

Modifying a DataSet

In addition to the Data Form Wizard, VB .NET offers another wizard you can use to modify or generate DataSet objects such as objdsAuthors. This wizard is known as the Data Adapter Configuration Wizard. When it creates a new DataSet object, it automatically renames the DataSet by appending 1 to the first DataSet's name, 2 to the second, and so on (like the default names when you add controls to a form).

In this section, you see how to modify a DataSet using the Data Adapter Configuration Wizard. You already have a DataSet object, so let's modify it to display a grid showing the results from a different SQL query.

1. **Click the DataForm1.vb [Design] tab at the top of the design window.**

   The DataForm is displayed.

2. **Right-click OleDbDataAdapter1 in the tray below the form and choose Configure Data Adapter.**

   The Data Adapter Configuration Wizard appears.

3. **Click Next three times.**

4. **Click the Query Builder button.**

   Query Builder opens and you see the existing SQL query specifying the current DataSet. The query asks for the authors table, and every column in that table is selected.

5. **Right-click the title bar of the authors table box in the top pane and choose Remove.**

   The authors table box is removed as well as the SQL query, leaving behind an empty query (SELECT nothing FROM nothing).

6. **Right-click the top pane and choose Add Table.**

   The Add Table dialog box appears.

7. **Double-click the Jobs table.**

   A box is created displaying the Jobs table in the top pane of Query Builder.

8. **Click the Close button.**

   The Add Table dialog box closes.

9. **In the Jobs box, click the All Columns option.**

   Now the SQL statement changes to the following:

   ```
   SELECT    jobs.*
   FROM      jobs
   ```

   This means, put all columns (*) in this table into the DataSet.

10. **Click OK to close Query Builder, and then click Next.**

    The Wizard generates various functions and mappings and performs other wizard-type activities behind the scenes.

11. **Click Finish.**

    The Wizard closes.

12. **Right-click the OleDbDataAdapter1 icon in the tray and choose Generate DataSet.**

    The DataSet is *regenerated*. The Jobs table is added to the existing Authors table in the DataSet object.

13. **To prove to yourself that a single DataSet can contain more than one table, right-click the objdsAuthors icon in the tray and choose View Schema.**

    The schema (structure) of the DataSet is displayed. Now two tables are in this DataSet, as shown in Figure 4-6.

    During design time, while you (or a wizard) are writing the programming for your DataSet, you specify the connection (the pubs database) and the structure (the tables and columns) of the DataSet. However, the data itself isn't loaded into the DataSet object until you run the program.

14. **Click the DataForm1.vb [Design] tab at the top of the design window.**

    The DataForm is displayed.

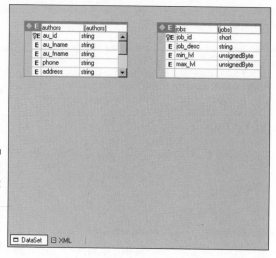

Figure 4-6:
A DataSet
can contain
more than a
single table.

15. **You now want to bind this DataGrid to the Jobs table, so click the DataGrid in the design window and press F4.**

    The Properties window opens, displaying the DataGrid's properties.

16. **Click the DataSource property, and then click the down arrow and select objdsAuthors.Jobs as the DataSource.**

    The headers in the DataGrid change to reflect the column names of the Jobs table.

17. **Press F5 to run the program, and then click the Load button on the form.**

    The DataGrid fills with this new set of data, as shown in Figure 4-7.

Figure 4-7:
Your
modified
DataGrid
displays its
contents.

	job_id	job_desc	min_lvl	max_lvl
▶	1	New Hire - Jo	10	10
	2	Chief Executi	200	250
	3	Business Op	175	225
	4	Chief Financi	175	250
	5	Publisher	150	250
	6	Managing Edi	140	225
	7	Marketing Ma	120	200
	8	Public Relatio	100	175
	9	Acquisitions	75	175
	10	Productions	75	165
	11	Operations M	75	150
	12	Editor	25	100
	13	Sales Repres	25	100
	14	Designer	25	100

DataForm1

Load   Update

Cancel All

The Single-Row DataForm Style

The Wizard constructed some interesting source code for the Load, Update, and Clear buttons, but you explore that in a future chapter. In this section, you turn your attention to the alternative DataForm style, the one that uses TextBoxes instead of a DataGrid. Follow these steps:

1. **Choose Project⇨Add New Item, and then double-click the Data Form Wizard icon.**

   The Wizard is displayed, and DataForm2 is added to your project. You're creating a new DataForm so that you can start with a clean slate and not worry about any code left over from the Wizard's activities in DataForm1.

2. **Click Next.**

   You are asked which DataSet you want to use.

3. **Click the Create a New DataSet Named option, type** dsEmployee **as the name of your new DataSet, and then click Next.**

   You're asked to choose a connection to a database.

4. **Click the down-arrow button, select the *computername*.pubs.dbo connection, and then click Next.**

   (Your computer's name will be listed as the first part of the pubs.dbo name.) The tables in this database appear.

5. **Double-click the Employee table.**

   The table moves from the left pane to the Selected Item(s) pane on the right.

6. **Click Next.**

   You can now specify the columns you want to display.

7. **Leave all columns selected (the default) in the Employee table, and then click Next.**

   You're now asked which of the two types of Data Form Wizard displays you want to use.

8. **Choose the Single Row in Individual Controls option.**

   You see a series of buttons that help the user maneuver through the DataSet.

9. **Leave all the checkboxes selected, and then click Finish.**

   The Data Form Wizard closes. The Wizard put a slew of controls on the form, as shown in Figure 4-8.

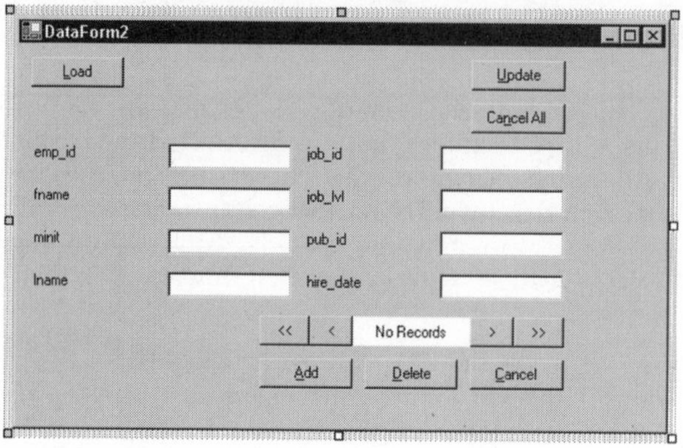

Figure 4-8:
The busy
Wizard has
put quite a
few controls
on this form
for you.

Next, make DataForm2 the Startup object:

1. **Right-click the project name (dataWiz) in Solution Explorer and choose Properties.**

   The Project Property Pages dialog box appears.

2. **Change the startup object to DataForm2, and then click OK.**

3. **Press F5 to see the results of the Wizard's labors.**

4. **Click the Load button.**

   The DataSet, and consequently the DataForm, are filled with rows of data, as shown in Figure 4-9.

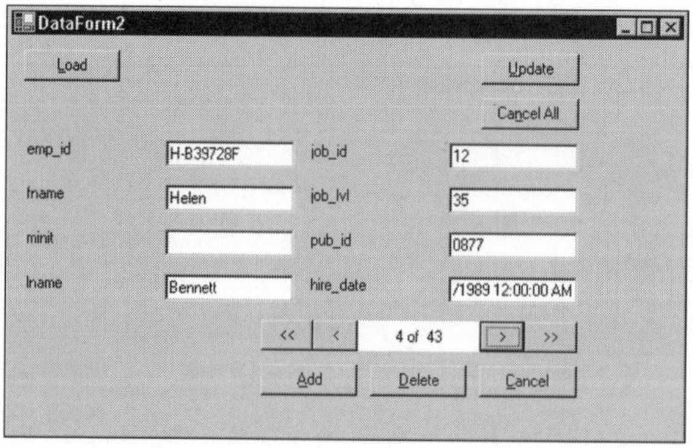

Figure 4-9:
The
alternative
DataForm
style
displays one
row of data
at a time.

A Brief Tour of Some Interesting Code

The Wizard has written interesting source code in this form as well as in DataForm1. Of special interest are the code that moves up and down through the rows, the code that displays the current row number and total rows in the DataSet, and the code that adds and deletes rows. All these topics, though, must await their turn and are covered in future chapters.

The Count property

Oh, well, who can resist? As a preview, here's the code that calculates the current row:

```
Me.BindingContext(objdsEmployee, "employee").Count.ToString
```

The key item here is the Count property of the `employee` table object. You look briefly at the sometimes useful `BindingContext` object in Chapter 3, and it comes up again in more detail in Chapter 7.

The ToString method

That `ToString` command? VB .NET is strict about data types. It doesn't like to treat numeric objects (such as the count property) as if they were text (string) data. The `ToString` method (which zillions of objects have at their disposal) casts, or changes, a numeric or other data type into a string that you can then assign to a Label or TextBox or otherwise use as a string.

So , just remember that if you ever get a `SystemInvalidCastException` error message when you're testing a project, you're attempting to cast one variable into a type it can't be changed into. *Exception* in VB .NET means *error*. But exception sounds nicer, doesn't it?

You can usually correct this kind of error by adding `.ToString` following the problem data, as in `Count.ToString`.

The Position property of the BindingContext object

The button on DataForm2 with the > symbol on it moves the user up one row in the DataSet. Here's a portion of the code you see when you double-click that button:

```
Me.BindingContext(objdsEmployee, "employee").Position =
        (Me.BindingContext(objdsEmployee,
        "employee").Position + 1)

Me.objdsEmployee_PositionChanged()
```

`Me` means the current form (DataForm2 in this example). The `BindingContext` object of this form contains a DataSet object named `objdsEmployee` that you're currently using. That DataSet object contains a table named `employee`. The `BindingContext` object maintains a Position property that specifies the current location . By *current location,* I mean which row: Is it row 3? Or the first row? The last row? Or what row? You can read or change the current position. Using the new += operator, you can simplify the preceding code so that you don't have to repeat the entire object definition:

```
Me.BindingContext(objdsEmployee, "employee").Position += 1
```

Deleting a row

The essential code to delete the current row follows:

```
Me.BindingContext(objdsEmployee,
        "employee").RemoveAt(Me.BindingContext(objdsEmploy
        ee, "employee").Position)
```

Another way to delete a row is to use the `Remove` method of a DataTable's Rows collection, like this (*dt* has previously been declared with the `Dim` command as a DataTable object in a DataSet):

```
dt.Rows.Remove(dt.Rows(CurrentRow))
```

But more on this in Chapter 9. This is just a taste of things to come.

Adding a row

The essential code to add a new row to the DataSet uses the `AddNew` method:

```
Me.BindingContext(objdsEmployee, "employee").AddNew()
```

If you want, continue on your own this tour of the source code that the Wizard has written under the Update, Cancel, Cancel All, MoveToLast (>>), and Load buttons. You need not understand it all right now. Taking introductory tours of wizard code is one of the best ways to begin to familiarize yourself with VB .NET database programming technique.

When you've finished touring the source code, check out the next section, where you see how to use the OleDbDataAdapter object to build a stored procedure.

Working with Stored Procedures

As I explain in detail in Chapters 18 and 19, you can use SQL to create *SQL queries*. These queries specify the types and ranges of data that you want to extract from a database. A database can contain also stored procedures, which are similar to SQL queries.

The difference between using an SQL statement (query) to generate a DataSet (as you did in the previous examples in this chapter) and using a stored procedure is that the latter is prewritten. It's *stored* (get it?) as part of the database and need only be invoked. By contrast, an SQL query is not part of the database but is applied to it from the outside — it's part of your application. Also, stored procedures can include more advanced programming (calculations, looping, and so on) than ordinary SQL queries.

One use of stored procedures is to prevent users from having total read access to your database. You can permit them to use several stored procedures (that you wrote and stored) to view or even edit *limited areas* in your database. Users aren't permitted to write their own stored procedures. Stored procedures can also ensure that data is updated in the database in a consistent and safe way.

Another primary difference between a stored procedure and an SQL statement in a typical VB .NET database project is that the stored procedure resides in the database, whereas an SQL statement resides in the object or application that contacts that database. This means if you find a stored procedure you can use, you don't have to write an SQL query in your application.

And because stored procedures are precompiled, they're faster than queries. Stored procedures can contain more than a single SQL statement, as well as flow control language (including branching commands such as IF-THEN). A stored procedure can also do the kind of job that a function would do in ordinary VB .NET source code, such as adding all outstanding debts listed in the database and returning the total. If you want to get fancy, you can even trigger one stored procedure from another.

Creating a stored procedure

To build a stored procedure, follow these steps:

1. **Click the DataForm2.vb [Design] tab at the top of the design window.**

   The DataForm that you used in the preceding example is displayed.

2. **Right-click OleDbDataAdapter1 in the tray below the form and choose Configure Data Adapter.**

   The Data Adapter Configuration Wizard appears.

3. **Click Next twice.**

   You can now choose the query type.

4. **Click the Create New Stored Procedures option, and then click Next.**

   You see the query that you defined using Query Builder in the preceding example. If you don't see it displayed in the Wizard, type the following SQL query in the TextBox labeled What Data Should the Data Adapter Load into the DataSet?

   ```
   SELECT emp_id, fname, minit, lname, job_id, job_lvl,
          pub_id, hire_date FROM employee
   ```

5. **Click Next.**

   You see the page displayed in Figure 4-10. You can rename the procedures or choose not to add them to the existing database.

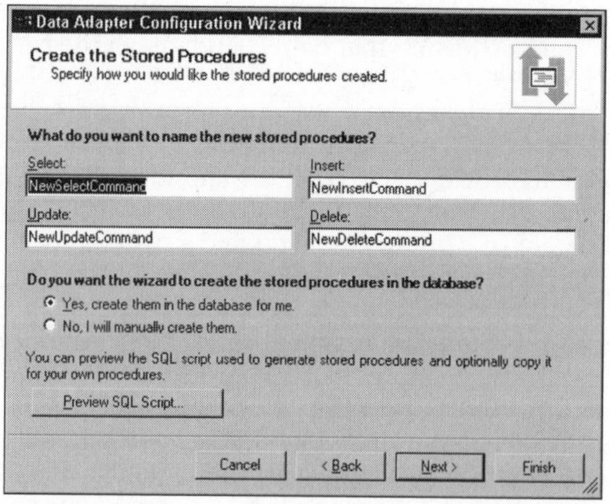

Figure 4-10: Here are the four stored procedures that the Wizard will create for you.

6. Click the Preview SQL Script button to see (or modify) the code that generates these procedures.

(Some experts use the word *script* to describe what you write in a programming language that isn't quite as sophisticated as a true language, where you write *code*. Script languages, such as VBScript, are used for specialized programming and also often tend to be a subset of a larger language.)

You see the following code, or script, if you prefer to call it that. This is just the portion of the code that defines NewInsertCommand:

```
IF EXISTS (SELECT * FROM sysobjects WHERE name =
        'NewInsertCommand' AND user_name(uid) = 'dbo')
        DROP PROCEDURE dbo.NewInsertCommand;
GO

CREATE PROCEDURE dbo.NewInsertCommand
(
        @emp_id nvarchar(50),
        @fname varchar(20),
        @minit char(1),
        @lname varchar(30),
        @job_id smallint,
        @job_lvl tinyint,
        @pub_id char(4),
        @hire_date datetime,
        @Select_emp_id nvarchar(50)
)
AS
        SET NOCOUNT OFF;
INSERT INTO employee(emp_id, fname, minit, lname, job_id,
        job_lvl, pub_id, hire_date) VALUES (@emp_id,
        @fname, @minit, @lname, @job_id, @job_lvl,
        @pub_id, @hire_date);
        SELECT emp_id, fname, minit, lname, job_id,
        job_lvl, pub_id, hire_date FROM employee WHERE
        (emp_id = @Select_emp_id);
GO
```

7. Click Close, and then click Next.

The Preview SQL Script window closes, and the Wizard tells you that it will now save your work to the DataSetCommand control.

8. Click Finish.

The Wizard closes.

In the component tray below the design window, click the OleDbDataAdapter1 icon and then press F4 to display the Properties window. Note that your four new procedures have now become part of the Properties window. Expand the InsertCommand procedure by clicking the small + next to its name. You see that procedure's properties.

Now click Parameters (Collection) located under InsertCommand in the Properties window, and then click the ellipsis (...) so you can see the OleDbParameter Collection Editor, as shown in Figure 4-11. Don't touch! You're just browsing. Click OK to close the Editor.

Figure 4-11: This is where you can edit the properties of your procedure's contents.

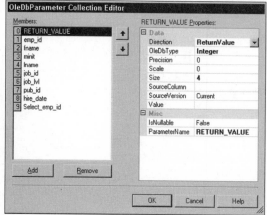

You can see your new stored procedures in the pubs database. Open Server Explorer in VB .NET (press Ctrl+Alt+S), and then drill down the tree of items under Data Connections. Look in *computername*.pubs.dbo, Stored Procedures. The four new stored procedures should be there.

Using Enterprise Manager

If you want to get deeply into stored procedures, explore the Enterprise Manager tool. Locate it by choosing Start⇨Programs⇨Microsoft SQL Server⇨Enterprise Manager. After opening Enterprise Manager, drill down in the tree in the left pane until you see the pubs database, as shown in Figure 4-12.

Explore the many tools available in Enterprise Manager, so you'll know where to go when you want to accomplish a particular job in the future. Don't forget to right-click various locations (the right pane, left pane, and names of objects) to see lists of tools in the various context menus.

For example, right-click Databases in the left pane and choose New Database. You'll find a tool there that permits you to do what its name promises.

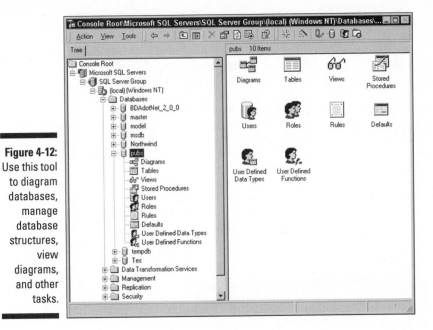

Figure 4-12:
Use this tool
to diagram
databases,
manage
database
structures,
view
diagrams,
and other
tasks.

Then, to create a new table in the pubs database, for instance, right-click Tables (under pubs) in the left pane and choose New Table. You see the dialog box shown in Figure 4-13.

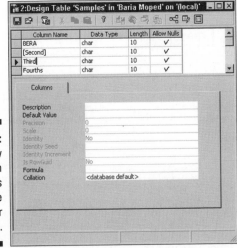

Figure 4-13:
Design new
tables with
this
Enterprise
Manager
tool.

Some tools in Enterprise Manager operate eccentrically — or at least they sometimes don't conform to customary Windows behaviors. For example, the Design Table dialog box permits you to add new columns to your table by pressing the Enter key, although it doesn't by default display all the columns you've thus entered. Repeatedly pressing Enter moves you through the four primary fields and then moves you down to the next row where you can specify a new column. This response to the Enter key is typical of the way data-entry applications work: The typist's hands never have to leave the keyboard. Nonetheless, you should know that you can drag the top pane (the pane with the scrollbars) to increase its size so that you see the various columns you've defined, as shown in Figure 4-13.

If you want to create a stored procedure and then test it, right-click Stored Procedures (under pubs) and choose New Stored Procedure. You see the tool shown in Figure 4-14. You can write your new procedure, and then click the Check Syntax button to see whether there are any errors in your SQL code.

Figure 4-14:
Create and
test new
stored
procedures
here.

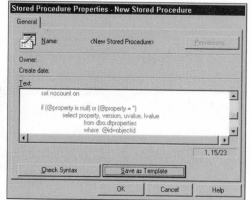

Some of the tools offered by Enterprise Manager are available also in the VB .NET Server Explorer window by right-clicking various objects in that window: Create a New Database, Add Table, and so on. Server Explorer is covered in the next section.

An in-depth explanation of how to use the many tools available in Enterprise Manager is beyond the scope of this book. However, here are the primary jobs it can assist you with:

- Create or modify SQL Server databases, tables, columns, keys, and relationships

- Diagram databases

- Create and test SQL scripts (for stored procedures) using the New Stored Procedure dialog box

✔ Take advantage of the several SQL Server wizards

✔ Modify SQL Server options, including permissions, logins, user groups, and other security features

✔ Register new servers and define server groups

Working with Server Explorer

Server Explorer, which is new in Visual Studio .NET, contains information about all available servers and their contents. (These days, databases almost always reside on servers so that more than one person can easily access the database.)

You can use Server Explorer to connect to servers, view what the servers contain, create database connections for your current project, drag and drop procedures or tables onto your forms, and otherwise manage a client-server relationship between your project and a server or servers.

Displaying Server Explorer

Server Explorer is available any time you're working in the VB .NET IDE. To see how Server Explorer works, follow these steps:

1. **Choose File⇨New Project.**

2. **Name your new project** SE.

3. **Double-click the Windows Application icon.**

   Your new project opens in the Visual Studio .NET IDE (Integrated Design Environment — the editor you work with while creating VB .NET programs).

4. **Choose View⇨Server Explorer.**

   Server Explorer appears, as shown in Figure 4-15.

If you want to keep Server Explorer readily available to a project, right-click the Server Explorer's toolbar and choose Auto Hide. Now Server Explorer appears as a tab on the left side of the design window whenever you're not working with it. Just click the tab to revive it. I use Auto Hide for almost all frequently used VB .NET tools (Properties window, Output window, TaskList, Toolbox, and so on).

Figure 4-15:
Server
Explorer is a
new and
valuable
tool for VB
.NET.

Adding or removing servers

When you first open Server Explorer, you see any database connections you've defined, as well as any servers (or databases) you've made available to your computer. If you want, you can specify which items are displayed in Server Explorer.

Notice that Server Explorer has two primary categories: Data Connections and Servers. Right-click Data Connections to see an option named Add Connection. If you select Add Connection, the DataLink Properties dialog box appears.

If you use your computer as a client/server simulation, you'll want to name your computer as a server in Server Explorer (using the Connection tab of the DataLink Properties dialog box). The process is described in detail in the "Using SqlDataAdapter" section in Chapter 3). If you don't know the name of your computer, go to the Windows desktop, right-click the My Computer icon and choose Properties. Now click the Network Identification tab. There's your computer name, identified as *full computer name*. To remove a data connection or server, you right-click it in Server Explorer and choose Delete. *Don't panic!* This *doesn't* delete the database or server. It merely breaks the connection between your machine and that server. You can always define a new connection.

Visual Basic 6 included a Data View feature that you could use to view or modify the structure (tables and stored procedures) of a database. Right-click any table and the Table Designer utility appeared, all ready for your manipulations. Server Explorer offers capabilities similar to the old Data View but also goes beyond the limitations of Data View. For example, instead of looking at a single database, Server Explorer opens up a view of potentially many servers — along with all the databases that reside on them, as long as they're running on SQL Server.

If you right-click Servers in Server Explorer, you see the Add Server option. If you select this option, the Add Server dialog box appears. You can either type the name of your computer (or an address of a computer on a local network or the Internet) or click the Search for a Computer on the Network option.

All available SQL-Server-based databases appear in the Servers category on Server Explorer, and you need not create a connection to that database to see it. However, if you do create a connection to that database so that you can reference it in your programming (as described in Chapter 3 in "Connecting to a Database"), the database will appear also in the Data Connections category in Server Explorer. Databases that are not SQL-Server-based and that run on other platforms (such as UNIX) require that you specify a connection.

Data connections listed in Server Explorer are named by combining the server name with the database name. Server Explorer also lists any Web services available on your servers.

Chapter 5

A Collection of Connections

*B*y itself, a database file is merely an orderly collection of information. It's usually not an executable program that can, by itself, do anything. (Although you can create programs called stored procedures and put them in a database, along with the data.) For the most part, you need a database engine that can look at a request — such as "get me a list of the last names of all employees" — and then go to the database and extract that information for you. Think of a database as the books and a database engine as a smart research librarian.

A database engine manages a database and has direct access to the data it contains. When you think about working with databases, a primary question is: What type of database engine should I use? Jet? Oracle? Access? SQL Server? This chapter describes the uses of the Jet engine and then goes into other data engines as well.

Microsoft doesn't plan to revise or expand Jet, so the current version of the Jet engine (get it?) is doomed to be the last. At least, that's the plan. (Sometimes, Microsoft doesn't follow the plan, so you'll have to wait and see.) However, Microsoft will support it indefinitely. Why? Because Access and, to a lesser extent, Visual Basic, have used Jet for years, and vast numbers of users, developers, and programmers depend on it for small-scale, local database applications.

In spite of Jet's popularity, Microsoft has — correctly in my view — decided to move on to more robust database applications, specifically SQL Server. Because VB .NET focuses on the technologies in SQL Server, and because those technologies are increasingly valuable in Internet programming in particular, this chapter (and indeed the entire book) primarily covers SQL Server techniques. However, near the end of this chapter, you see how to work with a Jet database. If you are interested in Jet and the language and technologies supporting it, see the previous edition of this book, *Visual Basic 6 Database Programming For Dummies,* which focuses on Jet.

The Little Engine That Could

The Jet engine acts essentially like a high-level language (such as Basic itself). You provide Jet with a command, such as MoveNext, and it takes care of the low-level details necessary for performing the command, such as moving to the next record in the database.

Jet might be your engine of choice for several reasons:

- ✔ Jet is a solid, established technology.
- ✔ Jet has been the world's most popular database engine for several years.
- ✔ Jet works with Visual Basic and Access.
- ✔ Jet comes free with VB .NET so you don't have to pay anything extra for it.
- ✔ Jet is designed to be highly efficient with desktop and smaller intranet database applications.

Although Excel is not a real database, people use it like one, and it was until recently the most popular "database manager" around. Many people used Excel not as a spreadsheet but as a way of storing and organizing data. Access was number two in popularity.

However, for large-scale database applications and for Internet database programming, consider SQL Server or Oracle. Jet works great unless you go beyond, say, 600 records in a given table or DataSet or beyond approximately four or five users. Past that point, you're likely to run into some performance degradation and user-traffic problems. Beyond ten users, Jet is brought down. If you need a powerhouse, you should abandon Jet and move up to a client/server solution such as SQL Server (which comes with the Enterprise edition of Visual Basic 6 and is likely to be available with the advanced version of Visual Studio .NET). Some databases with 100,000 plus records have been reported to run smoothly under Jet, but don't push it by allowing more than a few users simultaneously. Multiuser traffic is not Jet's strong point.

Given that .NET, and much contemporary programming, is designed to work on the Internet, you must consider the issue of *scalability* (the capability to grow or shrink, as demand requires). One prominent aspect of scalability is the capability to go from handling a few users to many users suddenly. If your Web site succeeds, you could go rapidly from a few visitors to hundreds, thousands . . . why, the sky's the limit!

All about data sources

A little history is in order. In Visual Basic 5 and earlier versions, you had to put a data control on a form and then connect the data control to a database. Then, you would *bind*, or connect, other controls — such as a text box — to the data control.

In Visual Basic 6, you got a bit more flexibility. You could create a data source and bind any data-aware control directly to the data source, bypassing a data control entirely. You could even create a set of data sources, which could be in special data link files on the hard drive or reside in the Registry. A data source is not a control; instead, it is a description of a connection to a database. There was also a detachable recordset, but it had limited functionality.

Finally, in VB .NET, you can extract a table, or several tables, or a result of an SQL query and manipulate this extraction (or send it to someone), independent of the database from which it comes. This extracted packet of data, called a DataSet, is translated into XML (a plain-text, HTML-style file format). This approach avoids the twin bugaboos of managing databases for use with Internet sites: security and scalability. You can send XML packets past firewalls just as easily as you can send ordinary HTML (which firewalls are designed to ignore). And, although XML is considered a verbose language (it can be highly repetitive with all its recurring tags, nested elements, and other descriptive text), it is far less of a download hit than sending a big library of functions along with a whole table of data.

Should you even consider using a Jet-based database system when creating Internet programs? Jet *does* support multiple users, but each request is handled by the client computer making the request. Nothing on the server executes requests or returns the data that those requests want. All visitors to your Web site would have to run a Jet-based engine to access data from your site.

Technically, if your application uses a Jet database, users need not have Access installed on their hard drives. Instead, you can bundle the Jet libraries in a Visual Basic application, so people who use your database program have everything they need. But, the problem — for Internet sites anyway — is twofold. First, how many of those flighty Web surfers, flitting here and there like hummingbirds, are willing to sit and wait while the entire Jet library downloads, just so they can view the items in your company's catalog or place an order? Second, many people have set up their browser's security settings or installed a firewall to block incoming executable programs. A virus and a set of functions (the Jet library) are essentially indistinguishable to a firewall, so it would block them both.

With a client/server database engine, you have something called a *back end*. (No rude comments, please.) A back end simply means that programming resides on the server to provide security features, manage multiple users, and retrieve and temporarily store data. *That's* the approach you need to use, along with detachable DataSets that can be sent as HTML to get past firewalls and other security systems on the user's machine). Another important virtue of detachable DataSets is that the database on your server isn't required to maintain simultaneous connections for each of the thousands of Web surfers who might be reading your database's information at once. Detaching your catalog and uploading it to these surfers obviously greatly improves the efficiency of your Web site.

Good old Jet, though, can work well in restricted environments such as relatively small intranets. To understand a bit more about what the Jet connection means to a VB database programmer, consider Jet in relation to Access. Access is a Microsoft application — part of the Microsoft Office suite of applications. Access is a standalone database manager that works with relational databases. Access uses both the Jet engine and, among others, the Data Access Objects (DAO) technology.

DAO is a library of objects that stands between Access or some other database manager application and the Jet engine, providing relatively high-level communication between the application and the down-and-dirty, low-level behaviors of the Jet engine itself.

The Main Connections

In this section, you look at one of today's premier database technologies: SQL Server. (At the end of this chapter, however, you see how to get connected to a Jet-based database.)

VB .NET gives you several ways to connect to a database:

- ✔ Using connection controls
- ✔ Using a DataSet command
- ✔ Using Server Explorer

Each approach has its uses. In this chapter, I show you examples of the connection controls and Server Explorer. (Chapter 4 describes the DataSetCommand and the DataForm control, which offer a somewhat different approach to creating a data source.)

Using a connection control

You can drop two connection controls into a VB .NET project: the OleDbConnection and SqlConnection controls. All data-related controls work with either a WinForm (Windows-style) or WebForm (Internet-style) VB .NET program. In the examples, you work with WinForms.

To see how to use the connection controls, follow these steps:

1. **Choose File⇨New ⇨ Project**

   The VB New Project dialog box appears.

2. **Double-click the Windows Application icon.**

   A standard VB project is started.

3. **Click the Data tab in the Toolbox.**

   The data controls appear.

4. **In the toolbox, double-click the OleDbConnection icon.**

   OleDbConnection1 is added to your project; you can see it in the component tray.

5. **Right-click the OleDbConnection1 icon and choose Properties.**

   The Properties window appears, displaying the properties of OleDbConnection.

6. **Click the down arrow next to the ConnectionString property in the Properties window.**

   A list appears, as shown in Figure 5-1.

Figure 5-1:
Choose an existing connection or create a new connection.

7. **Click <New Connection>.**

   The Data Link Properties dialog box for the data control appears.

8. **Click the Use Windows NT Integrated Security option.**

   Because you're focusing on creating a data connection, you won't go through any special security steps here.

9. **Click the down arrow next to Select or Enter a Server Name, and select your computer's name in the list.**

10. **Click Select the Database on the Server, as shown in Figure 5-2.**

11. **Click pubs (or some other database listed on your machine).**

Data Link Properties

Provider Connection Advanced All

Specify the following to connect to SQL Server data:

1. Select or enter a server name:

DELL ▼ Refresh

2. Enter information to log on to the server:

◉ Use Windows NT Integrated security
○ Use a specific user name and password:
User name:
Password:
☐ Blank password ☐ Allow saving password

3. ◉ Select the database on the server:

master
model
msdb
Northwind
pubs
tempdb

○

Test Connection

OK Cancel Help

Figure 5-2:
Here you can choose among existing databases on the server.

12. **Click the Test Connection button.**

A message box displays Test Connection Succeeded.

13. **Click OK to close the dialog box and the Data Link Properties window.**

You now have a connection string that defines a link between your project and a database. The connection string — which this Wizard just wrote for you — looks something like this in your source code window. (You can see it also in the Properties window, next to ConnectionString.)

```
Provider=SQLOLEDB.1;Integrated Security=SSPI;Persist Security
        Info=False;Initial Catalog=pubs;Data
        Source=DELL;Use Procedure for Prepare=1;Auto
        Translate=True;Packet Size=4096;Workstation
        ID=DELL;Use Encryption for Data=False;Tag with
        column collation when possible=False
```

Aren't you glad you didn't have to write that code yourself? As platform-independent, self-describing, firewall-jumping, distributed programming becomes increasingly important, source code becomes increasingly verbose.

You can also use the SqlConnection control on the toolbox in the same way to create a similar connection string.

You can build a connection string directly to a database file. Locate a file with an .MDF (SQL Server) extension on your hard drive or server, and then follow the steps in the preceding example, except when you get to Step 10, click Using the Filename. Then type the path to your .MDF file or click the ... (ellipsis) button to browse your hard drive for the .MDF file. (This option is hidden by the drop-down list in Figure 5-2.)

Using Server Explorer

The new Server Explorer allows you to generate connections and even includes a drag-and-drop facility. To see how Server Explorer works as a connection source, start a new Windows Application project as described in the preceding example. Then follow these steps:

1. **Choose View⇨Server Explorer.**

   Server Explorer contains two primary sections: Data Connections and Servers. You can use elements in either of these categories to generate a connection between your project and a data source.

2. **Click the + next to Data Connections to open that section. Look for a pubs.dbo connection, as shown in Figure 5-3.**

Figure 5-3: You can use any of these existing connections in your project.

3. **Locate and open a Tables listing underneath the** pubs **database. Then open the authors table.**

   You can see all the columns in each table and all the tables in each data connection. In other words, Server Explorer displays the entire structure of a data connection.

4. **Drag the *computername*.pubs.dbo connection from Server Explorer and drop it on the VB .NET form.**

   Substitute the name of your computer for *computername*. A connection name is made up of your computer's name plus the name you gave this connection when you defined it in Chapter 3 plus *.dbo*.

An SqlConnection1 object is added to the component tray. In the Properties window for the SqlConnection1 object, the following connection string has been generated for you automatically:

```
initial catalog=pubs;integrated security=SSPI;persist
        security info=False;workstation id=DELL;packet
        size=4096
```

You can also find a list of databases under the Servers category in Server Explorer (look for the SQL Servers entry and click the + to open that node).

Dragging and dropping tables, views, or stored procedures from Server Explorer works the same way as described for the Data Connections area inside Server Explorer.

Accessing Jet Databases

So far in this chapter, I've assumed that you've created connections to SQL databases because you specified Microsoft OLE DB Provider for SQL Server as described in Chapter 3. You can, however, choose various other database types.

To see how to access other database types, follow these steps:

1. **Choose Tools⇨Connect To Database.**

   The familiar Data Link Properties dialog box appears.

2. **Click the Provider tab.**

3. **Click the Microsoft Jet 4.0 OLE DB Provider entry, and then click Next.**

   You see the Connection tab (shown in Figure 5-4). However, this Connection tab page differs from the Connection tab page displayed when you were working with SQL Server 2000 previously in this chapter. Notice that you can browse your hard drive or server for an .MDB database. In the samples that come with Visual Studio .NET, you should find several .MDB files, including a version of pubs.MDB as well as the grocertogo database.

4. **Browse your hard drive to select an .MDB filename, and then click OK to close the Data Link Properties dialog box.**

   You should now see your new database connection in Server Explorer, as shown in Figure 5-5.

5. **Drag one of the tables from your new Jet database connection in Server Explorer and drop it into a VB .NET form.**

   If you're using the grocertogo sample database, drag and drop the Products table.

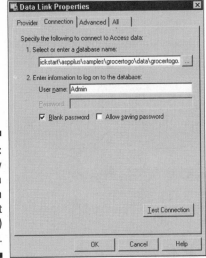

Figure 5-4:
Here's how
you create a
connection
to a Jet
(.MDB)
database.

Figure 5-5:
Your new
connection
is now
available in
Server
Explorer.

Be patient. You continue this example in the next section.

Seeing Some Data

After following the steps in the preceding section, you'll see an
OleDbConnection1 object and an OleDbDataAdapter1 object on the tray
beneath your form. Now it's time to view the data available from your new
connection:

1. **In the design window, right-click the *background* of Form1 and
   choose Generate DataSet. (Alternatively, you can choose Data⟳
   Generate DataSet.)**

2. **Click the New option in the Generate DataSet dialog box, and then click OK.**

   The dialog box closes and a new DataSet1 icon appears in the tray.

3. **Right-click the form again and choose Preview Data.**

   The Data Adapter Preview dialog box appears.

4. **Click the Fill DataSet button.**

   You should see a grid fill with records, as shown in Figure 5-6.

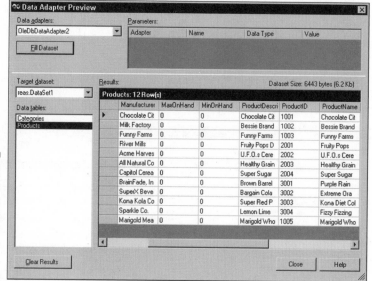

Figure 5-6:
You can see the data in a data source in this Preview window.

Creating Data Connections in Control Panel

If you've been reading along from the beginning of this chapter, you're probably thinking that I've covered all possible ways to create a database connection, aren't you? Well, you have one more way: You can create data connections (and manage existing ones) from the Control Panel! Let's see how to start the ODBC Manager from Control Panel.

In Windows 95 and 98, you'll see an icon named ODBC(32bit); in NT 4, it's named ODBC Data Sources; and in other machines, it's named 32bit ODBC. In Windows 2000, the icon is called Data Sources (ODBC) — hey, why try for consistency when renaming elements in each new OS is such fun? Also, in Windows 2000, the icon has been moved to the Administrative Tools folder in Control Panel, so it's hidden from view unless you open that folder. Just to keep us all guessing, this renaming did *not* take place in Windows XP. The icon bears the same name and is located in the same place as in Windows 2000. It just goes to show that you never know *what's* going to happen. Working with computers is Big Fun.

Whatever it's called and wherever it's found, the icon opens an organizer for data connections. To use this feature in Windows 2000 or Windows XP, follow these steps:

1. **Choose Start**⇨**Settings**⇨**Control Panel.**

2. **Double-click the Administrative Tools folder.**

3. **Double-click the Data Sources (ODBC) icon.**

    The ODBC Data Source Administrator dialog box appears, as shown in Figure 5-7.

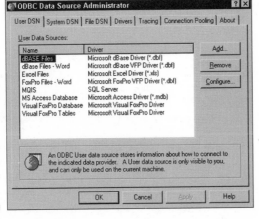

Figure 5-7: Use this utility to manage connections to various database types.

4. **Click the first three tabs in turn: User DSN, System DSN, and File DSN.**

(DSN stands for Data Source Name.) You see each type of data connection listed in separate pages in the Administrator.

Each of the first three tabs includes Add, Remove, and Configure buttons. The Add button displays a Create New Datasource Wizard that allows you to specify a driver for your connection. The Configure button gives you quite a bit of latitude in managing and defining an existing connection (various wizards appear, depending on which connection you want to manipulate). The Remove button is self-explanatory.

The Drivers tab lists all the database engines registered on your computer. The Tracing tab features tools to assist you in debugging. You can create a log file of calls to ODBC functions and then look at that file to see how one of your database connections is working with those functions. The Connection Pooling tab enables you to specify that a particular database engine can use existing handles, to save time. You can also request performance monitoring on this tab. Finally, the About tab lists the primary ODBC dynamic link libraries.

Part III
Contacting the User

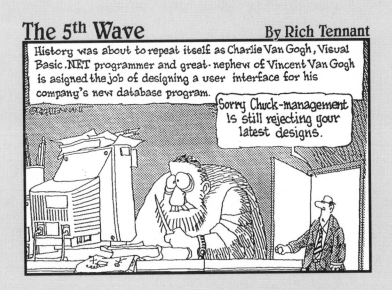

The 5th Wave   By Rich Tennant

History was about to repeat itself as Charlie Van Gogh, Visual Basic .NET programmer and great-nephew of Vincent Van Gogh is asigned the job of designing a user interface for his company's new database program.

Sorry Chuck-management is still rejecting your latest designs.

In this part . . .

If you need to make databases work for other people, you want to know how to design effective, friendly user interfaces. Your database needs to be filled with data, so you have to provide bulletproof ways for users to enter data. And after the database is filled with data, you often have to generate reports, displaying subsets of the data in an organized, easily understood manner.

The chapters in Part III show you how to get good data into your databases and how to get good data out of them. Always remember the programmer's axiom: What goes in must come out.

Chapter 6

Simple ASP.NET Data Binding and Web Controls

ASP.NET is the technology you use to write VB. NET code that resides in a server. Your server communicates with visitors to your Web site. ASP.NET enables you to connect to data in a variety of ways and send an HTML page back to the visitor's browser, which then displays that data.

Part V goes into greater detail about ASP.NET, but you get your first taste of it in this chapter. ASP.NET is as important a technology as VB .NET in some ways. ASP.NET *uses* VB .NET to write programming that works on the Internet. (And we all know how important *that* kind of programming is becoming.)

So, as the Nova Scotians say, put on your gum boots and let's go explorin'.

First, you write server code that you can run and test in the Internet Explorer browser. This testing process will imitate a Web page on the Internet (the server ASP.NET code) responding to a user visiting that page (the browser). By going back and forth between these two entities, you can successfully reproduce the intercourse between a Web server and people contacting that server over the Internet. In many cases when programming an Internet Web page, you'll be adding data to the Web page (server-side) and displaying that data to the visitor (browser-side). The chapter concludes with an overview of Web server controls.

Creating Your First WebForm

In Chapter 3, you install a virtual directory using the IIS Virtual Directory Management for SQL Server utility. Now it's time to put one of these virtual directories to work. The directory will *pose* as a server that handles visitors contacting your "Web site" from somewhere out there on the Internet. (If you have not yet created these directories, do so now by turning to Chapter 3 and following the instructions there.)

In this example, you see how easy it is to test an ASP.NET application written to deal with Internet traffic. You get to test it in the good, old VB way: Just press F5 and the page that the visitor to your Web site sees is displayed in all its glory in Internet Explorer (IE).

If you press F5 and test a WebForm page in the VB .NET IDE by clicking a button on the Web page, for example, the results of that click are sent from IE to the server (the virtual directory that you create in Chapter 3).

During the testing process, if you click a button in the browser and the results arrive at the virtual server inside your machine, your ASP.NET code (in the "server") composes an HTML response, and the response is sent back to IE for you to see. As you can see, Internet Explorer poses as a browser somewhere on the Internet that "visits" your virtual server.

The process of testing ASP.NET code is all smooth and easy to do when you press F5 to test a WebForm in VB .NET. The process mimics Internet communications, for example between a guy in Oregon surfing the Web and visiting a Web site server located in England. This little VB .NET virtual server is also known as the *local host*.

Anyway, if you've got your gum boots on now, follow these steps:

1. **Start VB .NET and choose File➪New➪Project.**

2. **Double-click the ASP.NET Web Application icon.**

   VB .NET tells you that it's creating a new Web, as shown in Figure 6-1.

   After VS .NET creates the WebForm and its support files, you see a message in the design window informing you that you are currently in *grid layout mode*. In other words, any controls you add to this page will be located exactly where you put them (like on a traditional Windows form). You can drag the controls around anywhere on the page. You are told that you can use flow layout instead, if you want. Flow layout mode is the lame way that traditional HTML positions everything against the left side of the page. To switch to that mode, you would change the document's PageLayout property to FlowLayout (but why would you do that?).

   For now, stick with the default grid layout mode, which gives you the freedom to put anything anywhere on the page.

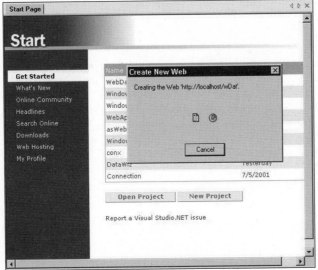

3. **You should now be viewing the design window. Click the HTML button (on the bottom of the main document window) to get to the HTML code window.**

   A WebForm (a Web application's equivalent to the traditional VB form) uses *two* types of code in two separate code windows: HTML code (which you're looking at now) and a VB-like code window (which you explore later).

4. **Erase all the default code that VB .NET put in the HTML code window.**

   You're experimenting now with data-related, hand-coded programming, so you'll build the entire HTML code yourself.

5. **Type the following into the (now-blank) HTML code window:**

```
<html>
   <head>
   <script language="VB" runat="server">
       Sub Page_Load(sender As Object, e As EventArgs)
           Page.DataBind
       End Sub

       ReadOnly Property CountryName() As String
           Get
               Return "Canada"
           End Get
       End Property

       ReadOnly Property Population() As Integer
           Get
               Return 12000000
           End Get
```

```
        End Property

        ReadOnly Property Languages() As Integer
            Get
                Return 3
            End Get
        End Property

    </script>
    </head>
    <body>

    <form runat="server" ID="Form1">
        Country: <b>
            <%# CountryName %>
        </b>
        <br>
        Pop.: <b>
            <%# Population %>
            <br>
        </b>Number of Spoken Languages:
        <b>
            <%# languages %>
        </b>
    </form>

    </body>
</html>
```

6. Press F5 to test this program.

Internet Explorer displays this result:

```
Country: Canada
Pop.: 12000000
Number of Spoken Languages: 3
```

This example illustrates that you can create properties within your HTML code and then later use the `<%# PropertyName %>` code to read and display the data in a property. The `runat="server"` command announces that this code will be executed at the server in the Web site's computer, not in the computer (the browser) of the visitor to this Web site.

If you have experience creating classes in VB .NET, you'll recognize the classic syntax for creating a property:

```
ReadOnly Property Population() As Integer
    Get
        Return 12000000
    End Get
End Property
```

Note that the property names are not case sensitive (both *Languages* and later *languages* refer to the same property). Finally, note what happens when this page first loads after you press F5:

```
Page.DataBind
```

You can use the `DataBind` method to bind not only to traditional data sources (such as a database), but also to simple properties (as illustrated in this example), controls' properties, expressions, collections, or the results of methods.

The data is not evaluated (`<%# CountryName %>` replaced with `Canada`) until the Page's `DataBind` method is executed, which occurs in this case in the `Page_Load` event. Many ASP.NET server controls also have their own DataBind property. As you see next, however, the binding need not take place immediately when the page loads.

Notice that ASP.NET data being bound must use the `<%# %>` punctuation to indicate where the data will appear.

Binding to get data from a control

The next example illustrates how you can use the `DataBind` method in locations other than the `Page_Load` event. You also see how data can be extracted from a control. Delete everything in the HTML code window and then type this:

```
<html>
    <script language="VB" runat="server">

    Sub Button1_Click(sender As Object, e As EventArgs)
              Page.DataBind
    End Sub

</script>
<body>
  <form runat="server">
    <asp:DropDownList id="TheirChoice" runat="server">
       <asp:ListItem>Bach</asp:ListItem>
       <asp:ListItem>Beethoven</asp:ListItem>
       <asp:ListItem>Sam Johnson</asp:ListItem>
    </asp:DropDownList>
    <asp:button Text="Click Me" OnClick="Button1_Click"
       runat="server" />
    You chose
    <asp:label text='<%# TheirChoice.SelectedItem.Text
       %>' runat="server" />
  </form>
</body>
</html>
```

The primary line of code to notice here is this one:

```
<asp:label text='<%# TheirChoice.SelectedItem.Text %>'
           runat="server" />
```

This data is bound from the selection the user makes in the ListBox. But the actual binding doesn't take place until the user clicks the button. Press F5 to try it. You'll see results like those shown in Figure 6-2.

Figure 6-2:
The black rectangle at the bottom of the browser window is your clue that info has been sent on a round trip from the browser to the server and back.

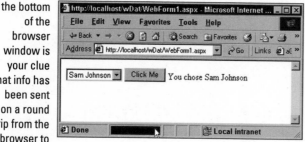

When you click the button labeled Click Me (shown in Figure 6-2), information about the currently selected item in the ListBox is sent back to the server. The server binds the data, finding out which item is currently in the `SelectedItem` property of the ListBox and then displaying it in the Label. All this is then translated into an HTML page that is sent back to the visitor's browser.

Binding to an ArrayList

The following example illustrates how you can bind to a collection or an array of data. You can create a hardwired array with the VB .NET `ArrayList` structure, like this:

```
Dim MyArray as new ArrayList

myArray.Add ("one")
myArray.Add ("two")
myArray.Add ("three")
```

This holds the data inside your Visual Basic program. (Because the programmer writes this data, it's embedded in the .exe file. That means it can't change, which is why the data is said to be *hardwired* into the program.)

This approach is good for lists that are short and do not change. (Because the data is hardwired in your programming, changing that data would require that the program itself be modified in the source code and then recompiled.) But often there is no real advantage to using this technique. Why create an ArrayList when you can just use the Add method of a ListBox's Items collection instead, like this:

```
listbox1.items.Add("one")
listbox1.items.Add("two")
```

Using this type of programming, you don't need an ArrayList at all. However, as you'll soon see, you'll want to bind data. And the ArrayList example illustrates how this can be accomplished. You can use the DataBind method to fill a ListBox in one quick command, as illustrated in the following example. Delete everything in the HTML code window and then type this code:

```
<html>
    <script language="vb" runat="server">
    Sub Page_Load(Sender as Object, E as Eventargs)

Dim MyArray as new ArrayList

myArray.Add ("Red")
myArray.Add ("Green")
myArray.Add ("Blue")
myArray.Add ("Brown")
myArray.Add ("Puce")

ListBox1.DataSource = MyArray
ListBox1.DataBind()

end Sub

    </script>
    <body>
      <form id="WebForm1" method="post" runat="server">
        <asp:ListBox id="ListBox1" runat="server" Width="145"
            Height="200"></asp:ListBox>
      </form>
    </body>
</html>
```

When you run this example, the ListBox becomes filled with the contents of the ArrayList, thanks to the DataBind property of the ListBox. Recall that many ASP.NET server controls also have their own DataBind property.

Binding to the Results of an Evaluated Expression

The next example illustrates how you can execute a function and then bind that function's results to an object. In this case, you fill a list with answers to the question, "Is the word longer than four letters?"

Delete everything in the HTML window and then type the following:

```
<html>
  <head>
  <script language="VB" runat="server">

    Sub Page_Load(sender As Object, e As EventArgs)

      Dim MyWords as ArrayList= new ArrayList()

        MyWords.Add ("abacus")
        MyWords.Add ("worm")
        MyWords.Add ("cat")
        MyWords.Add ("catfish")
        MyWords.Add ("fishbait")
        MyWords.Add ("free")

        DataList1.DataSource = MyWords
        DataList1.DataBind

    End Sub

    Function WordSize(passedword As String) As String
        If (len(passedword)> 4) Then
          Return "longer than 4 letters"
        Else
          Return "shorter than, or equal to, 4"
        End If
    End Function

  </script>
  </head>
  <body>
    <form runat="server" ID="Form1">
      <asp:DataList id="DataList1" runat="server"
        BorderWidth="2" BorderColor="red" CellPadding="4"
        CellSpacing="0">
        <ItemTemplate>
          The word "<%# Container.DataItem %>" is
                <%# WordSize(Container.DataItem) %>
        </ItemTemplate>
      </asp:DataList>
    </form>
  </body>
</html>
```

An `ArrayList` named `MyWords` is built. It contains a group of words of varying lengths that will be tested in the `WordSize` function. When this page is loaded, `ArrayList` is filled and the following code binds data into `DataList`:

```
DataList1.DataSource = MyWords
DataList1.DataBind
```

As each word is bound, it is first displayed in an ordinary sentence in the data list (notice how you can add quotation marks around a string):

```
The word "<%# Container.DataItem %>" is
```

The real action happens in the following, as the `WordSize` function evaluates each word and places the results in the data list:

```
<%# WordSize(Container.DataItem) %>
```

Binding in WinForms

Don't make the mistake of thinking that data binding works only in WebForms. It's a useful technique in WinForms (traditional Windows applications) as well. The next two examples prove this point. However, to save time, I'm going to recommend something unique in this book: *don't try these next two examples*. They merely provide a contrast with the WebForm data binding examples earlier in this chapter. So just read the source code and don't bother going to the trouble of shutting down the current WebForm project in VB .NET and starting up a WinForm-style project to test these next two examples. You'll go back to the WebForm quickly in the section titled "Understanding Server Controls."

Binding to a WinForm ComboBox

To get an idea of some of the differences between binding data in a WinForm and a WebForm, consider how you can add data to a ComboBox. When binding a data source in a WinForm, you can use the DataSource property, like this:

```
Private Sub Form1_Load(ByVal sender As System.Object, ByVal e
            As System.EventArgs) Handles MyBase.Load

    Dim MyArray As New ArrayList()

    MyArray.Add("abacus")
    MyArray.Add("worm")
```

```
    MyArray.Add("cat")
    MyArray.Add("catfish")

    ComboBox1.DataSource = MyArray

End Sub
```

If you put a ComboBox control on a WinForm (Windows-style form), you can bind data to it quite easily by setting its DataSource property, as this example illustrates.

Adding properties in a WinForm

You can't actually use the DataBind method with a Windows form, in the way that you use Page.DataBind to bind a Web page (WebForm). For example, if you want to insert a property's value into a ComboBox, you would use the ComboBox's Add method:

```
ReadOnly Property CountryName() As String
    Get
        Return "Canada"
    End Get
End Property


Private Sub Form1_Load(ByVal sender As System.Object, ByVal e
        As System.EventArgs) Handles MyBase.Load

ComboBox1.Items.Add(CountryName)

End Sub
```

These are code snippets — short illustrative pieces of source code. The Property definition, for example, would be located within a class. For a comparison and to understand the Property procedure, see the "Creating Your First WebForm" section earlier in this chapter.

Understanding Server Controls

You've used several server-side controls in this chapter. In this section, you take a closer look at the various types of controls you can use when you're working in a VB .NET WebForm.

The HTML controls are traditional elements that have been available for years to the HTML programmer. Here's an example demonstrating how three of these classic Internet-style controls work:

1. Choose Project ➪ Add Web Form.

You see the Add New Item dialog box.

2. Double-click the Web Form icon in the dialog box.

A new WebForm is added to your project.

3. In the Toolbox, click the HTML tab.

4. Double-click the Submit Button, Table, and CheckBox controls to add them to your WebForm.

The order in which the definitions for these controls appear in the HTML code depend on the order in which you add the controls to your WebForm.

5. Click the HTML tab at the bottom of the code window.

You see the HTML code that VB .NET has added to create your Web page and the three controls you placed on it:

```
<%@ Page Language="vb">
<!DOCTYPE HTML PUBLIC "-//W3C//DTD HTML 4.0
        Transitional//EN">
<HTML>
<HEAD>
    <title></title>
    <meta name="GENERATOR" content="Microsoft Visual
        Studio.NET 7.0">
    <meta name="CODE_LANGUAGE" content="Visual Basic
        7.0">
    <meta name="vs_defaultClientScript"
        content="JavaScript">
    <meta name="vs_targetSchema"
        content="http://schemas.microsoft.com/intel-
        lisense/ie5">
</HEAD>

<body MS_POSITIONING="GridLayout">

<form id="Form1" method="post" runat="server">

<INPUT style="Z-INDEX: 101; LEFT: 27px; POSITION:
        absolute; TOP: 136px" type="submit"
        value="Submit">

<TABLE style="Z-INDEX: 103; LEFT: 24px; WIDTH: 300px;
        POSITION: absolute; TOP: 24px; HEIGHT: 75px"
        cellSpacing="1" cellPadding="1" width="300"
        border="1">
    <TR>
        <TD style="HEIGHT: 29px">
        </TD>
        <TD style="HEIGHT: 29px">
        </TD>
        <TD style="HEIGHT: 29px">
```

```
                    </TD>
                </TR>
                <TR>
                    <TD>
                    </TD>
                    <TD>
                    </TD>
                    <TD>
                    </TD>
                </TR>
                <TR>
                    <TD>
                    </TD>
                    <TD>
                    </TD>
                    <TD>
                    </TD>
                </TR>
            </TABLE>

            <INPUT style="Z-INDEX: 102; LEFT: 35px; WIDTH: 20px;
                    POSITION: absolute; TOP: 193px; HEIGHT: 20px"
                    type="checkbox">

        </form>
    </body>
</HTML>
```

6. Press F5 to see the results in Internet Explorer.

You can discover several things from this code. The mystery stuff at the top, such as DHTML 4.0 Transitional and Intellisense and *especially* that stuff about Java, are just notes that VB .NET and ASP.NET make to themselves about how to handle this WebForm. You can ignore these notes. Just don't modify any of that code.

However, do consider this line:

```
<body MS_POSITIONING="GridLayout">
```

With this, you can position the controls anywhere on the WebForm. Each control will have a TOP and LEFT attribute, defining its location on the Web page. This specification is in pixels (px, picture elements) by default. Also, each control has a POSITION attribute defining it as *absolute*. The alternative PageLayout property in VB .NET is FlowLayout, where controls are positioned relative to each other on the WebForm (and end up flush left by default).

If you change the document's PageLayout property to FlowLayout, and then again examine the HTML code, you will find that VB .NET strips the MS_POSITIONING attribute and leaves the code much simpler (it's actually classic HTML code), like this:

```
<body>
  <P>
    <INPUT type="submit" value="Submit">
  </P>
  <P>
    <INPUT type="checkbox">
  </P>
  <P>
     
  </P>
  <P>
    <TABLE cellSpacing="1" cellPadding="1" width="300"
           border="1">
    <TR>
  </P>
</body>
</HTML>
```

The TR and TD elements for the table are the same in both PageLayout styles, so I won't repeat them. But notice how much simpler the HTML code is when you use the traditional HTML flow layout style. Simpler, though, isn't necessarily better — from the point of view of both the programmer and the user. You'll likely find that positioning controls is easier, and certainly more flexible, if you stick with the default grid layout.

You'll find that selecting or moving the HTML Table control is difficult. To select it, drag the mouse outside its perimeter. The control displays handles (small squares), indicating that you can delete it, copy it, change its properties, or otherwise manipulate it in the design window. To move the control, position the mouse pointer on top of the table. You see a small, strange, cross icon — an icon never seen before in VB. Drag this icon to reposition the table, as shown in Figure 6-3.

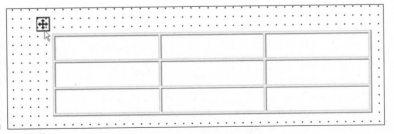

Figure 6-3:
The drag handle for an HTML table control.

If you click the HTML tab, you can then get to the HTML code window and modify the HTML. But, as computer languages go, HTML is crude and simple (some argue that it's not a computer language at all).

Instead, you probably want to use the code-behind technique, which is more familiar to VB programmers. Follow these steps:

1. **Click the Design tab.**

2. **Double-click the Submit button.**

   A message tells you that to write server-based code for this element (the button), it must be converted to a server control.

3. **Click OK.**

4. **Right-click the Submit button and choose Run as Server Control.**

   A small, green triangle is added to the Submit button's icon (see Figure 6-4).

Figure 6-4:
The small arrow icon on top of the button icon indicates that this is a server-side HTML control.

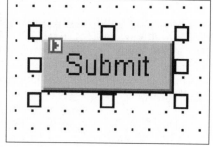

VB .NET changed the Submit button's HTML code from this:

```
<INPUT style="Z-INDEX: 101; LEFT: 27px; POSITION: absolute;
       TOP: 136px" type="submit" value="Submit">
```

to this:

```
<INPUT style="Z-INDEX: 101; LEFT: 21px; POSITION: absolute;
       TOP: 112px" type="submit" value="Submit"
       id="Submit1" name="Submit1" runat="server">
```

Note the three attributes that were added. The runat attribute is a directive to ASP.NET that this element should be manipulated in the server, not the browser. The id provides a way to identify this control if you need to refer to it in your HTML code.

However, in addition to the id element, there is also the name element. Where is it used? ASP.NET provides *a second, different window of source code* in addition to the HTML code you see when you click the HTML tab at the bottom of the design window. This second window holds VB .NET source code that can be used *with this same WebForm*. The VB source code is called *code behind*.

To see the VB code-behind window, follow these steps:

1. **Click the Design tab.**

2. **Right-click the Submit button and choose Run as Server Control.**

3. **Double-click the Submit button.**

   A new WebForm1.aspx.vb code window opens, showing you the code behind this WebForm page.

The name element allows you to change the control's properties, invoke its methods, or create an event for it. In other words, you can work with the control in the code-behind VB source code file just as if you were working with the control as a traditional VB .NET control, as opposed to an HTML control. I have much more to say about code-behind ASP.NET programming in Part V.

Now follow these steps:

1. **Click the Design tab, and then double-click the Submit button again.**

   This time you're taken to the code-behind window (the code window displaying the contents of the .ASPX.VB file for this WebForm). This should remind you of a traditional VB programming code window:

```
Public Class WebForm1
    Inherits System.Web.UI.Page

Protected WithEvents Submit1 As
        System.Web.UI.HtmlControls.HtmlInputButton


    Private Sub Page_Load(ByVal sender As System.Object,
        ByVal e As System.EventArgs) Handles MyBase.Load
        'Put user code to initialize the page here
    End Sub

    Private Sub Submit1_ServerClick(ByVal sender As
        System.Object, ByVal e As System.EventArgs)
        Handles Submit1.ServerClick

    End Sub
End Class
```

You have a WebForm class declaration, containing an HTMLInputButton declaration. Then you have Page_Load and Submit1_ServerClick procedures — events to handle a page and a button object's events, respectively. Note that your HTML Table and CheckBox controls are conspicuously absent from this source code page. They have not been converted into server-side controls.

2. **In the** `ServerClick` **event, type the following:**

```
Private Sub Submit1_ServerClick(ByVal sender As
        System.Object, ByVal e As System.EventArgs)
        Handles Submit1.ServerClick

        Response.Write("Clicked indeed.")

End Sub
```

Recall that you can't use a MsgBox when running inside a browser. So typically, you assign a text response to a label or a textbox or simply write it right there on the background of the WebForm with `Response.Write` (`Response.Write` can be useful particularly during debugging.)

3. **Press F5. When the browser appears, click the Submit button.**

Clicked indeed appears on the WebForm.

4. **Click the WebForm1.aspx tab at the top of the code window, and then click the HTML tab at the bottom of the window.**

Notice this line at the top of the code, highlighted in yellow:

```
<%@ Page Language="vb" AutoEventWireup="false"
        Codebehind="WebForm1.aspx.vb"
        Inherits="WebApplication6.WebForm1"%>
```

This tells you which file in the Solution Explorer contains the code-behind source code.

5. **Right-click this WebForm1.aspx file in Solution Explorer and then choose View Code.**

The Style Builder Dialog Box

You'll want to know about an interesting Style Builder dialog box that is not widely advertised but can come in handy. Here's how to get it up and running.

Click the WebForm1.aspx tab at the top of the design window, and then click the Design tab at the bottom of the design window. Right-click the Submit button on your Web Form (left over from the preceding example) and chose Build Style. (Normally, you would expect this option to say Properties, but the Properties option simply displays the Properties window, as if you'd pressed F4.)

The Build Style option displays up a properties dialog box, as shown in Figure 6-5.

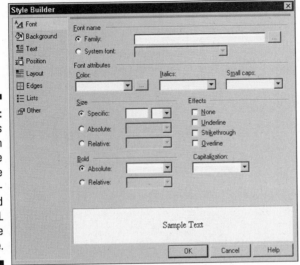

Figure 6-5:
Changes
you make in
this Style
Builder are
automatic-
ally added
to the HTML
source
code.

Choose a nice baby blue color and change the font to Arial. Look at the HTML code window and you'll see that VB .NET has added some HTML code:

```
<INPUT id="Submit1" style="Z-INDEX: 101; LEFT: 21px; COLOR:
    #3399ff; FONT-FAMILY: Arial; POSITION: absolute;
    TOP: 112px" type="submit" value="Submit Button"
    name="Submit1" runat="server">
```

The Style Builder is a good way to modify the look of HTML controls. However, this dialog box doesn't work with VB's WebForm controls. You modify those the classic way: using the Properties window.

Chapter 7

Designing a User Interface

. . . .

In This Chapter

▶ Using classic components

▶ Adding Textboxes to a form

▶ Binding multiple controls

▶ Moving through rows

▶ Using the DataGrid

▶ Using CheckBoxes, Labels, and ListBoxes

▶ Working with specialized, data-aware controls

. . . .

Creating a user interface ranks as one of the more important jobs that any computer programmer or developer undertakes. The interface should make it easy for a user to view and, sometimes, change information.

Don't neglect the important job of designing the user interface. Having those controls sitting there on the VB Toolbox, right next to that naked, vulnerable form, is just too tempting for many programmers. Instead of thinking through the user interface and making practical decisions, they just start populating the form with whatever components they think they need and position them merely where they look good. Good design is a science and an art that is all-too-often ignored.

The tools the user sees on-screen should be, as much as possible, self-explanatory and easy to use. To that end, Microsoft has created dozens of user-interface tools called *controls,* or *components*. Microsoft's user-interface experts have carefully thought out these predesigned objects, such as the TextBox and the DataGrid, constructing them with familiar tools such as scrollbars and buttons that open list boxes so that the user can easily see how they work and what they do.

This chapter focuses on the components most useful for database work. Some components that you can drop into your Visual Basic projects have been around for years; others are brand-new in VB .NET.

Using the Classic Components

Visual Basic's classic components are the controls that old hands at VB have seen for years: Labels, TextBoxes, ListBoxes and the like. In VB 6, of the 20 classic VB components, 7 were *data-aware* — capable of being linked to a data control or a DataSet. The data-aware classic controls were

- TextBox
- Label
- CheckBox
- PictureBox
- Image
- ComboBox
- ListBox

Recall that in VB .NET, these controls are all data-aware (the Image control has been dropped from the language), but so are *all other* visible controls, even the Scrollbar and Button (formerly CommandButton), which are seemingly unrelated to database interfaces.

Nonetheless, in VB .NET, you'll find that all visible controls have a DataBindings collection (found at the very top of the Properties window), which means they can be bound to a data source. Controls with no visible surface, such as Timers, are the exception. They have no DataBindings collection.

Technically, DataBindings is a collection (not a property) because there can be several properties and objects contained under the name DataBindings. However, call it a property if you want — Microsoft isn't consistent about categories such as *property* and *object*. For example, several properties are contained under the name Font, but Font is still considered a property, not a collection. My advice is to relax and not ask for too much consistency in computer language grammar and diction. You'll be disappointed.

All the properties of each control can be bound to the data source — not just the obvious properties such as Text, but also bizarre ones (at least bizarre in the context of data binding) such as BorderStyle! This is a bit mind-boggling, but it could be of use. It means that you can take charge of the control's appearance and some of its behavior from data in a data source, such as a database or a DataSet. This raises some interesting possibilities.

Attaching a Data-Aware Control

The TextBox is one of the VB workhorses. It's a mini word processor, enabling users to view or edit text. In Chapter 3, you see how to attach a TextBox to a database by setting the properties within the TextBox's DataBindings collection to point to a DataSet. Then you point to a specific column in a table in that database to bind to the TextBox's Text property.

You begin this chapter by finding out how to bind multiple controls (three TextBoxes) at the same time and how to move through the DataSet.

To try the following examples, you should have already followed the instructions in Chapter 3 to create an SQL Server connection to the Pubs sample database. Such connections live outside your VB .NET projects, so the connection still exists even if you start a new VB .NET project.

To attach a TextBox to a DataSet, follow these steps:

1. **Create a new project in VB.NET by choosing File⇨New ⇨ Project.**

   The New Project dialog box appears.

2. **Name your new project whatever you want.**

3. **Double-click the Windows Application icon.**

   VB .NET builds the default components of a WinForm project.

4. **Open VB .NET Server Explorer.**

5. **Click + next to Servers, click + next to SQL Servers, and then click + next to your computer's name.**

   You see a list of the SQL Server connections.

6. **Click + next to the Pubs database.**

   You see the tables in the Pubs database.

7. **Drag the Jobs table from Server Explorer and drop it onto your VB .NET form.**

   VB .NET adds an SqlConnection1 control and an SqlDataAdapter1 control to your tray.

8. **Right-click the SqlDataAdapter1 control in the tray and choose Configure Data Adapter.**

   The Data Adapter Configuration Wizard appears.

9. **Click Next.**

10. **Choose the Pubs.dbo connection, and then click Next.**

11. **Choose the Use SQL Statements option, and then click Next. Click Next again.**

    You are offered a textbox where you can type in an SQL query. Because you already selected the Jobs table by dropping it on your form, you will likely see that table and all of its columns already defined in Query Builder.

12. **If the Jobs table and its columns are already defined in Query Builder, skip to Step 18. If not, continue with the next step.**

13. **Click the Query Builder button.**

14. **In the Add Table dialog box, double-click Jobs.**

    The Jobs table is added to the Query Builder window.

    If you don't see the Add Table dialog box, right-click the background of Query Builder and choose Add Table.

15. **Click Close.**

    The Add Table dialog box closes

16. **In the Jobs window in Query Builder, click All Columns.**

    You've chosen to use all the columns in this table. The correct SQL statement is displayed for this choice:

    ```
    SELECT    jobs.*
    FROM      jobs
    ```

17. **Click OK to close Query Builder.**

18. **Click Next.**

    The Wizard generates several methods for you, including the important Insert, Update, and Delete methods.

19. **Click Finish.**

    The SqlDataAdapter1 is now configured and ready to create a DataSet object based on the SQL statement you created (or rather, the statement you helped Query Builder create).

Creating a Jobs DataSet

Now it's time create a DataSet to hold the data you can display to the user in your TextBoxes. To create your DataSet, follow these steps:

1. **Right-click the SqlDataAdapter1 icon and choose Generate Dataset.**

   The Generate DataSet Class dialog box appears.

2. **Name your new dataset dsJobs.**

3. **Choose the Add This DataSet to the Designer option.**

   You want to add a DataSet named `dsJobs1` to this project. You'll bind your TextBoxes to `dsJobs1` so you can display various columns of data (one column per TextBox) to the user.

4. **Click OK**

   The `DsJobs1` DataSet object appears in your tray.

You're now ready to create the user interface so people can view (and edit if you permit them to) the data in your DataSet.

Binding multiple controls and properties to a DataSet

Here's one way to attach, or *bind,* VB .NET controls to a DataSet. Recall that some controls (such as the DataGrid) have their own wizard. When you add one of those controls to a form, the wizard pops up, takes over, and does the binding for you by asking you to fill in some information.

This example, however, shows you how to bind by hand. And it works for any control that you want to display data in. To see how to bind controls and their properties to a data source, follow these steps:

1. **Add three TextBoxes to your form, as shown in Figure 7-1.**

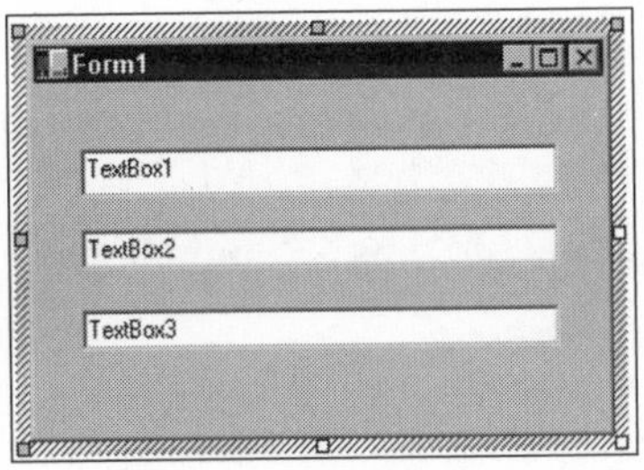

Figure 7-1:
Each TextBox will display a different column from the database.

2. **Click TextBox1 and then press F4 to display the Properties window.**

3. **Click the small + next to the DataBindings collection (it's at the very top of the Properties window).**

   The DataBindings collection expands. Notice that for a TextBox, VB.NET assumes you probably want to bind data to the Text property. That's sensible. You deal with the Advanced option shortly.

4. Click the down-arrow button next to the Text property.

A list displays all the data sources currently in your project. In this case, the only data source is your DataSet, dsJobs1.

5. Click the + next to Jobs to expand it.

You see all the available columns in the Jobs table, as shown in Figure 7-2.

6. Double-click jobs.job_desc.

The job description column is attached to TextBox1.

It took me a while to realize that I had to click the words *jobs.job_desc* rather than the icon to its left in the Properties window. By the time the book goes to print, perhaps this will be corrected and you can click either the icon or the words (which is typical Windows behavior).

7. Click TextBox2 to select it and repeat Steps 5 through 7, but this time choose jobs.min_lvl.

The minimum annual salary level is attached to TextBox2.

8. Click TextBox3 to select it and repeat Steps 5-7, but choose jobs.max_lvl.

The maximum annual salary level is attached to TextBox3.

At this point, you might think you're finished and ready to press F5 to test your bindings. Not so fast! There's one more little job. You have to tell this program to fill the DataSet when the program runs. The three controls on the tray already know what table and columns in that table you want. In fact, a DataSet schema (structure) is already in place in the DataSet object (DsJobs1) on the tray.

Recall that the DsJobs1 object already contains the structure, the empty categories. The actual data is pulled out of the database and poured into those empty categories when the program runs. You must write some new code in the Form_Load event:

1. **Double-click the form in the Design window to get to the code window.**

   To fill the DataSet object with the data from the Jobs table in the Pubs database, you must trigger, or call, the Fill method of the SqlDataAdapter1 object.

2. **Type the following into the** Form_Load **event:**

```
Private Sub Form1_Load(ByVal sender As System.Object,
          ByVal e As System.EventArgs) Handles MyBase.Load

    SqlDataAdapter1.Fill(DsJobs1)

End Sub
```

3. **Now go ahead and press F5.**

   Three columns from the first row in the DataSet are displayed in the three TextBoxes, as shown in Figure 7-3.

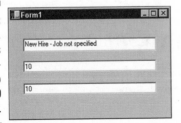

Figure 7-3: Here you go. This "unspecified" job pays $10,000 a year.

Binding to other properties

As promised, you can bind virtually any properties to a database. To see for yourself, follow these steps:

1. **Click any TextBox in your form in Design view to select it, and then press F4 to display the Properties window.**

2. **Click the + next to the DataBindings collection.**

3. **Click the Advanced property to select it.**

4. **Click the ... (ellipsis) button at the right side of the Advanced property.**

   The Advanced Binding dialog box appears, as shown in Figure 7-4.

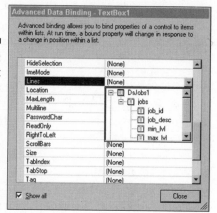

Figure 7-4:
This isn't
your father's
Visual
Basic. You
can bind
almost any
property to
a data
source.

Binding the ForeColor property of the TextBox to the `job_id` number in the data source might produce some colorful text, but would be unpredictable and, let's be honest, peculiar. However, storing specifications for properties in a data source could come in handy. For example, you might want to turn the text color (ForeColor) property red if someone misses a rent payment. That way, you could look down the list of all your tenants and instantly see which were in arrears. Then you could make your move and set things right.

Moving through the DataSet's Rows

The user will want to be able to see various rows and conveniently navigate through the information in the DataSet. In previous versions of VB, you would move forward and back through data using commands such as these:

```
Data1.Rowset.MoveNext
Data1.Rowset.MovePrevious
Data1.Rowset.MoveLast
```

No more. A DataSet resides in RAM, not in a database on a hard drive. All rows are instantly available. Microsoft has decided to treat a DataSet's data like an array, rather than like a traditional (meaning relatively sequential) list of pieces of information. The data in a DataSet still consists of pieces of information, but you can access them randomly (like moving around to different tracks on a CD) rather than sequentially (like searching for a track on a cassette tape). Actually, this distinction is a bit strained, but you get the point. Just remember: no more `MoveNext`.

The old-style move commands were technically called cursor access because they worked in a way similar to moving a cursor through a bunch of text with the arrow keys. Now, with VB .NET's array style, you move around in the data more like you were clicking.

In fact, a DataSet is like an intelligent array. That is, a DataSet, like an array, is an ordered collection of information. To move, you do it yourself (no `MovePrevious`, `MoveNext`, or similar commands are available). To "MoveNext," you can establish a global variable and increment it to keep track of where you are in the DataSet.

At the top of your code window, locate the `Class` declaration for Form1. Just below this line, declare a public variable named `Pointer`. (You can choose whatever name you want for the variable, but to follow this example, name it `Pointer`):

```
Public Class Form1
   Inherits System.Windows.Forms.Form
   Public Pointer As Integer
```

Then add a Button to your form. Use the Properties window to change the Button's Text property to Next. Each time the user clicks this button, you'll display data from the next row "up" in the DataSet. Double-click the button to get to its `Click` event, and then type the following:

```
Private Sub Button1_Click(ByVal sender As System.Object,
          ByVal e As System.EventArgs) Handles Button1.Click

    Pointer += 1

    Dim r1 As String
    Dim r2, r3 As Byte

    Try
         r1 = dsJobs1.Jobs(Pointer).job_desc
         r2 = dsJobs1.Jobs(Pointer).min_lvl
         r3 = dsJobs1.Jobs(Pointer).max_lvl

         textbox1.Text = r1
         textbox2.Text = CStr(r2)
         textbox3.Text = CStr(r3)
    Catch er As Exception
         MessageBox.Show("Error" & er.ToString)
    Finally
    End Try

End Sub
```

The first thing that happens is that the index (Pointer) to the DataSet's array is incremented. `VarName += 1` is the VB .NET equivalent to traditional VB's `VarName = VarName + 1`.

Next, you declare three variables to hold data from each column in the row. Then you assign the data to each variable. Here's what the first assignment line:

```
r1 = dsJobs1.Jobs(Pointer).job_desc
```

dsJobs1 is the name of the DataSet; Jobs is the name of the table in that DataSet that you're interested in; pointer is the index to the dsJobs1.Jobs array; and job_desc is the column of data you are retrieving.

Note that the job description column is a string variable type in the DataSet, but both the minimum and maximum salary columns are byte (numeric) types. I didn't know that in advance when I wrote this program. I thought all three might be strings, so I originally wrote:

```
Dim r1, r2, r3 As String
```

But the VB .NET compiler didn't like this and displayed the following error message:

```
Option strict disallows implicit conversions from System.Byte
            to System.String.
```

In Beta 1 of VB .NET, Option Strict was on by default. Now, in Beta 2 (and presumably in the final public version of VB .NET), Option Strict is off by default. Many programming experts suggest that you always turn Option Strict on. Put this at the top of your code window (by itself on the very first line):

```
Option Strict On
```

I agree that Option Strict provides a safety net, warning you while you are testing your projects of possible (and hard-to-catch) errors caused by incorrectly converting one variable type to another. But I'm easy. I think people should have as much freedom as possible, even if it means freedom to err. So, although I suggest you turn Option Strict on, I'm happy that you have the choice of leaving it off if that's your preference.

So, the Option Strict error message told me I must first declare variables r2 and r3 (using Dim r2 and r3 As Byte). Finally, the Try-Catch-Finally-End Try structure replaces VB's traditional On Error Resume technique for trapping runtime errors. I discuss Try-Catch in Chapter 20 and also in the section titled "Error Handling Revised" in the appendix at this book's Web site, which is located at http://www.dummies.com/extras/VBNetDataProg/.

Press F5, and then click the Next button repeatedly to move through the entire set of rows.

If you click the button 14 times, you see an error message (and a long one at that) informing you that there is no row at position 14. You should add the following code to the button to prevent this awkward message from ever being displayed to the user:

```
Private Sub Button1_Click(ByVal sender As System.Object,
        ByVal e As System.EventArgs) Handles Button1.Click

    Pointer += 1

    If Pointer > DsJobs1.jobs.Rows.Count Then Pointer -= 1 :
        Exit Sub

    Dim r1 As String
    Dim r2, r3 As Byte
```

There is also a `BindingContext` object you can use to maintain a pointer to the current row in a DataSet. This object is introduced in Chapter 3. In a Button object designed to move "up" one row to the next row in the DataSet, you can use code like the following in the Button's `Click` event:

```
Private Sub Button1_Click(ByVal sender As System.Object,
        ByVal e As System.EventArgs) Handles Button1.Click

    Me.BindingContext(DsJobs1, "jobs").Position() += 1

End Sub
```

Or to move "down" one row:

```
Private Sub Button1_Click(ByVal sender As System.Object,
        ByVal e As System.EventArgs) Handles Button1.Click

    Me.BindingContext(DsJobs1, "jobs").Position() -= 1

End Sub
```

The `BindingContext` object keeps track of the first and last row positions, so you don't have to worry about going outside the bounds of the available rows. This is a simpler, easier way to both maintain a pointer to the current position in the rows collection in a DataSet as well as move displayed data in the bound controls as the user (or some other agent) changes the current row. However, I showed you how to manage the job yourself because it's often useful to know how to do important programming tasks. By hand programming, you understand the objects, properties, and methods involved in a given job. That can come in handy if you need to add features that are not available from more automatic, built-in functionality such as the `BindingContext` feature.

A Few More Words about the DataSet

Recall that you can think of a DataSet as a mini-database detached from the parent database(s) from which it was extracted. A DataSet has one or more tables, columns, rows, constraints, and relations. You can write programming that reads or changes the elements of a DataSet (either its structure or its data). A DataSet has properties and methods. It has several collections (similar to traditional arrays). There are collections of tables, relations, rows, and columns.

I've covered this issue before, but it's worth repeating. By default, a DataSet is *typed*, meaning that it has an associated schema file, which has an .XSD extension. The schema file specifies the names of the tables and columns, along with the data type used in each column. If you create a DataSet using a VB .NET tool (such as the OleDbCommand control), an .XSD file is created automatically.

It's a bit easier to write programming code for typed DataSets because the lines are slightly less verbose, though perhaps a bit less readable and less descriptive. A typed DataSet permits this kind of coding:

```
r1 = dsJobs1.Jobs(Pointer).job_desc
```

An untyped DataSet does the same thing with this code:

```
r1 = dsJobs1.Tables("Jobs")(Pointer).Columns("job_desc")
```

However, a typed DataSet includes automatic type checking, which makes it easy to ensure that data of the wrong type does not get stored in the DataSet.

Now that I've reminded you about a few DataSet details, it's time to work with some higher-level stuff — the DataGrid control.

The Splendid DataGrid

The DataGrid is one of the best controls for displaying large amounts of data to the user. It's highly efficient, flexible, easy for the user to work with, and offers several different styles.

To see how to use the DataGrid, follow these steps:

1. **Remove the three TextBoxes and the Button you used in the preceding example.**

   Leave the SqlDataAdapter, SqlConnection, and DataSet objects on the tray as they were (connected to the Jobs table).

2. **On your clean, uncluttered form, add a DataGrid from the Toolbox.**

   The DataGrid is on the Windows Forms tab in the Toolbox.

3. **Press F4 to display the Properties window.**

4. **Locate the DataGrid's DataSource (not DataBindings) property, click the down-arrow button to display the list of data sources that VB.NET knows about, and then click** dsJobs1.jobs.

   (You could use DataBindings, but this example illustrates an alternative approach.)

5. **Press F5 to run the program.**

   A filled DataGrid is displayed, as shown in Figure 7-5.

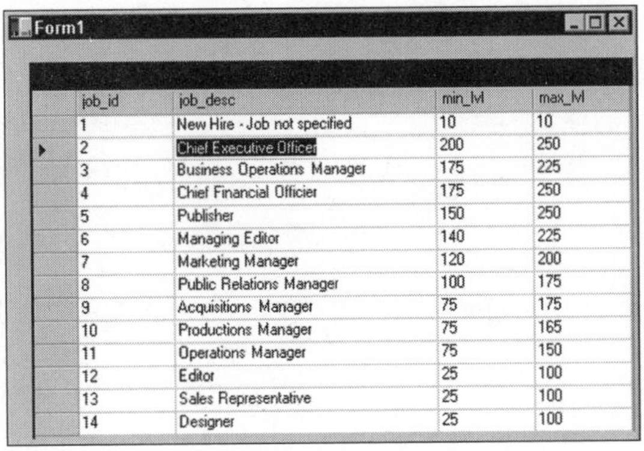

Figure 7-5:
The DataGrid control is a highly efficient way to display a table of information.

The DataGrid is filled with data only because you previously added this code to the Form_Load event:

```
Private Sub Form1_Load(ByVal sender As System.Object, ByVal e
            As System.EventArgs) Handles MyBase.Load

    SqlDataAdapter1.Fill(DsJobs1)

End Sub
```

So don't think you can simply drop a DataGrid onto a form, add the three database-related objects on the tray (the SqlDataAdapter, SqlConnection, and DataSet objects), and then press F5. You must *fill* the DataSet before any bound control can display the data.

You can also change the format of the DataGrid. To do so, first stop the project from running by clicking the x in the upper-right of the DataGrid's form. Then, follow these steps:

1. **Back in the VB.NET design window, right-click the DataGrid and choose Auto Format.**

   The AutoFormat dialog box appears, as shown in Figure 7-6.

2. **Chose Professional 1 and then click OK.**

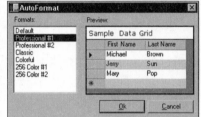

Figure 7-6: Use this dialog box to select from a variety of DataGrid formats.

3. **Press F5.**

   You see a nice, well-designed variant of the default DataGrid appearance.

   Also try the one called Colorful. It's particularly easy to read and work with, as shown in Figure 7-7.

	Job_id	job_desc	min_lvl	max_lvl
▶	1	New Hire - Job not specified	10	10
	2	Chief Executive Officer	200	250
	3	Business Operations Manager	175	225
	4	Chief Financial Officier	175	250
	5	Publisher	150	250
	6	Managing Editor	140	225
	7	Marketing Manager	120	200
	8	Public Relations Manager	100	175
	9	Acquisitions Manager	75	175
	10	Productions Manager	75	165
	11	Operations Manager	75	150

Figure 7-7: The Colorful DataGrid style is perhaps the most ergonomic of them all.

You can also customize the fonts, colors, and other elements of any DataGrid format, as shown in Figure 7-8.

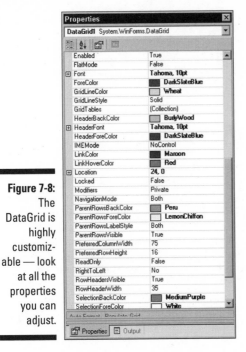

Figure 7-8:
The
DataGrid is
highly
customiz-
able — look
at all the
properties
you can
adjust.

Working with Other Classic Controls

Clearly, using data-enabled controls such as the DataGrid, TextBox, and Label makes a lot of sense. They are obvious choices when designing a user inter-face in which a user interacts with a data source. But remember, nearly all VB .NET controls are data-enabled (they have a DataBindings collection or a DataSource property). In this section, you consider possible uses for some of the other VB .NET controls when displaying data to users.

How about CheckBoxes?

You might think that the CheckBox has little utility as a data display device. After all, it has only two states: checked or unchecked. However, you can use it to let the user define certain kinds of data. For example, in a reservation form for a hotel, you might set a CheckBox's Text property (caption) to Non-smoking. By clicking that box, the user demands a room so wholesome, so uncontaminated, that no one has ever lit tobacco in it. (The way people jump to sue these days, a wise hotelier would include additional CheckBoxes to exclude peanuts and fish.)

Using Labels for read-only displays

You may also wonder about the utility of the Label control. However, if you want to display data that the user can't change, the Label is one way to do it. A Label also uses fewer resources than a TextBox.

Understanding ListBox limitations

Applications usually display a ListBox as a kind of menu, from which the user selects an item by clicking it. After that, your application can expand the selection. This feature can be useful in database work because you could, for example, show a list of product names. When the user clicks a particular product, the application can display details about its price, availability, weight, color, and so on. You can also use a ListBox to provide options when someone is filling out a form. For example, you could provide a list of four shipping options, with their different costs, from which the user can select.

However, ListBoxes (and their cousins, ComboBoxes) have several limitations when used with databases:

- They can't hold unlimited amounts of data.

- They will attempt to display thousands of rows, if that's what's asked of them — until they shut down the application (at the very least). Although VB.NET controls are supposed to be capable of holding data to the limit of the computer's memory, I wouldn't want to test this theory with a ListBox.

- They don't display data automatically when attached to a data source (as does, for example, a TextBox). Instead, you must write programming to populate a ListBox.

Visual Basic does include a database-specialized DBList control, which does automatically display a column from the first row and can handle huge lists. If you use the DBList control, however, you must supply it when you distribute your project because it's not an intrinsic component of VB. (Right-click the Toolbox and choose Customize Toolbox, and then locate the Microsoft DBList control in the Com Controls tab of the Customize Toolbox dialog box.)

To populate a standard VB .NET ListBox with the Job Description (job_desc) column of the dsJobs1 DataSet, follow these steps:

1. **Add a ListBox to Form1 in the VB .NET project you've been using for all the examples in this chapter.**

2. **Double-click the form to get to the code window.**

3. **Check the Form_Load event to ensure that the following line of code, which populates your DataSet, is still there:**

```
SqlDataAdapter1.Fill(DsJobs1)
```

4. **Click the Form1.vb [Design] tab on the top of the Design window.**

   The code window closes and the Design window opens.

5. **Click the ListBox to select it and then press F4.**

   The Properties window opens, showing the ListBox's properties.

6. **Click the DataSource property, click its down-arrow button to display a list of possible data sources, and then select dsJobs1.jobs.**

7. **Click the DisplayMember property, click its down-arrow button to display a list of possible columns within the data source you selected in Step 6, and then select Job_Desc.**

8. **Press F5.**

   Your ListBox is populated with the Job Description column of data, as shown in Figure 7-9.

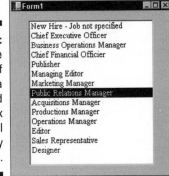

Figure 7-9:
For some
types of
data, a
standard
ListBox
works well
as a display
device.

Exploring Specialized, Data-Related Controls

Over the last few years, VB has added various database-related components. These components generally endeavor to display rows in a more flexible or elaborate fashion than as single-row TextBox clusters or single-column ListBox lists. The DataGrid is an example of this more sophisticated data-display device group. In this section, you take a quick look at some of the data-display components that by default are not part of the Toolbox. (You can, however, add them to the Toolbox.)

Unlike classic (intrinsic) VB components, specialized, data-aware components must be distributed along with your VB project when you give it to others for their use. The VB .NET deployment features usually make this process relatively painless. The deployment process detects the use of any nonstandard components and ensures that they are included in the setup or deployment package. The only problems I've run into with add-on, specialized components is that they are sometimes replaced with newer (and incompatible) versions, which can present problems. It's sometimes safer to stick with the intrinsic components, despite their limitations.

To see all the controls that are available to the VB .NET programmer but are not by default part of the Toolbox collection of controls, follow these steps:

1. **Right-click the Toolbox and choose Customize Toolbox.**

   The Customize Toolbox dialog box appears, containing massive lists of available controls. Dozens and dozens of controls, as shown in Figure 7-10.

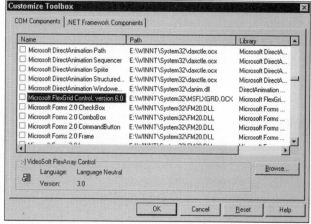

Figure 7-10: Surprised? You can add scores of extra controls to a VB .NET project.

2. **Click the COM Controls tab.**

   The COM Controls tab lists controls available to VB 6; some are even older than that.

3. **Locate and select one of the Version 6.0 controls.**

   (What you see in the COM Components tab depends on which libraries are installed on your computer.)

4. **Click the .NET Framework Components tab.**

5. **Select DataViewManager or some other .NET control.**

6. **Click OK to close the Customize Toolbox dialog box.**

Scroll all the way down to the bottom of the WinForms tab on the Toolbox. There they are! The two controls you just added.

Part IV
Building a Database

The 5th Wave
By Rich Tennant

"Our automated response policy to a large company wide data crash is to notify management, back up existing data and sell 90% of my shares in the company."

In this part . . .

*O*ften, you'll just work with existing databases, generating reports or managing the data. But there comes
a time in every database programmer's life when he or
she is called upon to climb the stairs to the next level.
When that happens to you, you'll be ready if you use the
information in Part IV. The chapters here show you how to
design and build a DataSet from scratch.

You get to know VB's excellent DataSet support tools and
controls by experimenting with building new DataSets and
seeing how easy it is to modify the structure of existing
ones. You also discover how to use indexes to speed up
searches for data and how to check data entry to make
sure that users don't enter an area code when they're supposed to enter a zip code. When you've finished this part,
you'll feel confident about specifying new structures (or
schemas, as they're now called) for data and modifying
existing structures.

Chapter 8

Creating a DataSet

● ●

In This Chapter

▶ Discovering more about DataSets

▶ Creating a database

▶ Creating a user interface

● ●

The key to understanding the ADO.NET technology is the DataSet. In this chapter, you focus on how to create, save, and load a DataSet. To better understand the DataSet concept — and to give yourself maximum flexibility — you go through these various tasks *programmatically*. That means you'll write the code rather than leave it up to a wizard.

More about DataSets

The DataSet is a brand new .NET item, similar to the traditional recordset used for years by database programmers. A *DataSet* is a copy of some data (containing as many tables as you want) that is held in memory or stored as two XML files on a hard drive. To simplify the contents of each XML file, the structure (the names of the tables, columns, and other features) of the DataSet is stored in one file, while the actual *data* (the specific rows of information) is stored in a separate file.

A DataSet does not require an active connection to a database. A DataSet object is fairly self-sufficient — it contains a variety of commands (methods) and properties you can employ to manage its data.

Typically, you connect to a large database and then extract a DataSet from that database. This way, you need not maintain a constant connection between your machine and the database (which might be on the Internet somewhere else in the world). Instead, you can work all you want with the DataSet in your computer and then return the DataSet for merging with the big database. Recall that this kind of *disconnectedness* (also known as *distributed applications* or *distributed programming*) is perhaps the primary distinction between traditional programming and programming designed to work on the Internet.

If 2000 people are simultaneously connected to your company's catalog database, your little server computer will probably start *smoldering*! To take the load off, each person can have his or her own little disconnected portion of information from the catalog. In other words, send each visitor his or her own DataSet (requiring only a brief connection to the database to extract a DataSet).

Visitors can even update the database with, say, their new phone number or something. Then they can click a Submit button and the DataSet is sent back to your server and merged with the database (requiring only a brief reconnection for the update). With disconnected DataSets, all 2000 visitors don't have to maintain continuous connections to the database, which would put a huge strain on your resources.

When they hold the annual family reunion picnic in Limping Turkey, West Virginia, all 457 cousins don't converge on the big stew pot and push and shove to stick in their forks. No. Everyone gets their own plate and goes off to eat on their own tree stump or perhaps on a rock down by the river. That way, no one starts one of them feuds. Good manners make for good reunions, that's our motto.

Building Your First DataSet

DataSets are stored in XML files, so they are especially useful for transmitting data over networks, such as the Internet. DataSets can be extracted from existing databases, or you can just create a new DataSet that isn't derived from a larger database. In this chapter and the next, you see how to create an independent DataSet that isn't extracted from some larger database. And you work within a WinForm, not a WebForm (an Internet Web page document). The programming techniques illustrated in this chapter and Chapter 9 will, nonetheless, serve you well when you go to use a DataSet with Internet programming and an existing database.

You'll create a little DataSet that mimics a cookbook. It will have one table (named recipes). This table will be the equivalent of an entire cookbook. The table will have two columns (named title and desc, for description). Each row (think of a row as a single recipe in your cookbook) will therefore be divided into two sections: the title section holding the recipe's title and the desc section holding the recipe itself. Let's get cooking.

Some global variables and namespaces

First off, you want to import some namespaces (to make referring to database objects and their members easier). Follow these steps:

1. **Start a new VB .NET project (File⇨New⇨Project).**

2. **Name the project** Ds **for DataSet.**

3. **Double-click the Windows Application icon in the New Project dialog box.**

4. **Double-click the form in the design window to get to the code window.**

5. **Go to the very top of the code window. Put the following** Imports **statements at the very top of the code window (and I mean up above** *all code,* **including** Public Class Form**). Type this:**

```
Imports System.Data
Imports System.Data.OleDb
Imports System.Data.SqlTypes
Imports System.Data.SqlDbType
Imports System.Data.SqlClient
```

Chapter 14 explains why you might want to always attach all these Imports when working with data in VB .NET. For now, just go ahead and add them as listed.

You also want to declare some of your own global variables. In VB .NET, global variables can be placed in a module (Project⇨Add Module) and thus be made available to the entire project (all the forms and other containers in the project). Or, if you just need to make the variables global to an individual form, you can do what you'll do now.

6. **A few lines down, just below the line that** Inherits System. Windows.Forms.Form, **type the lines that appear here in boldface:**

```
Public Class Form1
    Inherits System.Windows.Forms.Form

    Dim ds As New DataSet(), dr As DataRow, dt As
        DataTable

    'holds a deleted record
    Dim titlehold As String, descriptionhold As String

    'holds the current filenames
    Dim schemafilepath As String, datafilepath As String

    'holds the total records and current record number
    Dim TotalRows As Integer, CurrentRow As Integer
```

You've just created your global variables.

These variables will be used by more than one procedure (subroutine) in your project, so you want them to be *global* — to retain their contents even when the program isn't executing within the procedure where they were declared (with the `Dim` command). Solution? Declare them *outside* any particular procedure, in what's called the *General Declarations* section of the class (the form).

Put a form's global variables between the `Inherits` line and the `Sub Form_Load` line (or the first `Sub`, whatever it is) in `Class Form`.

Building a DataSet in code

Now it's time to create the DataSet. Although you can create a DataSet using the database controls in VB .NET (the OleDbDataAdapter and SqlDataAdaper controls, among others), sometimes you might want to let the user create his or her own DataSet files from scratch. This is one of those times. To do that, you need to create the DataSet not with controls during program design, but within your source code during program execution.

Scroll all the way down to the bottom of the code window and just above the `End Class` line. Type the following `Test` subroutine:

```
Sub Test()

    'TEST THE DATASET OBJECT:

    'Create a new table named Recipes with title and desc (the
            description of the actual recipe) columns.

    dt = New DataTable("Recipes")
    dt.Columns.Add("title", GetType(String))
    dt.Columns.Add("desc", GetType(String))
    ds.Tables.Add(dt)

    ' stick some data into the first row's two columns
    dr = dt.NewRow()
    dr!title = "First Test Recipe"
    dr!desc = "Instructions on making popular pies..."
    dt.Rows.Add(dr)

    'save the structure (schema) of this dataset
    ds.WriteXmlSchema("c:\RecipesDataSet.xml")
    'save the actual data that's currently in this dataset
    ds.WriteXml("c:\RecipesData.xml")

    Debug.WriteLine("DataSet Loaded. ")
    Debug.WriteLine("Number of Tables: " & ds.Tables.Count)
```

```
Dim s As String

s = ds.Tables(0).Columns.Count.ToString

Debug.WriteLine("Table 1 has " & s & " columns")

s = ds.Tables(0).Rows.Count.ToString()

Debug.WriteLine("Table 1 currently has " & s & " rows" &
        "(" & s & " records of data)")
dt = ds.Tables(0)
For Each dr In dt.Rows

  Debug.WriteLine("ColumnName: " & dt.Columns(0).ColumnName
        & "  Data: " & dr(0).ToString)
  'Debug.WriteLine(" ")

  Debug.WriteLine("ColumnName: " & dt.Columns(1).ColumnName
        & "  Data: " & dr(1).ToString)
Next

End Sub
```

This subroutine will be removed from your project later; you're using it now to see how to work with a DataSet.

Now scroll back up in the code window, locate the Form1_Load event, and type the following boldface line so that it will be the first thing that happens when you run the application:

```
Private Sub Form1_Load(ByVal sender As System.Object, ByVal e
        As System.EventArgs) Handles MyBase.Load

  Test() : End

End Sub
```

Press F5. The test runs and the program stops by itself (thanks to that End command).

To see the results of your experiment, follow these steps:

1. **Open the VB .NET Output window by choosing View⇨Other Windows⇨Output).**

2. **Make sure the Debug option appears in the drop-down box in the Output window. (If you don't see Debug just under the title bar in the Output window, click the down-arrow button at the top right of the Output window and select Debug.)**

   You should see the following results at the bottom of the Output window — you have to scroll down in the Output window to see this:

```
DataSet Loaded.
Number of Tables: 1
Table 1 has 2 columns
Table 1 currently has 1 rows(1 records of data)
ColumnName: title  Data: First Test Recipe
ColumnName: desc  Data: Instructions on making popular
          pies...
The program '[1256] ds.exe' has exited with code 0 (0x0).
```

When you're working on a program in VB .NET, you might want to get some feedback. If you need to see only one or two things, MsgBox works okay:

```
MsgBox ("Number of Tables: " & ds.Tables.Count)
```

But if you need to see several items, the MsgBox approach can be a pain — each MsgBox halts execution and you have to keep clicking the OK button to close each box. Instead, use the Debug.Write or Debug.WriteLine technique illustrated in the example. That way, you get your report all neat and listed in the Output window, without having to click OK to shut a bunch of message boxes. (Debug.WriteLine causes VB .NET to move down a line in the Output window.)

Creating global object variables

In this example, you've seen how to create a new DataSet and define a table and columns within it. Also included is the code necessary to read information from and store information in a DataSet's rows. Each of the various tasks that were accomplished in this code is described by comments within the code. However, consider some of the highlights.

```
Dim ds As New DataSet(), dr As DataRow, dt As DataTable
```

With this line, you created global object variables for a DataSet object (ds), a DataRow object (dr), and a DataTable object (dt). The DataRow object will contain a collection of all the individual rows (or what used to be called *records*) of data, however many there may be. The number of rows can grow or shrink — depending on whether new data units (rows) are added or deleted from the DataSet.

Defining the schema

You began by creating a table named recipes (so far, this is just a table object; it hasn't been made part of the DataSet yet):

```
dt = New DataTable("Recipes")
```

Note that you can create as many tables as you want, but you're going to use only one in this DataSet.

Then you created two columns (formerly known as *fields*). These are named title and desc, but you could have named them anything you wanted to. At the same time you created them, you added them to the Columns collection of the Recipes table object:

```
dt.Columns.Add("title", GetType(String))
dt.Columns.Add("desc", GetType(String))
```

You can add as many columns as you want to your table, but you're going to use only two categories in your recipe DataSet: the title of each recipe and the description (the recipe itself). So, given that you have two categories of information in this table, you should just use two columns.

Then, pleased with yourself, you added the recipes table to the Tables collection of the DataSet named ds:

```
ds.Tables.Add(dt)
```

Adding some rows (the actual data)

You specified the tables and columns in your DataSet. In other words, you've defined a structure for the DataSet. (It's as if you had a book full of blank pages, wrote RECIPES on the cover, and on each page drew a vertical line from top to bottom, dividing each page into two zones. Then you labeled the two zones Title and Description.) A DataSet's structure is called its *schema*.

Then you stored an actual row in the DataSet. A DataSet contains both categories (tables, and within tables, columns) as well as rows (records of data). You created a new row:

```
dr = dt.NewRow()
```

Then you added some data to each of the two columns:

```
dr!title = "First Test Recipe"
dr!desc = "Instructions on making pies..."
```

And finally, the new row is added to the Rows collection of the table (which already resides in the DataSet, so this row becomes part of the DataSet):

```
dt.Rows.Add(dr)
```

Then you used the WriteXMLSchema command to save the structure into one file:

```
ds.WriteXmlSchema("c:\RecipesDataSet.xml")
```

and used the WriteXML command to save the data (the rows) in a separate file:

```
ds.WriteXml("c:\RecipesData.xml")
```

Note that a DataSet need not be saved to the hard drive as a file. It's more common to simply keep the DataSet in the computer's memory while the user reads it or modifies it. Then, when the user is finished, any changes can be merged back into the original database and the DataSet itself simply left to die. However, to show you how you can manipulate independent DataSets, in this example you store them to disk. I simply chose the location and filenames for convenience. You can change `c:\RecipesData.xml`, for example, to whatever path and filename you want. There is no special place where you must store a DataSet, nor is there a special filename that you must give it.

The following code finds out how many columns and rows (individual records of data) are in a DataSet:

```
Dim s As String

s = ds.Tables(0).Columns.Count.ToString
s = ds.Tables(0).Rows.Count.ToString()
```

Finally, you used a technique that extracts all the data in your table:

```
For Each dr In dt.Rows

    Debug.Write("ColumnName: " & dt.Columns(0).ColumnName & "
        Data: " & dr(0).ToString)
    Debug.WriteLine(" ")

    Debug.Write("ColumnName: " & dt.Columns(1).ColumnName & "
        Data: " & dr(1).ToString)
    Debug.WriteLine(" ")
Next
```

This is the kind of code you could use to fill a ListBox with all the titles — `dr (0)` — in the DataSet. Then the user can click one of those titles to choose that particular row, and you could display both the title and the description in a pair of TextBoxes, for example.

By the way, to add more rows, you just repeat the code that created the first record, changing only the actual data that you're putting into the new rows:

```
dr = dt.NewRow()

dr!title = "2nd Test Recipe"
    dr!desc = "All about fish"
    dt.Rows.Add(dr)
```

Playing around

Perhaps you feel like playing around with this example a little (try adding a second table, for example) and working with the `Debug.WriteLine` command to find out how to generate mass quantities of debugging information. You can see the results in the Output window.

When you've finished playing around, delete the entire `Sub Test` from your source code, and also remove this line from the `Form1_Load` event:

```
Test() : End
```

The `Test Sub` was for experimentation only. You're going to create new code for this project, so delete the Sub Test and this line in Form1_Load.

Now that you understand the basics of DataSets, it's time to move on to some real-world examples that make use of DataSets.

Creating a Menu

Now you're closer to giving the user of your application the capability to create a new DataSet (and save it to the hard drive) or to open an existing DataSet (located on the hard drive). But hold your horses; you first need to provide the user with a way to initiate those tasks.

Typically, New, Save and Open options are located on a File menu. So this is a good time to find out how to use the new VB .NET menu-maker utility. Give the new VB .NET MainMenu control a try:

1. **Double-click the MainMenu icon in the Toolbox.**

   This control makes creating a menu structure a snap. The tray opens below your form, displaying a MainMenu icon. A box at the top left of the form reads, Type Here.

2. **Click the Type Here box with your mouse to select it and then type &File, as shown in Figure 8-1.**

   The & causes VB .NET to underline the following letter (F in this case), thus providing the user with a shortcut key. The user can now open this menu by pressing Alt+F, rather than by clicking it with the mouse.

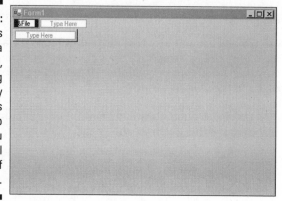

The menus across the top are called *root* menus (or sometimes *parent* menus). They are always visible. Their only job is to drop down a list of sub-menu items. And they already know how to do their job, so you don't write any code for them.

Each submenu item, on the other hand, *does* have a `Click` event where you must write the programming to respond if the user chooses that menu item:

1. **In the box just below the one you captioned File, type** &New.

   Note again that various adjacent empty boxes open up, where you can type additional submenus, if you want.

2. **Just below &New, type** &Open.

3. **Then, below &Open, type** &Save.

What I'm calling submenus and secondary menus are referred to officially as *child menus*. And every child (or group of child menus) has a parent. Notice that when clicked, parent menu items *do nothing except display their child (or children)*. So you don't write any programming code in the parent menu's event — you write your code in the child item events.

Double-click the New item in your menu system to get to its `Click` event in the code window. You'll see that VB .NET has provided this `Click` event:

```
Private Sub MenuItem2_Click(ByVal sender As System.Object,
        ByVal e As System.EventArgs) Handles
        MenuItem2.Click

End Sub
```

If you are creating a menu system of any size, you'll doubtless want to use more descriptive names than `MenuItem2`, `MenuItem3`, and so on for events. Here's a trick:

1. **Click the Form1.vb [Design] tab on the top of the design window to get back to the form editor.**

2. **Right-click the New item in your menus and choose Edit Names.**

   You see a transformation: Each menu item has not only the label section you've already filled in but also a section enclosed in brackets showing the default name that VB .NET gave to all the `Click` events.

3. **Type** mnuNew **as the name for the New item, and then press the Enter key.**

   You're now positioned to type mnuOpen and then mnuSave.

4. **Type** mnuOpen **for the Open item, and then press Enter.**

   The *mnu* prefix reminds you that the event in your source code involves a menu.

5. **Type** mnuSave **for the Save item, and then press Enter.**

6. **Right-click mnuNew on the form and choose Edit Names**.

   This deselects (deactivates) it, so you again see only the labels.

In Chapter 9, you can see how to make these menu items do their jobs: creating, saving, and opening DataSets.

Chapter 9

Managing DataSets

● ●

In This Chapter

▶ Discovering more about DataSets

▶ Creating a new database

▶ Creating a user interface

● ●

1 n this chapter you discover how to permit a user to create, save, and load a brand new DataSet. This DataSet is independent and disconnected from any database.

Creating a DataSet

In this example, you write programming that lets users create a new DataSet whenever they want, as many times as they want. You will first want to add a SaveFileDialog from the Toolbox to the form you created in Chapter 8. And while you're at it, go ahead and add an OpenFileDialog as well (you'll use it later when you give the user the capability to Open an existing DataSet). These dialog boxes are not visible on the upper part of the Toolbox; click the small down-arrow icon on the bottom right of the Toolbox to scroll it.

Type this in the `mnuNew_Click` event in the code window:

```
Private Sub mnuNew_Click(ByVal sender As System.Object, ByVal
        e As System.EventArgs) Handles mnuNew.Click

    'Create a new DataSet with a table named Recipes that
        includes a title and a desc column.

    'first get user's name for the new DataSet
    Dim userFilePath As String

    SaveFileDialog1.FileName = "MyData"
    SaveFileDialog1.InitialDirectory = "C:\"
    SaveFileDialog1.RestoreDirectory = True
    SaveFileDialog1.Title = "Create a New PDM DataSet"
```

```
        SaveFileDialog1.Filter = "PDM|*.PDM"
        SaveFileDialog1.ShowDialog()
        userFilePath = SaveFileDialog1.FileName

        Dim l As Integer = Len(userFilePath)

        If Mid(userFilePath, l - 3, 1) = "." Then
            'they've added an extension, so remove it
            userFilePath =
            Microsoft.VisualBasic.Left(userFilePath, l - 4)
        End If


        dt = New DataTable("Recipes")
        dt.Columns.Add("title", GetType(String))
        dt.Columns.Add("desc", GetType(String))
        ds.Tables.Add(dt)

        Try
            'save the structure (schema) of this dataset
            ds.WriteXmlSchema(userFilePath & "schm.xml")
            'save data that's currently in this dataset
            ds.WriteXml(userFilePath & "data.xml")

    'store these filenames in global variables for saving later
            schemafilepath = userFilePath & "schm.xml"
            datafilepath = userFilePath & "data.xml"

            'save a file to display their filename:
            ds.WriteXml(userFilePath & ".PDM")

        Catch er As Exception 'if there was a problem opening
            this file
            Throw(er)

        Finally

        End Try

        dt = ds.Tables!Recipes ' set dt to point to this
            table

    End Sub
```

All you want to do here is establish a new (empty) DataSet and save its structure (one table, two columns) to the hard drive. You use the names Recipes, title, and desc for the structure, but that's okay because the user will never see these internal labels — any more than they will see your variable names.

All you need to get from the user is their choice of a filename. You will use this name twice. First you'll append `schm.xml` for the schema file and any data in a file of the same name. Second, you'll append `data.xml` for a separate file that holds the data. Finally, to make things less confusing for the user (when they go to open one of their DataSets on the hard drive), you'll create a third file with the extension PDM. This last file has no other purpose than to provide users with an easily recognizable filename when they use the Open menu option. *PDM* stands for *Personal Data Manager*.

You use the SaveFile dialog box to get the user's choice of directory and filename. It's a straightforward request, but you always need to anticipate ways that users might foul things up. In this case, they might get excited and add a file extension such as TXT to their filename. You don't want that — you're actually creating three files to which you'll add special extensions. So, if the user adds an extension, you remove it in code, like this:

```
If Mid(userFilePath, 1 - 3, 1) = "." Then
    'they've added an extension, so remove it
    userFilePath = Microsoft.VisualBasic.Left(userFilePath, 1
        - 4)
End If
```

Note that you have to add the "compatibility namespace" `Microsoft.VisualBasic` reference to use the `Left` command in this code. Simply referring to the name of this in your code, separated by a period, makes the `Left` command work fine.

After the users give you a valid filename and file path, you create their new DataSet using the WriteXmlSchema method and save a separate .XML file that will hold the data.

Understanding Collections

Note that many objects contain collections. *Collections* are similar to arrays. A DataSet contains a tables collection, and, in turn, each table has a columns collection, which tells you how that table is subdivided, and a rows collection, which contains the actual items of data in the collection. You can usually query or edit individual elements in a collection two ways. You can refer to them by index number (starting with zero) or by their name. For example:

```
dt = ds.Tables!Recipes 'by name
dt = ds.Tables("Recipes") 'same, but an alternative
        punctuation
dt = ds.Tables(0) 'same, but here we use the table's index
        number rather than its name.
```

Whichever of these options you use, the global dt variable now points to the particular DataSet and table that the user created with the `mnuNew_Click` event. I chose to use this version in the previous code:

```
dt = ds.Tables!Recipes ' set dt to point to this table
```

It's easy to read because it includes the name of the table.

Opening an Existing DataSet

What if the user wants to open an existing PDM DataSet located on the hard drive? Begin by putting two TextBoxes on your form:

1. **Click the Form1.vb [Design] tab on top of the code window, to get to the design window.**

2. **Use the Toolbox to add two TextBoxes, one above the other.**

3. **Set the MultiLine property of the lower TextBox to True. Then change the Name property of the lower TextBox to txtDesc and the Name property of the upper TextBox to txtTitle.**

4. **Delete the value `TextBox1` from the Text properties of both TextBoxes.**

   You want the TextBoxes to be blank. (To delete these values, click the TextBox, and then press F4 to display the Properties window. Select *TextBox1* in the Text property by dragging your mouse across it. Press the Del key to remove it, and then press Enter.)

   Your form should look something like the one shown in Figure 9-1.

   Notice in Figure 9-1 that the Task List and Output windows are merely tabs on the bottom of the IDE. These two windows will pop up whenever you press F5. And they *stay visible* after you're through with them. They take up valuable space onscreen when you merely want to work with the code or design window. To get around this problem, right-click the title bar of the Task List window and choose Auto Hide. Do the same for the Output window. Now the windows automatically shrink down into tabs (as shown in Figure 9-1) whenever you click the design or code window — thereby freeing up lots of screen space. I normally Auto Hide all the windows except for the design and code windows. I even Auto Hide the Properties and Solution Explorer windows.

5. **Locate the `mnuOpen_Click` event by clicking the Form1.vb [Design] tab on top of the code window and then double-clicking the Open item in the menu structure.**

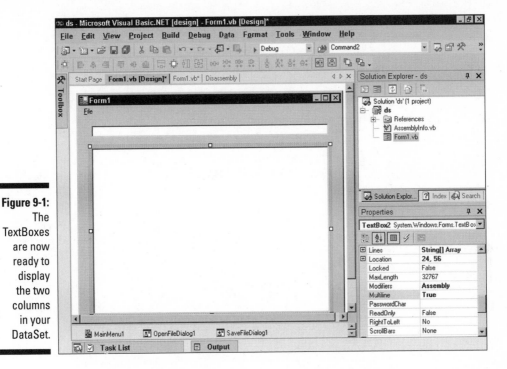

Figure 9-1:
The
TextBoxes
are now
ready to
display
the two
columns
in your
DataSet.

6. **Type the code that opens existing DataSet files:**

```vb
Private Sub mnuOpen_Click(ByVal sender As System.Object,
        ByVal e As System.EventArgs) Handles
        mnuOpen.Click

    Dim userFilePath As String
    Dim userfilenameonly As String, userpathonly As String

    OpenFileDialog1.FileName = "PDM"
    OpenFileDialog1.Filter = "PDM Files|*.PDM|All files
        (*.*)|*.*"
    OpenFileDialog1.InitialDirectory = "C:\"
    OpenFileDialog1.RestoreDirectory = True
    OpenFileDialog1.Title = "Open a PDM DataSet"

    If OpenFileDialog1.ShowDialog() = DialogResult.OK Then
        userFilePath = OpenFileDialog1.FileName

        'extract path and filename
        Dim l As Integer, m As Integer

        Dim position As Integer
```

```
         Do
             position = m
             m = InStr(m + 1, userFilePath, "\")
         Loop Until m = 0

         l = Len(userFilePath)

         userfilenameonly =
             Microsoft.VisualBasic.Right(userFilePath, l -
             position)
         userpathonly =
             Microsoft.VisualBasic.Left(userFilePath, posi-
             tion)

         'strip any extension from filename:
         If InStr(userfilenameonly, ".") Then userfilename-
             only = Microsoft.VisualBasic.Left(userfilename-
             only, Len(userfilenameonly) - 4)
         End If

     Try
         'get the structure file
         ds.ReadXmlSchema(userpathonly & userfilenameonly &
             "schm.xml")
         'get the data file
         ds.ReadXml(userpathonly & userfilenameonly &
             "data.xml")

         schemafilepath = userpathonly & userfilenameonly &
             "schm.xml"
         datafilepath = userpathonly & userfilenameonly &
             "data.xml"

     Catch er As Exception 'if there was a problem opening
             this file

         Throw (er)

     Finally

         dt = ds.Tables!Recipes ' set dt to point to this
             table

     End Try

     TotalRows = dt.Rows.Count
     CurrentRow = 0

     txtTitle.Text = dt.Rows(CurrentRow).Item(0)
     txtDesc.Text = dt.Rows(CurrentRow).Item(1)

 End Sub
```

In this procedure, you first showed the users an OpenFile dialog box and allowed them to double-click a filename (ending in .PDM). You get their choice of DataSet: It might be COOKBOOK.PDM or ADDRESSBOOK.PDM or COINCOLLECTION.PDM or whatever DataSet they've previously created. Their choice is returned to your program as the FileName property of the FileOpen dialog box:

```
userFilePath = OpenFileDialog1.FileName
```

After you have the filename (which actually includes the entire path — the disk name\directory name\filename, such as: C:\MyCoins.PDM), you have to separate the path from the filename (C:\ from MyCoins.PDMs in this example). You need these separate strings because you must open two XML files: the schema (structure definition) file (MyCoinsSchm.XML in the example) and the data file (MyCoinsData.XML).

This code finds where the path ends and the filename begins by searching for the \ symbol in C:\MyCoins.PDM:

```
'extract path and filename
Dim l As Integer, m As Integer
Dim position As Integer

Do
    position = m
    m = InStr(m + 1, userFilePath, "\")
Loop Until m = 0
```

When this loop is finished, the variable named position contains the location of the rightmost \. Why look for more than one \? Because if users stored their database in a subdirectory, more than one \ will be in the file path, like this: C:\MyData\PDM\MyCoins.PDM.

When you exit this loop, you can then extract the file path and put it in a variable named userpathonly, like this:

```
userpathonly = Microsoft.VisualBasic.Left(userFilePath,
           position)
```

getting, for example:

```
C:\MyData\PDM\
```

And you can extract the file name, getting:

```
MyCoins.PDM
```

Now you're ready to open your schema and data files, by appending your special extensions to the filename, like this:

```
'get the structure file
ds.ReadXmlSchema(userpathonly & userfilenameonly &
        "schm.xml")
'get the data file
 ds.ReadXml(userpathonly & userfilenameonly & "data.xml")
```

And, as you did in the mnuNew code, you must save the filenames in global variables so that you can save the data back to these files when the user chooses the Save option in the File menu or clicks the Exit button to shut down the program:

```
schemafilepath = userpathonly & userfilenameonly & "schm.xml"
datafilepath = userpathonly & userfilenameonly & "data.xml"
```

Technically, you need to keep saving the structure file (scmn.xml). The PDM doesn't contain any features for adjusting the structure by adding new tables or columns. However, saving doesn't hurt anything — and the capability is in place if you ever decide to expand the PDM and let users add tables.

Next you point the datatable variable (dt) to your newly opened DataSet:

```
dt = ds.Tables!Recipes ' set dt to point to this table
```

Then you put the total number of records into the global variable TotalRows, set the CurrentRow pointer to 0 (the first record):

```
TotalRows = dt.Rows.Count
CurrentRow = 0
```

and display the current record in your two TextBoxes:

```
txtTitle.Text = dt.Rows(CurrentRow).Item(0)
txtDesc.Text = dt.Rows(CurrentRow).Item(1)
```

Adding and Removing Data

You've finished the New and Open code, so now you can figure out how to add records to and remove records from a DataSet.

Adding data to a DataSet

To add data to your DataSet, follow these steps:

1. **Use the Toolbox to put a Button on the form.**

2. **Change the Button's Name property to btnAdd and its Text property to Add Record.**

3. **Double-click the Button to get to its** `Click` **event. Change it to look like the following:**

```
Private Sub btnAdd_Click(ByVal sender As System.Object,
        ByVal e As System.EventArgs) Handles btnAdd.Click
        'if they have no active DataSet, refuse to allow
        a new record:
If ds.Tables.Count = 0 Then MsgBox("Please Open a
        DataSet, or create one using the New option in
        the File menu--before attempting to add a new
        record.") : Exit Sub


    'if they have an incomplete record, refuse:
    If txtTitle Is "" Or txtDesc Is "" Then MsgBox("One
        of your TextBoxes has no data. You must enter
        something for the title and something for the
        description.") : Exit Sub


    ' stick the new data into the first row's two columns
    dr = dt.NewRow()
    dr!title = txtTitle.Text
    dr!desc = txtDesc.Text
    dt.Rows.Add(dr)
    TotalRows = TotalRows + 1
    CurrentRow = CurrentRow + 1

Me.Text = "Record " & TotalRows & " Added..."

End Sub
```

The first line tests whether or not the users have a currently active DataSet. If not, you post a message and exit this subroutine without executing any additional code. If the users haven't yet created or opened a DataSet, they shouldn't be trying to add a record to this non-existent data. Also, you don't want an incomplete record.

However, if the users do have a new record (text in the TextBoxes) that they want to save to the DataSet (*committing it*, as the saying is), you let them.

You use the `NewRow` method to notify your DataSet that a new row of data is coming. Then you fill the new row's two columns (`title` and `desc`) with the data in the TextBoxes. Then the `Add` method commits the data to the DataSet. You increment your total records counter and your current row pointer.

And, because users don't like to click a button and see *nothing* happen, you place a reassuring message in the form's title bar, telling them that the record has been added and showing them the total number of records currently in the DataSet.

Removing data from a DataSet

Users must be able to delete, as well as add, records from your DataSet. Here's code that can be used to remove the "current" record:

```
dt.Rows.Remove(dt.Rows(CurrentRow))
```

If you look in VB .NET's Help, you might think that there are two methods for deleting a row in a DataSet: `Delete` and `Remove`. However, the `Delete` method doesn't actually get rid of a row; it simply marks the row for later deletion when (or if) the programmer uses the `AcceptChanges` method. Marking a row is useful for such jobs as permitting an Undo option, restoring the row. In this example, however, you use the `Remove` method, which gets rid of the row completely, right then and there.

Saving a DataSet

The Save feature stores the DataSet to a file on the hard drive. Double-click the Save menu item to get to its `Click` event in the code window. Then type the following in the `mnuSave_Click` event:

```
Private Sub mnuSave_Click(ByVal sender As System.Object,
        ByVal e As System.EventArgs) Handles
        MenuItem4.Click

    If ds.Tables.Count = 0 Then ("Please use the New option
        to first create a new DataSet"): Exit Sub 'nothing
        to save

    'otherwise, save the dataset
    ds.WriteXmlSchema(schemafilepath)
    ds.WriteXml(datafilepath)

End Sub
```

If the DataSet has no tables, the users don't have any data to save yet, so you just quit this subroutine. However, if there is a DataSet, you use the two `WriteXML` methods to save the DataSet's structure and its data.

Testing . . . Testing

Now you can test your project to make sure that the XML files are being created on the hard drive. In addition, you can see the interesting way that a DataSet's schema and data are saved. Follow these steps:

1. **Press F5 and then choose File⇨New in your PDM project's menus.**

   The file saving dialog box appears, as shown in Figure 9-2.

2. **Click the Save button in the dialog box to create the default MyData files.**

   Recall that the program creates three files for the price of one. Now you have an active DataSet in your project. In the next step, you add a few records to it.

3. **In the Title TextBox (on top) in your form, type a title. In the lower TextBox, type a description.**

   In the example, I typed *Coin One* for the title and *Original Authentic Coin with Claudvius's Portrait on it* for the description.

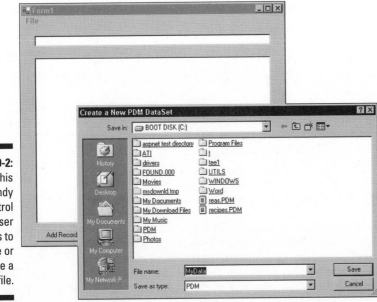

Figure 9-2:
Use this handy control when a user wants to save or create a disk file.

4. **Click the Add Record Button.**

   Notice that your message Record Added appears in the title bar of the form.

5. **Now replace the Title field with another title and change the description TextBox as well.**

   In the example, the title is *Second_Coin* and the description is *Of unknown origin, but looks just like Livia.*

6. **Click the Add Record button again.**

7. **Choose File⇨Save to store these two records on the hard drive.**

8. **Close the application by clicking the X icon in the top right of the form.**

Now take a look at the files, to see how a DataSet is saved in XML. Use Windows's Notepad to open the MyDatadata.XML file on your hard drive (Start⇨Programs⇨Accessories⇨Notepad.) This XML file is where the DataSet's actual rows (records) were stored.

The data should look like this in Notepad, if you typed the example text:

```
<?xml version="1.0" standalone="yes"?>
<NewDataSet>
  <Recipes>
    <title>Coin One</title>
    <desc>Original Authentic Coin with Claudvius's Portrait
          on it</desc>
  </Recipes>
  <Recipes>
    <title>Second Coin</title>
    <desc>Of unknown origin, but looks just like Livia</desc>
  </Recipes>
</NewDataSet>
```

Then use Notepad to open the schema XML file (MyDataschm.XML). You'll see the DataSet defined in a kind of nesting process, with the two rows nested inside the Recipes table, which itself is nested in the DataSet.

Moving through the DataSet

Users often want to scroll up or down through a set of data. When working with an older ADO RecordSet, you could use the MoveNext, MovePrevious, MoveFirst, and MoveLast methods to maneuver users through their records. The newer ADO.NET DataSet, however, has no such methods. It's up to you, the programmer, to organize and navigate the data "rows" inside the DataSet. That's why you created TotalRows and CurrentRow global variables — to keep track of where the user is located in the set of rows. (Technically, TotalRows isn't necessary; the DataSet does know that and you could ask it any time with ds.Tables(0).Rows.Count.)

Put two more Buttons on the form and change their Name properties to btnNext and btnPrevious. Change their Text properties to Next and Previous, respectively.

The btnNext and btnPrevious buttons will allow the user to move forward or backward through the currently loaded DataSet. Type this in the btnPrevious Click event:

```
Private Sub btnPrevious_Click(ByVal sender As System.Object,
        ByVal e As System.EventArgs) Handles
        btnPrevious.Click

    If CurrentRow = 0 Then Exit Sub

    CurrentRow = CurrentRow - 1

    txtTitle.Text = dt.Rows(CurrentRow).Item(0)
    txtDesc.Text = dt.Rows(CurrentRow).Item(1)

    Me.Text = CurrentRow + 1.ToString

End Sub
```

You first must check to see whether the users are viewing the "lowest" record. If CurrentRow = 0, there are no additional records to be viewed "below" the currently displayed one. So, if that's the case, you merely exit the subroutine.

I put the word *lowest* in quotes because in a *relational* set of data, there is no "lower" or "higher" any more than in relativistic astrophysics there is a "lower" or "higher" planet or star. It all depends on your point of view. A DataSet, which is relational, has no particular order. The records (rows) are added and deleted from the DataSet without regard to their alphabetical order. If you want to present an alphabetized DataSet to the user, you must alphabetize it yourself. (A VB .NET ListBox has an automatic alphabetizing feature if you set its Sorted property to True.)

So, back to your code: If there *is* a record to display (you're not at the "lowest" record in the DataSet), you adjust the CurrentRow variable, grab the text from the DataSet, and assign it to the two TextBoxes. Again, you display something to the user in the form's title bar; in this case, you show them the record number. How would you show them the record number *and* the total number of records?

```
Me.Text = CurrentRow + 1.ToString & " of " &
        TotalRows.ToString
```

Moving forward (or *up*, if you prefer) through the records is accomplished in the btnNext procedure:

```
Private Sub btnNext_Click(ByVal sender As System.Object,
            ByVal e As System.EventArgs) Handles btnNext.Click

    If CurrentRow = TotalRows - 1 Then Exit Sub

    CurrentRow = CurrentRow + 1

    txtTitle.Text = dt.Rows(CurrentRow).Item(0)
    txtDesc.Text = dt.Rows(CurrentRow).Item(1)

    Me.Text = CurrentRow + 1.ToString

End Sub
```

Just as in the btnPrevious code, you must first see whether the user is asking to see a record that doesn't exist. If the CurrentRow isn't the "highest" row, you proceed to adjust CurrentRow up by 1 and then display that record. The rest of the code is identical to the btnPrevious code.

Why must you use -1 when getting information from the TotalRows global variable in the PDM's code? Why can't you just hold the actual total number of rows in your TotalRows variable? Why must you subtract 1? That's because of a grievous fault in computer programming languages that I've mentioned previously: Some arrays and collections start with an index of 1 and others start with an index of 0. As the PDM program illustrates, you have to deal with both ways of counting when using a DataSet. The Count property of a DataSet's Tables().Rows collection begins with 1 but the DataRecords collection of a DataSet begins with 0. So, to keep things working correctly — to keep the TotalRows and CurrentRow variables in sync — you must subtract 1 from TotalRows each time you use it.

Try testing these new buttons. Press F5 and use your project's File⇨Open feature to load the DataSet named MyData that you created previously. It has two rows, so click the Previous and Next buttons to test them.

Searching a DataSet

Any good database program permits users to search through the entire group of records and return those that match a specific criterion. The PDM has this feature, too. The user can type a string (text) of any length. A ListBox then displays all records that contain that text anywhere in their description (desc) field. Then the users can click the title of the record that they want to display in the TextBoxes. Follow these steps:

1. **Put a ListBox on your form.**

   It's okay if the ListBox partially covers the TextBoxes.

2. **Change the ListBox's Name property to lstResults and its Visible property to False.**

3. **Put a Button on the form, too, and change its Name property to btnSearch and its Text property to Search.**

4. **Set the btnSearch Click Event to look like this:**

```
Private Sub btnSearch_Click(ByVal sender As
        System.Object, ByVal e As System.EventArgs)
        Handles btnSearch.Click


    'if they have no active DataSet, refuse:

    If ds.Tables.Count = 0 Then
        MsgBox("Please use the File menu to Open a
        DataSet, or create a New one first.") : Exit Sub
    End If

    Dim s As String, re As String
    Dim i As Integer, x As Integer


    s = InputBox("Enter Your Search Term", "Search")

    If s = "" Then Exit Sub

    s = LCase(s) 'make it case-insensitive

    lstResults.Items.Clear() ' clean out the ListBox

    For i = 0 To TotalRows - 1
        re = ds.Tables(0).Rows(i).Item(1) ' get desc
        column
        If InStr(LCase(re), s) Then
lstResults.Items.Add(ds.Tables(0).Rows(i).Item(0))'add
        title field
            x = x + 1
        End If
    Next

        If x = 0 Then MsgBox("We found no matches for " &
        s) : Exit Sub

        lstResults.Visible = True


End Sub
```

First, you see whether the current DataRow (dr) contains nothing. If so, there are no records and therefore nothing to search. So you let the users know that they can't search until they've created or opened a DataSet.

Next you use an InputBox to get the user's string. If the variable s is empty (" "), the user clicked the Cancel button and provided no string, so you exit the procedure.

Now you want to make the search ignore capitalization (either in the user's search string or in the records being searched). So you use the LCase method to reduce both the user's string and the records to all-lowercase characters. This means, for example, that *ROMAN* matches *Roman, roman, RoMaN,* and the like. The characters themselves, not their capitalization, trigger hits.

You empty any contents in the lstResults ListBox with the Clear command (in case some records are still listed from a previous search).

A loop is then used to search from 0 to TotalRows -1 (the entire set of records). You use the InStr function to see whether s (the string the user typed in) is found in any of the records in the entire DataSet. If so, you've found a match as you store the Title field of that record in the ListBox.

A variable x counts any hits. If x is 0 when you finish with the loop, you display a message to the user that no matches were found and exit the subroutine at that point.

Otherwise, the lstResults ListBox is displayed so that the users can choose the record they want to see (by clicking its title in the ListBox).

Go ahead and test this. You can load the MyData test file by choosing File⇨Open and then clicking the Search button. To list both records in the MyData DataSet, type **origin** in the InputBox (that term is in the description field of both records).

Selecting a Search Hit

For mysterious reasons, a ListBox's SelectedIndexChanged event is the default event — so if you click the ListBox, VB .NET types that event in the code window. You want the Click event instead, so follow these steps:

1. **In the drop-down list at the top left of the code window, choose lstResults.**

2. **In the list at the top right of the code window, choose Click.**

3. Type the following code in the lstResults `Click` event to permit the user to click a title and view the entire record in the TextBoxes:

```
Private Sub lstResults_Click(ByVal sender As Object,
        ByVal e As System.EventArgs) Handles
        lstResults.Click

    lstResults.Visible = False

    Dim i As Integer
    Dim s As String
    s = lstResults.SelectedItem.ToString

    'find their choice

    For Each dr In dt.Rows
        i = i + 1
        If dr(0).ToString = s Then
            txtTitle.Text = dr(0).ToString
            txtDesc.Text = dr(1).ToString
            CurrentRow = i
            Exit For
        End If
    Next

End Sub
```

First you make the ListBox invisible, and then you put the user's choice (the Title field that the user selected) into the variable s. Then you go through all the records until you find a match in the Title field (dr(0)). When the match is found, you put the text from that record into the two TextBoxes. You also update the CurrentRow variable.

Chapter 10

Validating and Indexing Your Data

● ●

In This Chapter

▶ Validating user input at the source

▶ Validating through programming

▶ Indexing your data for faster searching

● ●

*T*he old saying "garbage in, garbage out" is the truth. Most so-called computer errors are either programming or data entry errors. Data validation attempts to ensure that a database contains useful, accurate data. I use the phrase *attempts to ensure* because no amount of data validation can prevent someone from entering, say, Nggg as his or her name.

Indexing is important to database design, too. It speeds things up, as you'll see, in much the same way that an index in a book speeds up finding specific information. When you specify that a field (column) should be indexed, you're requesting that the data in that field be maintained in an organized, easily searched list.

In this chapter, you see how to validate in data-input forms as well as how to use various validation controls. You also find out why and how to index some fields in a table. You may be tempted to index all the fields, but don't. Too much of a good thing, as they say.

Validating User Input at the Source

The following example will not work on your computer unless you have followed the steps in Chapter 3 to turn your computer into a self-contained client/server simulation. Follow the steps in the "Connecting to a Database" section in Chapter 3.

Chapter 11 goes more deeply into Web applications (WebForms), but for now you can see how to employ validation techniques using controls available to a WebForm. To try a validation control and see how it works, follow these steps:

1. **Start VB .NET and choose Create New Project.**

   The New Project dialog box appears.

2. **Double-click the ASP.NET Web Application icon.**

   When you start your Web application, you see a different kind of design window than the one you've used with Windows applications. Just stay calm.

3. **Open the Toolbox and use the down-arrow icon to scroll through the controls available on the Web Forms tab.**

   Eventually, you'll come upon a set of validation controls, symbolized by check box icons, as shown in Figure 10-1. The validation controls help you avoid some programming because they test the user's input for you.

Figure 10-1:
Here's the set of validation controls you can use in your WebForm projects.

4. **Click the tab at the top of the design window that says WebForm1.aspx.**

   This is your design file.

5. **Also click the Design tab at the bottom of the design window.**

   It's now possible to place controls onto the WebForm.

6. **Double-click the RangeValidator control to place it on your WebForm. Then double-click a TextBox, a Label control, and a Button control to place them on your WebForm.**

These controls will overlap each other, so you'll want to drag them so that you can easily see and work with them.

7. **Click the RangeValidator control in the design window to select it, and then press F4 to display the Properties window.**

8. **In the Range Validator's Properties window, enter the following values:**

Maximum Value: 39

Minimum Value: 3

ErrorMessage: Your number must be between 3-39

ControlToValidate: TextBox1

(When the user types a number in the TextBox, the number will be validated.)

Type: Integer

(A numeric type, rather than the default text string.)

9. **Change the Button Text property to ClickThis.**

10. **Change the Label ID property to lblResponse**

11. **Click the HTML tab at the bottom of the design window to see the HTML code that VB .NET has written for your WebForm.**

12. **Locate the Button code and add an** OnClick **element to it by typing the following code that appears in boldface:**

```
<asp:Button id="Button1" style="Z-INDEX: 103; LEFT: 75px;
        POSITION: absolute; TOP: 144px" runat="server"
        onclick="Button1_Click" Text="Click
        This"></asp:Button>
```

This says to run the Button1_Click event when the user clicks this button.

13. **Open Solution Explorer, right-click WebForm1.aspx, and choose View Code.**

14. **Type the following code for the** Click **event:**

```
Public Sub Button1_Click(ByVal sender As Object, ByVal e
        As System.EventArgs) Handles Button1.Click

    RangeValidator1.Validate()

    If Page.IsValid = True Then
        lblResponse.Text = "Your entry is valid"
    End If

End Sub
```

This is the code-behind programming window, where you can write what appears to be traditional VB .NET code in a traditional VB .NET style (as opposed to HTML in an HTML code window). Recall that at the top of the HTML code there was a reference to this file:

```
Codebehind="WebForm1.aspx.vb"
```

The `Validate` method of the RangeValidator control is first fired, and then the Page object's IsValid property is tested. If it's True (the user entered a valid number), you display a `valid` message in the label. If the user types in a number that's out of range (such as 2 or 55), the RangeValidator's ErrorMessage property is displayed. Don't test this project just yet. You have a few more changes to make to the HTML.

It's not strictly necessary to type the `RangeValidator1.Validate()` code. When the user clicks the button, the form is sent back to the server (submitted, or posted back, as they say). The validation controls automatically test (validate) whenever a post-back occurs.

15. Click the WebForm1.aspx tab at the top of the code window to get back to the HTML code window.

16. Type the following boldface HTML, putting it just above the TextBox element in the HTML code:

```
<h3>Type in a number:</h3>
<asp:TextBox
```

This is just a level-3 headline in HTML that tells the user what to do.

Now you should be ready to test your WebForm:

1. Press F5.

It might take VB .NET a bit of time to get this WebForm page together before displaying it in your browser, so be patient. You should see an HTML page in your browser like the one shown in Figure 10-2.

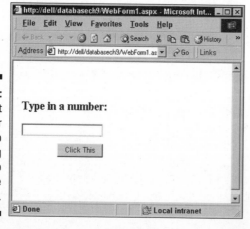

Figure 10-2: Your input validator system is up and running and ready to test the user's input.

2. Type 2, **which is an invalid number, and then click the button.**

You see the result shown in Figure 10-3.

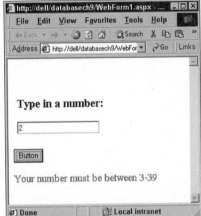

Figure 10-3:
The Range
Validator
control will
not permit
the user to
enter the
number 2.

3. When you're finished, close Internet Explorer.

If you don't get the results shown in Figure 10-3, check your HTML code against this correct code. (Some values in your code will differ, such as the numbers specifying the TOP and LEFT positions.)

```
<%@ Page Language="vb" AutoEventWireup="false"
         Codebehind="WebForm1.aspx.vb"
         Inherits="WebApplication2.WebForm1"%>
<!DOCTYPE HTML PUBLIC "-//W3C//DTD HTML 4.0
         Transitional//EN">
<HTML>
  <HEAD>
    <title></title>
    <meta name="GENERATOR" content="Microsoft Visual
         Studio.NET 7.0">
    <meta name="CODE_LANGUAGE" content="Visual Basic 7.0">
    <meta name="vs_defaultClientScript" content="JavaScript">
    <meta name="vs_targetSchema"
         content="http://schemas.microsoft.com/intellisense
         /ie5">
  </HEAD>
  <body MS_POSITIONING="GridLayout">
    <form id="Form1" method="post" runat="server">
      <asp:RangeValidator id="RangeValidator1" style="Z-
         INDEX: 101; LEFT: 8px; POSITION: absolute; TOP:
         8px" runat="server" ErrorMessage="Your number must
         be between 3-39" MaximumValue="39"
         MinimumValue="3" ControlToValidate="TextBox1"
```

```
Type="Integer"></asp:RangeValidator>
      <asp:Button id="Button1" style="Z-INDEX: 104; LEFT:
        100px; POSITION: absolute; TOP: 85px"
        runat="server" onclick="Button1_Click" Text="Click
        This"></asp:Button>
      <asp:Label id="lblResponse" style="Z-INDEX: 103;
        LEFT: 22px; POSITION: absolute; TOP: 68px"
        runat="server">Label</asp:Label>
      <h3>
          Type in a number:
      </h3>
      <asp:TextBox id="TextBox1" style="Z-INDEX: 102; LEFT:
        16px; POSITION: absolute; TOP: 16px"
        runat="server"></asp:TextBox>
    </form>
  </body>
</HTML>
```

Some might ask, "Why not just write the following code in the `Click` event?"

```
If CInt(TextBox1.Text) < 3 or CInt(TextBox1.Text) > 39 Then
   Response.write ("Must be between 3-39")
End If
```

(`CInt` forces the Text property to change from its default String data type to an Int.) This would work, but the validation controls offer you more flexibility. Also, if you have several controls on a page that you need to validate, the validation controls are probably your best route. Instead of writing lots of code, you just set a few properties.

Also, validation controls give you the ability to check either individual data (individual TextBox entries, for instance, using `RangeValidator1.IsValid`) or the validity of the entire page at once (using `Page.IsValid`). You can also specify the text, location, and appearance of error messages generated by the validation controls.

Using Validation Controls

For each input control you want to validate, you add a separate validation control. In the preceding example, you wanted to validate the TextBox, so you dedicated a RangeValidator control to that job. When the Web page is sent back to the server (in the example, when the user clicks the Button to submit the contents of the TextBox back to the server), the page object sends the text to the validation control that has its ControlToValidate property set to the TextBox.

You can attach more than a one-validation control to a single TextBox (or any control). For example, if you need to check for a range of numbers and make sure that the user didn't leave the TextBox empty, you could set the ControlToValidate properties of both the RangeValidator and RequiredFieldValidator controls to point to that TextBox. However, if you are permitting the user to enter more than one valid pattern (for instance, either 24456 or 24456-2242 might be a permissible, valid zip code pattern), you should not use multiple validation controls. In this situation, use the pattern-matching validation control (the RegularExpressionValidator, as it's called), and specify that two valid patterns are permitted.

When the page object sends data to a validation control for testing, the validation control sets a property that specifies whether or not the test was passed. For instance, in the preceding example, the IsValid property of the page object is set to either True or False. So you can test the condition of Page.IsValid and respond appropriately in your programming.

Note that if you have several validation controls active on a given page and any one of them fails some data, the Page.IsValid property will be set to False. So, you should normally first test the Page.IsValid property. Then, if the property is True, your programming could safely go ahead and save the user's input to a database:

```
If Page.IsValid = True Then
```

True means that you can be assured that the user has correctly entered the necessary data.

If the Page.IsValid property tests False, you would probably want to figure out which validation control or controls are individually set to False. To do that, you test their IsValid properties:

```
If RangeValidator1.IsValid = False Then
```

Alternatively, you could use a loop structure to test all the validators, using the Page.Validators collection, like this:

```
x = page.validators(0).IsValid
```

After you know which data is bad, you can display a message, asking the user to try again.

Some validation controls test more than one factor at a time. For instance, the following RangeValidator tests both for a range and that the data type is an integer:

```
<asp:RangeValidator id=RangeValidator1 runat="server"
          ErrorMessage="Your number must be between 3-39"
          minimumvalue="3" maximumvalue="39"
          controltovalidate="TextBox1" type="Integer">
</asp:RangeValidator>
```

The validation controls follow:

- ✔ **RequiredFieldValidator:** Makes sure the user fills in a required entry.

- ✔ **RangeValidator:** You specify an upper and lower boundary, and data outside that range is invalid. In the preceding example, you used a range of numbers, but you could also specify a range of dates or an alphabetic range (*a* through *f,* for instance).

- ✔ **CompareValidator:** Checks the user's entry against a property value in a different control on the page, against a value from a database, or against a literal value ("this" and 3 are literal values, as opposed to variables). You use comparison operators for this test: > for greater than, = for equals, and so on.

- ✔ **RegularExpressionValidator:** This (badly named) control is a pattern-matcher. Use it to compare what the user entered against a specified sequence of characters or digits. This works well when ensuring that the user entered a valid e-mail address (must have @ symbol), social security number, credit card number, zip code, phone number, and the like). Recall that you can specify two or more acceptable patterns simultaneously — such as two patterns of zip code numbers, one five digits long and a second style nine digits long with a hyphen.

- ✔ **CustomValidator:** Allows you to define the validation by writing custom code. Use this if you are getting information about the correct pattern at runtime. For instance, if the user clicks a CheckBox indicating he or she is Canadian, you would have code that changes your validation from zip code to the Canadian postal code pattern, which uses alphabetic characters.

Validating programmatically

Usually, you need to check data before it gets stored in a database. If someone types a three-digit zip code or forgets to enter a credit card number, your company can lose money because it can't process their order. Some database applications don't accept certain kinds of bad data.

When you're designing a database, you can sometimes use features of the database engine, such as the Jet engine's ValidationRule property, to accept or reject data. An alternative is to check the data at the point of entry — that is, the user-input form or any component that is used to permit the user to type data. In the preceding section, you saw how to use validation controls to trap problems in Web-page data entry. In this section, you consider some techniques for catching errors at the point of entry by writing a bit of programming.

The most common way to see whether a user has typed appropriate data (a zip code, for example, instead of an area code) is by simply checking the data when the user indicates that he or she has finished entering it. For example, you can write programming to test the length of a zip code, as follows:

```
Public Sub TextBox1_LostFocus(ByVal sender As Object,
        ByVal e As System.EventArgs) Handles
        TextBox1.LostFocus
    Dim L As Integer

    L = Len(TextBox1.Text)

 If L < 5 Then
    MsgBox("A zip code must be at least 5 characters long.
        But you! You entered only " & L & " characters. Do
        try again.")
 End If

End Sub
```

You can use the `LostFocus` event (of the control where the data is entered) to write the programming to validate data entry. If you do detect bad data, display an understandable error message to the user.

You could put your validation programming into whatever button on your data-entry form the user clicks to move to the next record. The button might be captioned Submit, Save, Add, Next — some way for the user to indicate, "I've finished entering this record, so save it to the database."

This approach works, but there are better methods for handling data validation. For one, this approach checks the record only after all the fields have been filled in and the user is ready to move to the next record or submit the entire form to your server. Instead, if possible, you should validate each field as soon as the user moves to the next field. This approach enables you to leave the insertion cursor still blinking in the problem field, so users don't have to move their hands from the keyboard to the mouse to click the invalid field and thus put the cursor back into that TextBox. To validate in this way, use the `LostFocus` event.

Validating a zip code

How does your application know that the user has typed a zip code and then pressed the Tab key to move to the next TextBox, which means that your application should now validate the zip code? In the past, some programmers used the `GotFocus` event of the next TextBox. The flaw in this approach is that users don't always proceed from TextBox to TextBox in a data-entry form, entering data in each field in order: Name, Address, City, State, Zip, and so on.

A better approach puts validation code in the LostFocus event of the zip code TextBox. With this approach, your application checks each field's entry when that field *loses focus* (is no longer the container where characters will be displayed when the user types). A field loses focus when the user presses the Tab key, moving to the next input component based on the TabIndex property, or when the user clicks any component capable of input.

Indexing Your Data

When you design a database, you can designate some of its fields as indexes. Information in a relational database is not automatically stored alphabetically (or by numeric order, if the field is numeric). When someone adds a new record to a database, it's just put at the end of a table. No attempt is made to place it in some particular position.

If you specify that a particular field or fields are to be indexed, however, they will be kept in an ordered list. This makes searching them far faster (for the same reason that you can find a particular topic faster in a book that has an index). For an in-depth discussion of indexes, see Chapter 2.

An index speeds up data access for the field that you index, so you usually design a database with at least one index. For example, if you usually display the names in your address book database sorted by the LastName field, you would want to index the LastName field. By doing so, you speed up the process of displaying this alphabetized list. Or, if you expect to frequently request specific records based on birthdays, you'd probably want to index the BirthDate field.

Why not index every field?

So, if you think data will be accessed primarily from several fields in a table, you can index each of these fields. "A-ha!" you say. "Why not index every field? Then, no matter what, the display of data must be ultimately swift." Nope, sorry. The use of indexes involves a tradeoff: If you index everything, you cancel the indexing efficiencies. So, use indexes only in moderation.

One reason why you don't index every field in a table is that sometimes a quick table scan is faster than analyzing a query, identifying the right index, loading that index, and querying against it. The main reason, though, is that whenever data is updated, the indexes relative to that data must be updated too. So, indexes speed up searches but always slow down updates.

Indexing a database properly is an art and requires performing a detailed analysis of your users' behaviors to detect what operations are performed more often — read or write — and adapting the application and configuring the database to reflect this.

The special primary index

One special index, called the *primary key,* ensures that the records in the database can be distinguished from each other. In other words, no two records can have identical data in the primary key field.

If you use a LastName field as your primary key, you can't enter two records with the same last name. Of course, that would be impractical. (If you create an index on a field such as LastName or FirstName, don't select the Unique property for either of those fields, which are likely to have duplicate values.) A more sensible field to use as the primary key is the taxpayer identification number because, by design, no duplicate numbers exist. Everyone gets a unique taxpayer identification number. For additional details on the primary key, read on or look at the discussion of indexing in Chapter 2.

Not only must each record have a distinct value (distinct content) in its primary key field, but each record must also have some content in the primary key field. This field can't be empty. (Technically, a field with no data is said to contain a *null value.*)

Every table should have a primary key field. Often, the most practical kind of primary key isn't some data about a person or object, but instead is generated at the time a record is added to the database. To obtain this number, each new record is given a number that is one higher than the preceding record. Usually, such a specialized, generated number is called an ID. The database itself can generate these serial ID numbers for each item of data.

Part V
The Internet Connection

"Give him air! Give him air! He'll be okay. He's just been exposed to some raw HTML code. It must have accidently flashed across his screen from the server."

In this part . . .

If you're swept up in Internet Madness (and who isn't?), Part V is for you. You find out how to use ASP.NET (Active Server Pages), how to port your classic Windows utilities and applications (you've written some great ones, haven't you?) into Web pages, and the best ways to use databases with a Web site. You'll create ASP but also take advantage of VB .NET's code-behind features — a way to program for the Internet using the familiar VB code window and language features. With the controls and tools VB .NET gives you, you'll wonder why people have been afraid of database programming in Internet applications.

Chapter 11

Translating Windows Applications to WebForms

*W*ebControls are a set of server-side controls that you can place on WebForms. When someone visits your Web site, those controls are translated into HTML on your server (by the ASP.NET technology), and then sent to the visitor's browser as pure HTML. That's why they're called server-side controls. The collection of WebControls is in the Toolbox when you are working with a WebForm in VB .NET and click the WebForms tab in the Toolbox.

ASP stands for *Active Server Pages* and refers to a technology whereby you can write scripting such as VBScript (or in ASP.NET, you can now use the full VB .NET language) to respond to, and interact with, visitors to a Web site. Chapter 13 goes into detail about ASP.NET, the latest incarnation of the ASP programming technology.

A *WebForm* is similar to the traditional VB form, and a WebControl is similar to the traditional VB control, so you're in a familiar environment, albeit inside an alien world. The familiar environment is the Visual Basic paradigm, and the alien world is the .NET framework.

When you work in the WebForm/WebControl model, you'll feel fairly at home. In many ways, this kind of programming is like traditional VB programming (events, the Property window, the form, the Toolbox, and so on). But when you add a WebControl to a WebForm, VB .NET instantly translates that control into HTML.

Some people say that HTML is a restrictive environment, limiting what can be displayed. They're correct. Forcing a control such as a RichTextBox into HTML is rather like shoving a wedding cake through a pipe. What comes out the other end is, technically, the same content as what was pushed into the pipe in the first place. But something — namely form — gets lost in the translation.

On the other hand, you're likely to be surprised at what Microsoft's busy programmers have been able to accomplish, given the restrictions imposed by browser architecture and by communication over the Internet.

In this chapter, you explore the WebControls and take a quick look at the set of VB .NET HTML controls as well.

Programming a DataSet in a WebForm

You'll find few differences between creating and displaying a DataSet on a *WebForm* (the new VB .NET Internet-page form) instead of a *WinForm* (the traditional Windows form). The fundamental programming in both cases is VB .NET. In this following example, you programmatically build a DataSet, and then display its schema in the browser within a DataGrid control. Recall that a *schema* is the structure (tables and columns) of a database, rather than its data (the *rows*).

To begin, follow these steps:

1. **Start a new VB .NET project and name it** WapWeb.

2. **Double-click the ASP.NET Web Application icon in the New Project dialog box.**

   This makes WapWeb a WebForm project, not a Windows project

3. **Click the Toolbox's Web Forms tab.**

4. **Double-click the DataGrid icon to add that control to the Design window.**

5. **Click the HTML tab at the bottom of the design window.**

   You should see this code:

```
<%@ Page Language="vb" AutoEventWireup="false"
        Codebehind="WebForm1.aspx.vb"
        Inherits="WappWeb.WebForm1"%>
<!DOCTYPE HTML PUBLIC "-//W3C//DTD HTML 4.0
        Transitional//EN">
<HTML>
  <HEAD>
    <title></title>
    <meta name="GENERATOR" content="Microsoft Visual
```

```
Studio.NET 7.0">
    <meta name="CODE_LANGUAGE" content="Visual Basic
        7.0">
    <meta name="vs_defaultClientScript"
        content="JavaScript">
    <meta name="vs_targetSchema"
        content="http://schemas.microsoft.com/intel-
        lisense/ie5">
  </HEAD>
  <body MS_POSITIONING="GridLayout">
    <form id="Form1" method="post" runat="server">
        <asp:DataGrid id="DataGrid1" style="Z-INDEX: 101;
        LEFT: 8px; POSITION: absolute; TOP: 8px"
        runat="server"></asp:DataGrid>
    </form>
  </body>
</HTML>
```

Note the code `Codebehind="WebForm1.aspx.vb"`. This tells ASP.NET that you have a code-behind (support source code) file written in VB .NET that should be looked at when evaluating this HTML page. The code-behind file could contain important information, such as events to trigger when the page loads or when the user clicks a button or otherwise interacts with the Web page.

In fact, let's provide some code-behind right now. This code will create a DataSet, connect to a database, fill the DataSet with a schema (the structure of data, its tables and columns), and then bind that DataSet to the DataGrid control in the HTML page. (Then, after that flurry of activity, the HTML page is sent off to the visitor to be displayed in his or her browser.) You'll get to view the results, just as if you were this visitor. Microsoft has a clever way of imitating the Internet, all within your single, local computer. You'll see.

Follow these steps:

1. **In Solution Explorer, right-click WebForm1.aspx and choose View Code.**

   You see this default code:

```
Public Class WebForm1
    Inherits System.Web.UI.Page
    Protected WithEvents DataGrid1 As
        System.Web.UI.WebControls.DataGrid

Web Form Designer Generated Code

Private Sub Page_Load(ByVal sender As System.Object,
        ByVal e As System.EventArgs) Handles MyBase.Load
    'Put user code to initialize the page here
End Sub

End Class
```

Note that a `WithEvents` reference to the DataGrid has been placed in the code. This means the DataGrid permits you to use some events. Also notice that a new tab has been added to the top of the code window: WebForm1.aspx.vb.

2. **At the very top of the code window, type the following boldface code:**

```
Imports System.Data
Imports System.Data.OleDb
Imports System.Data.SqlTypes
Imports System.Data.SqlDbType
Imports System.Data.SqlClient

Public Class WebForm1
Inherits System.Web.UI.Page
```

3. **Next, add this boldface code:**

```
Protected WithEvents DataGrid1 As
        System.Web.UI.WebControls.DataGrid

Dim ds As DataSet = New DataSet()

Private Sub Page_Load(ByVal sender As System.Object,
        ByVal e As System.EventArgs) Handles MyBase.Load

    filldatasetx()
    DataGrid1.DataSource = ds.Tables
    DataGrid1.DataBind()

End Sub

Public Sub filldatasetx()

    Dim pubConn As SqlConnection = New SqlConnection("Data
        Source=localhost;Integrated Security=SSPI;Initial
        Catalog=pubs")

    Dim selectCMD As SqlCommand = New SqlCommand("SELECT *
        FROM Authors", pubConn)
    selectCMD.CommandTimeout = 30

    Dim da As SqlDataAdapter = New SqlDataAdapter()
    da.SelectCommand = selectCMD

    pubConn.Open()

    da.Fill(ds, "Authors")

    pubConn.Close()

End Sub

End Class
```

This VB .NET source code used to create and display a DataSet in this WebForm (to define a database connection) is functionally identical to the source code you use in a WinForm to accomplish the same tasks.

4. Press F5.

You see the results shown in Figure 11-1.

Figure 11-1: This DataGrid displays the schema of the DataSet table.

Prefix	DesignMode	Namespace	HasErrors	MinimumCapacity	TableName	DisplayExpression	CaseSensitive
False			False	50	Authors		False

Notice that when you're programming in ASP.NET (in HTML code), you use an `Import` command to add a namespace, but when you're programming in VB .NET, you use an `Imports` command. Can't say why. Also, technically you don't need all those `Imports` statements. For example, you're using SQL-style database access in this example, so the `OleDb` namespace isn't necessary — none of your code uses it. All you really need is `System.Data` and `System.Data.SQLClient`. However, I simplified things by just importing all the data-access namespaces. That way, I don't have to bother deciding which ones to use each time I try an experiment while learning to use this new VB .NET ADO.NET programming.

If this is the first time you've programmed ASP.NET in VB .NET, you're likely to be startled by the results in Figure 11-1. When you press F5 after writing a WebForm project, you do not see the usual Form1 displayed by a Windows project. Instead of a form, the Internet Explorer browser starts running, and then it receives over the virtual Internet a Web page composed by VB .NET and ASP.NET in a virtual Web server. This is great for testing your ASP.NET projects. It mimics the communication that takes place between a Web surfer's browser and your ASP.NET project. It's a pretend Internet communication that works like the real thing.

To display the data in your DataSet (as opposed to the schema shown in Figure 11-1), replace the following line in the example:

```
DataGrid1.DataSource = ds.Tables
```

with this line:

```
DataGrid1.DataSource = ds
```

Here, you're not simply asking for Tables (the schema). You're asking for the DataSet, which you named ds in your source code when you declared it:

```
Dim ds As DataSet = New DataSet()
```

As you can see in Figure 11-2, the data is now visible in the DataGrid.

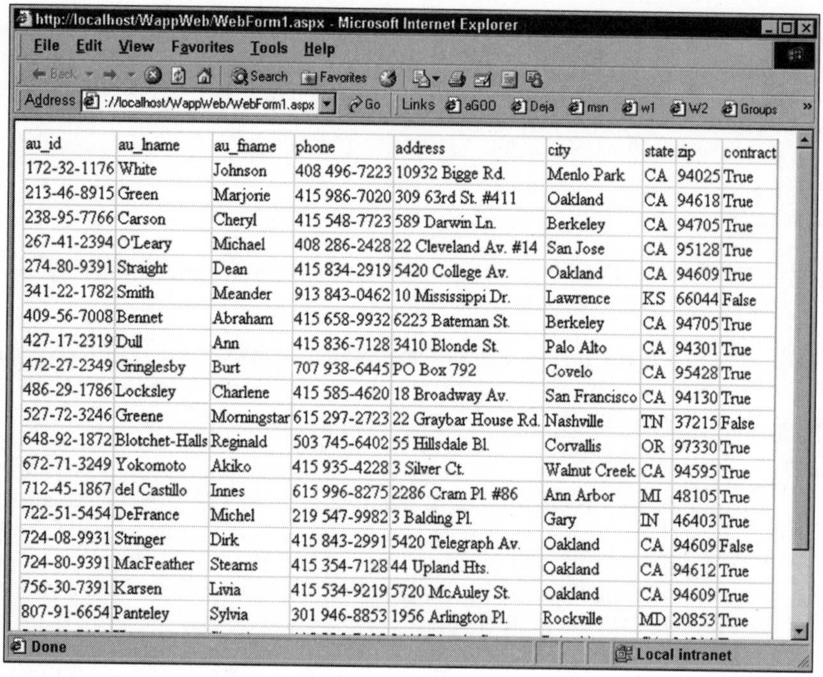

Figure 11-2:
To see the data, use the name of your DataSet as the DataGrid's DataSource.

au_id	au_lname	au_fname	phone	address	city	state	zip	contract
172-32-1176	White	Johnson	408 496-7223	10932 Bigge Rd.	Menlo Park	CA	94025	True
213-46-8915	Green	Marjorie	415 986-7020	309 63rd St. #411	Oakland	CA	94618	True
238-95-7766	Carson	Cheryl	415 548-7723	589 Darwin Ln.	Berkeley	CA	94705	True
267-41-2394	O'Leary	Michael	408 286-2428	22 Cleveland Av. #14	San Jose	CA	95128	True
274-80-9391	Straight	Dean	415 834-2919	5420 College Av.	Oakland	CA	94609	True
341-22-1782	Smith	Meander	913 843-0462	10 Mississippi Dr.	Lawrence	KS	66044	False
409-56-7008	Bennet	Abraham	415 658-9932	6223 Bateman St.	Berkeley	CA	94705	True
427-17-2319	Dull	Ann	415 836-7128	3410 Blonde St.	Palo Alto	CA	94301	True
472-27-2349	Gringlesby	Burt	707 938-6445	PO Box 792	Covelo	CA	95428	True
486-29-1786	Locksley	Charlene	415 585-4620	18 Broadway Av.	San Francisco	CA	94130	True
527-72-3246	Greene	Morningstar	615 297-2723	22 Graybar House Rd.	Nashville	TN	37215	False
648-92-1872	Blotchet-Halls	Reginald	503 745-6402	55 Hillsdale Bl.	Corvallis	OR	97330	True
672-71-3249	Yokomoto	Akiko	415 935-4228	3 Silver Ct.	Walnut Creek	CA	94595	True
712-45-1867	del Castillo	Innes	615 996-8275	2286 Cram Pl. #86	Ann Arbor	MI	48105	True
722-51-5454	DeFrance	Michel	219 547-9982	3 Balding Pl.	Gary	IN	46403	True
724-08-9931	Stringer	Dirk	415 843-2991	5420 Telegraph Av.	Oakland	CA	94609	False
724-80-9391	MacFeather	Stearns	415 354-7128	44 Upland Hts.	Oakland	CA	94612	True
756-30-7391	Karsen	Livia	415 534-9219	5720 McAuley St.	Oakland	CA	94609	True
807-91-6654	Panteley	Sylvia	301 946-8853	1956 Arlington Pl.	Rockville	MD	20853	True

Detecting Postback

Now that you see how to display data to a user, how do you detect a postback? *Postback* means sending information from a client (Web surfer's browser) to your server. For example, how can you identify and react if a user clicks one of the items in your ListBox to see some data? Or clicks a Submit button to send back a filled-in order form?

Recall that your entire page is *recreated* on the server in the Page_Load event, and then sent fresh to the user's browser. In this example, the user will click an item in the ListBox in his or her browser, shown in Figure 11-3. You, the programmer, must make two changes to the source code to be able to detect that click.

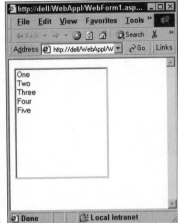

Figure 11-3:
When the user clicks an item in this ListBox, your server-side code must detect that click.

To see how this works, follow these steps:

1. **Click the WebForm1.aspx tab at the top of the code window, and then click the Design tab at the bottom of the window.**

   You see the WebForm (as opposed to your VB .NET code-behind code window).

2. **Click the DataGrid control you used in the preceding example, and then press the Del key to delete it.**

3. **In the Toolbox, click the WebForms tab (if necessary), and then double-click the ListBox icon to place it on your WebForm.**

4. **Drag the ListBox down a few inches from the top.**

   You don't want the ListBox covering the text you'll be printing on the form.

5. **Click the HTML tab at the bottom of the design window.**

6. **Add an autopostback element to the ListBox by adding** autopost-back="true" **(shown in boldface) to the ListBox code:**

```
<asp:ListBox id="ListBox1" autopostback="true" style="Z-
        INDEX: 101; LEFT: 91px; POSITION: absolute; TOP:
        8px" runat="server" Width="145px"
        Height="280px"></asp:ListBox>
```

   The various size and position properties are likely to differ in your HTML, but just ignore them. Adding the autopostback element causes this ListBox item to be posted back to your server when the user clicks it.

7. On your server, query the `IsPostBack` **property of the Web page to determine whether or not a postback has occurred. To do this, click the WebForm1.vb.aspx tab at the top of the code window, and then change the** `Page_Load` **event to this code:**

```
Private Sub Page_Load(ByVal sender As System.Object,
        ByVal e As System.EventArgs) Handles MyBase.Load
    If Not IsPostBack Then

        Dim MyArray As New ArrayList()

        MyArray.Add("One")
        MyArray.Add("Two")
        MyArray.Add("Three")
        MyArray.Add("Four")
        MyArray.Add("Five")

        ListBox1.DataSource = MyArray
        ListBox1.DataBind()

    Else ' it is a postback

        Response.Write("You clicked " &
            ListBox1.SelectedItem.Text)

    End If

End Sub
```

In this example, your code fills the ListBox with data from an array *only if this is the first time you are sending the page to the user.* That's what `If Not IsPostBack Then` means. If this page is not being posted (sent) back from the visitor, the visitor is seeing the page for the first time and you display some data in the ListBox. But if this is a postback, you don't need to refill the already-filled ListBox. Instead, you react to the choice that the user made by clicking one of the items displayed in the ListBox.

This example code can distinguish between a simple `Page_Load` (where the user has merely visited your page but not yet interacted with it by clicking) and a postback (where the user, in this case, clicked an item in the ListBox and therefore did interact with your page).

As you can see in Figure 11-4, a click sends the ListBox's SelectedItem.Text property back to the server, where you can grab the data and respond. Here you respond by printing a message with `Response.Write` in the visitor's browser. But in real life, you would send back a picture of the item the user selected, the price of the item, or some such useful information.

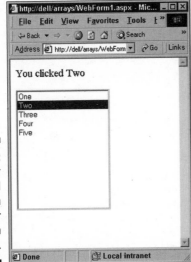

Figure 11-4:
The server detected which item the user clicked in this ListBox.

The Rich Data Controls

You've used the DataGrid and ListBox controls in previous examples in this chapter to connect to a data source and then display the data to the user. Now take a closer look at the VB .NET server-side controls, which are designed to be used with databases in WebForms. You start with a second look at the DataGrid.

The ASP.NET DataGrid

The DataGrid control is probably the most flexible of the new rich ASP.NET controls. You've worked with it in previous examples in this chapter, but there are more tricks it can perform that you might want to know about. In this example, you manipulate the DataGrid, using not the Pubs sample database but the Northwind database.

Follow these steps to continue your exploration of the DataGrid:.

1. **Start a new VB .NET project (choose Project⇨New).**

2. **In Solution Explorer, right-click WebForm1.aspx and choose View Code.**

3. **At the very top of the code window, type the following code (shown in boldface):**

```
Imports System.Data
Imports System.Data.SqlClient

Public Class WebForm1
Inherits System.Web.UI.Page
```

4. **Then type the following code into the** Page_Load **event:**

```
Private Sub Page_Load(ByVal sender As System.Object,
        ByVal e As System.EventArgs) Handles MyBase.Load

    Dim ds As DataSet = New DataSet()
    Dim pubConn As SqlConnection = New
        SqlConnection("Data Source=localhost;Integrated
        Security=SSPI;Initial Catalog=northwind")

    Dim selectCMD As SqlCommand = New
        SqlCommand("SELECT * FROM Customers", pubConn)
    selectCMD.CommandTimeout = 30

    Dim da As SqlDataAdapter = New SqlDataAdapter()
        da.SelectCommand = selectCMD

    pubConn.Open()

    da.Fill(ds, "Customers")

    pubConn.Close()

    DataGrid1.DataSource = ds
    DataGrid1.DataBind()

End Sub
```

5. **Click the WebForm1.aspx tab, and then click the Design tab in the main window.**

6. **Double-click the DataGrid control in the Toolbox to add the control to your WebForm.**

7. **Press F5 to run this program.**

   You see the results shown in Figure 11-5.

Now let's fiddle with the DataGrid, to make it more readable and professional looking. As a member of the so-called *rich* Control class, the DataGrid is wealthy in features and tricks it can perform for you and your Web site visitors. Among *many* other properties that you can adjust are the BackColor and AlternatingBackColor properties. If you change the BackColor property, every other row is displayed in the new color. The AlternatingItemStyle property's BackColor property remains the default color, making the table easier to read.

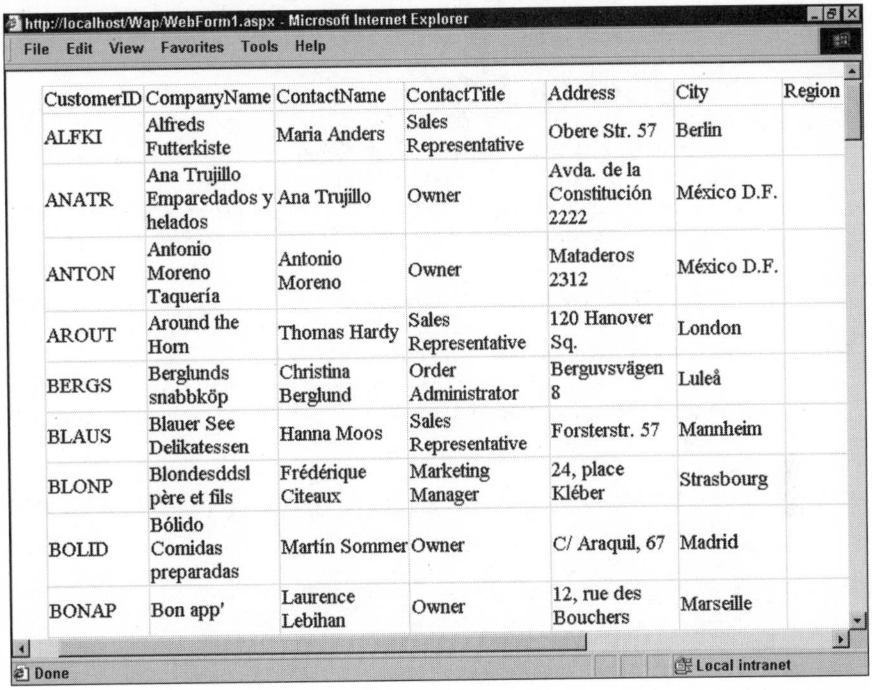

CustomerID	CompanyName	ContactName	ContactTitle	Address	City	Region
ALFKI	Alfreds Futterkiste	Maria Anders	Sales Representative	Obere Str. 57	Berlin	
ANATR	Ana Trujillo Emparedados y helados	Ana Trujillo	Owner	Avda. de la Constitución 2222	México D.F.	
ANTON	Antonio Moreno Taquería	Antonio Moreno	Owner	Mataderos 2312	México D.F.	
AROUT	Around the Horn	Thomas Hardy	Sales Representative	120 Hanover Sq.	London	
BERGS	Berglunds snabbköp	Christina Berglund	Order Administrator	Berguvsvägen 8	Luleå	
BLAUS	Blauer See Delikatessen	Hanna Moos	Sales Representative	Forsterstr. 57	Mannheim	
BLONP	Blondesddsl père et fils	Frédérique Citeaux	Marketing Manager	24, place Kléber	Strasbourg	
BOLID	Bólido Comidas preparadas	Martín Sommer	Owner	C/ Araquil, 67	Madrid	
BONAP	Bon app'	Laurence Lebihan	Owner	12, rue des Bouchers	Marseille	

Figure 11-5: Here's the database, displayed the way visitors to your Web site will see it in their browsers.

To create this effect, follow these steps:

1. **Click the WebForm1.aspx tab at the top of the design window.**
2. **Click the Design tab at the bottom of the design window.**
3. **Press F4 to open the DataGrid's Properties window.**
4. **Click the DataGrid to select it.**
5. **In the Properties window, click + next to ItemStyle to open its list of properties.**
6. **Click the BackColor property, and then click the down arrow symbol and choose a new BackColor from the palette.**
7. **Also fiddle with the AlternatingItemStyle's BackColor property.**

   You see the results in the design window immediately.

If you look at the HTML, you'll see that your adjustments in the Properties window are reflected in new HTML code:

```
<AlternatingItemStyle
          BackColor="#FFE0C0"></AlternatingItemStyle>

<ItemStyle BackColor="#C0C0FF"></ItemStyle>
```

Manipulating the DataGrid programmatically

Because the DataGrid in this example isn't bound to a data store (source) until runtime, you can't use the Properties window to adjust the headers and data (with the Columns collection). In this section, you see how to do it programmatically.

First, you'll change the `AutoGenerate Columns` attribute (property) of the DataGrid to False. This way the grid will not automatically fill with column heads and rows of data. You can either make this change using the Properties window in Design view, or you can click the HTML tab in the design window to make this change directly to the HTML code itself. Let's experiment with the latter approach.

Add this attribute (in boldface) to the HTML code's definition of the DataGrid:

```
<asp:DataGrid id=DataGrid1 autogeneratecolumns="false"
         runat="server" ForeColor="Black">
```

If you copy and paste code into the HTML editor window, you might see a red sawtooth line under the code you pasted. This means the HTML editor does-n't like what you inserted. Perhaps the code has a typo or isn't a member of the object you're working with, or perhaps you used curly quotation marks (") instead of plain ones ("). You should correct your code before testing your WebForm. Also, if you copy and paste source code from Word or another application that uses embedded codes, you'll likely see all kinds of problems with the pasted code. The solution is to paste the code into Notepad, which strips all embedded symbols and most special characters, and then copy and paste the code from Notepad to the VB .NET editor.

Now, look again at the HTML code defining the DataGrid, and add to the existing code this definition of which columns you want to display (shown here in boldface):

```
<asp:DataGrid id="DataGrid1" autogeneratecolumns="False"
         style="Z-INDEX: 101; LEFT: 76px; POSITION:
         absolute; TOP: 36px" runat="server" Width="243px"
         Height="280px">

<AlternatingItemStyle
         BackColor="#FFE0C0"></AlternatingItemStyle>
<ItemStyle BackColor="#C0C0FF"></ItemStyle>
```

```
<Columns>

<asp:BoundColumn HeaderText="Name" DataField="ContactName"
          ItemStyle-Font-Size="15"></asp:BoundColumn>

<asp:BoundColumn HeaderText="Title" DataField="ContactTitle"
          ItemStyle-Font-Size="11"></asp:BoundColumn>

<asp:BoundColumn HeaderText="City" DataField="City"
          ItemStyle-Font-Size="11"></asp:BoundColumn>

<asp:BoundColumn HeaderText="Phone Number" DataField="Phone"
          ItemStyle-Font-Bold="True"></asp:BoundColumn>

</Columns>

</asp:DataGrid>
```

As you see, you can use this technique to freely manipulate which columns are displayed (DataField), the header names, font size, boldface, and many other properties of each column.

Intellisense lists are displayed in the HTML code window of a WebForm. Just go to the end of an attribute in the HTML source code, such as the `HeaderText="Name"` attribute, and press the Spacebar. As soon as you insert a space character into the source code, up pops a list of all the additional attributes available for use with that element. (An HTML element is similar to an object. For example, a single `asp:BoundColumn` is an element. You can modify an element by adding *attributes* to its definitions between the < and </ symbols that surround the element specification in the HTML code.) You can find out more about the VB .NET Intellisense features at the end of the "Generating Your DataSet" section in Chapter 16.

Press F5 to see the results shown in Figure 11-6. You changed the order of the columns and their header text, changed the font size, and added boldface to two of the columns.

While in Design view, you can manipulate the DataGrid's properties as a whole in the Properties window. But you can also adjust the properties of each individual column. Just click the ... (ellipsis) next to the Columns property in the DataGrid Properties window. You see a wonderfully complete dialog box where you can adjust many elements of the DataGrid and its components.

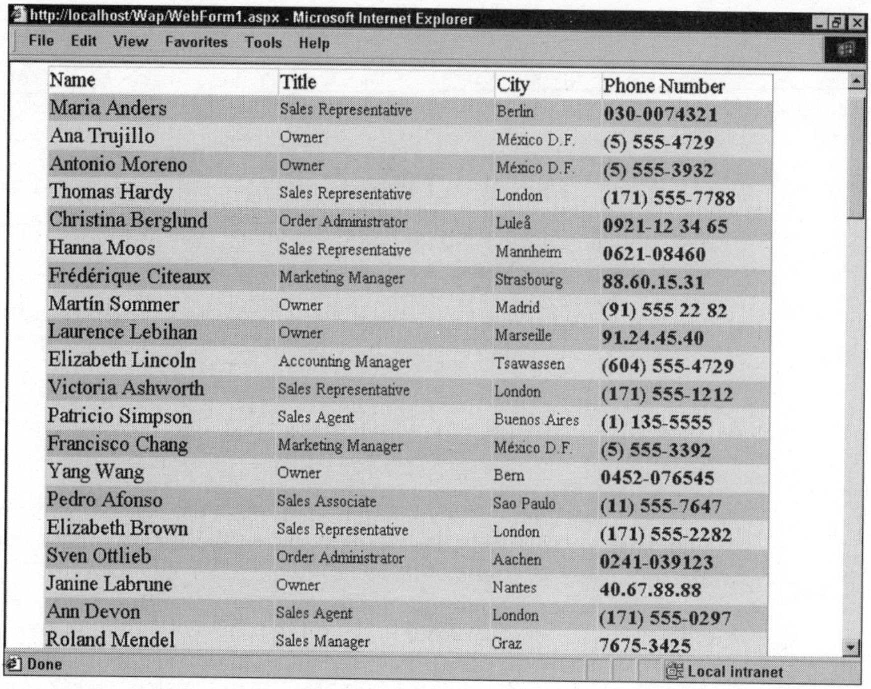

Name	Title	City	Phone Number
Maria Anders	Sales Representative	Berlin	030-0074321
Ana Trujillo	Owner	México D.F.	(5) 555-4729
Antonio Moreno	Owner	México D.F.	(5) 555-3932
Thomas Hardy	Sales Representative	London	(171) 555-7788
Christina Berglund	Order Administrator	Luleå	0921-12 34 65
Hanna Moos	Sales Representative	Mannheim	0621-08460
Frédérique Citeaux	Marketing Manager	Strasbourg	88.60.15.31
Martín Sommer	Owner	Madrid	(91) 555 22 82
Laurence Lebihan	Owner	Marseille	91.24.45.40
Elizabeth Lincoln	Accounting Manager	Tsawassen	(604) 555-4729
Victoria Ashworth	Sales Representative	London	(171) 555-1212
Patricio Simpson	Sales Agent	Buenos Aires	(1) 135-5555
Francisco Chang	Marketing Manager	México D.F.	(5) 555-3392
Yang Wang	Owner	Bern	0452-076545
Pedro Afonso	Sales Associate	Sao Paulo	(11) 555-7647
Elizabeth Brown	Sales Representative	London	(171) 555-2282
Sven Ottlieb	Order Administrator	Aachen	0241-039123
Janine Labrune	Owner	Nantes	40.67.88.88
Ann Devon	Sales Agent	London	(171) 555-0297
Roland Mendel	Sales Manager	Graz	7675-3425

Figure 11-6: You can programmatically adjust all the elements of a DataGrid.

Using a template

The Repeater control, like the DataGrid and DataList controls, is an ASP.NET server-side control. The Repeater is somewhat more primitive than the other two controls, but it is nonetheless flexible. It is designed to be used with a template because the Repeater itself has no built-in visual structure — no gridlines, no default shape.

Note that you can use templates with DataGrids or DataLists too, but only the Repeater *requires* a template for its visual output. A *template* is a group of HTML elements (and any controls you place in each element) that specify the look of an area (a single cell, for instance) of a container control. For instance, you can create a template that specifies how each row in a DataGrid looks.

Templates are distinct from styles. *Styles* describe such properties as color and font size for a control and can be used to change the defaults for these properties. You can use styles independently or in a template. A template specifies such elements as separators, headers, footers and alternating items (the DataGrid also supports a template for columns).

You use XML declarations to build a template in an .ASPX file. The `<template>` element includes a description of the look of the template and the `NAME` attribute is the template type. See "ASP.NET Server Controls Templates" in VB .NET Help for a list of which templates you can use with which ASP.NET controls.

The DataList control

Another ASP.NET database-related rich control to consider is the DataList. It's similar to the Repeater but the DataList can display data items in horizontal, as well as vertical, cells, whereas the Repeater is limited to a vertical display.

The DataList control is an interesting, somewhat customizable list control. You get to define a number of parameters, including the appearance of the following: the selected cell, alternating rows (you can give them a light-colored background, for example, so that the list is easier to read), or an edited cell.

Start a new WebForm project and put a DataList control on the WebForm. The control's icon contains a message, informing you that you should right-click the DataList icon. After you right-click, choose the Edit Template option, as shown in Figure 11-7.

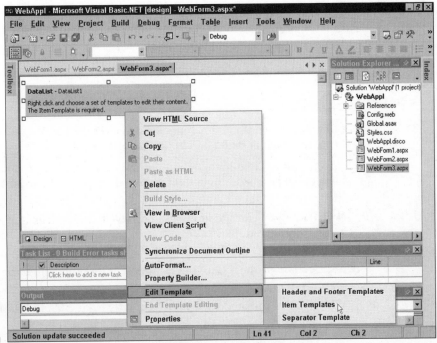

Figure 11-7:
The DataList Control — unique among the data-related controls — offers this Edit Template feature.

Stick with GridLayout

If you change a WebForm's GridLayout mode by switching the document's PageLayout property in the Properties window to FlowLayout, VB .NET stacks controls one below the other, arranged vertically down the page like a tower. You can't drag the controls horizontally to arrange them in more visually pleasing ways on your page. You *can* move them horizontally using HTML code, but why worry about coding it? Just stick with the default GridLayout for the easiest, simplest way to design a Web page.

Note that when you use a DataList, you *must* at the very least provide an ItemTemplate. Now let's see how to generate a template, and how to use the Template Editor. You create a template that defines what controls are included in the DataList as well as the appearance of the header, footer, divider, and individual cells.

To see how to create a template, follow these steps:

1. **Add a DataList control to your project.**

2. **In Design view, right-click DataList and choose Edit Template⇨Item Templates.**

3. **In the design windows, select the ItemTemplate area in the DataList.**

   An insertion cursor starts blinking.

4. **Double-click a TextBox in the Toolbox.**

   This places a TextBox in the ItemTemplate, so the user will see a TextBox for *each* item displayed in the DataList.

5. **Click the AlternatingItem Template area to select it. Add a TextBox here, too, but set its BackColor property to light gray.**

6. **Add two more TextBoxes — one for the currently selected item (perhaps make its BorderStyle light red) and one to indicate an Edited item.**

   Notice that you can add any other controls to these cells that make sense to you (buttons, images, whatever). You can also simply type words in the cell, and they, too, will be displayed to the user.

7. **Adjust some properties of the Header, Footer, and Separator elements, if you want.**

8. **When you're finished with your template, right-click DataList again and choose End Template Editing.**

   You return to the normal design mode.

9. Click the HTML tab on the bottom of the design window to see all the HTML that VB .NET has generated for you to define your DataList.

Note that the DataGrid and the Repeater are two similar, template-based, data-bound controls.

HTML Controls versus WebControls

There is some overlap between WebControls and the HTML controls in the VB .NET Toolbox. My advice is to choose the WebControls, when possible. They have several advantages, most important of which is that you get to program using the tested and familiar VB programming language (or at least what's left of it after the massive changes to VB in VB .NET).

You'll be able to use events, set properties in those events, and otherwise avoid the restrictive and often inefficient HTML programming model. (It's inefficient from a programmer's point of view. For example, to create a table, you must type many, many ⟨TD⟩ tags and other tags. HTML, like XML, employs a verbose code.)

HTML also suffers from having only a single data type, the string. This prevents the computer from assisting you with *type safety* (ensuring that data types are accurately represented and accurately translated into other types).

However, let's not throw out HTML controls entirely. They can be useful if you must split your programming, locating some on your server and writing other programming (known as *script* code) that will run in the user's browser. The reason: The control will be the same in both the server and the browser runtime environments, simplifying your job of writing the browser script.

HTML controls are also useful if you're merely updating an existing ASP or HTML page by transforming it into a WebForm. In this situation, by limiting yourself to HTML controls, you won't disturb the other elements on the original Web page.

Open the Toolbox, click the HTML tab, and take a look at the HTML controls. These are mostly traditional HTML (Web page) controls, such as the horizontal rule, table, image, and submit button. They are server controls, like WebControls, but they are classic, familiar HTML components.

At the top of the WebForms tab — as well as the Data, Components, HTML, and every other tab on the Toolbox — is a Pointer control. What's mysterious about this entry is that it has no purpose. You can't add it to a WebForm. It does nothing and has no properties. But there it is, a reminder that no matter how well-thought-out, every environment has its puzzles.

You often don't see the entire group of controls in any given tab in the Toolbox. Take a look at Figure 11-8 and notice that to see all the HTML controls, you must scroll the list by clicking the down-arrow icon near the bottom of the Toolbox (which the white mouse cursor is pointing to in the figure).

An HTML server-side control either contains the `runat="server"` HTML attribute or is enclosed with a form element with a `runat server` attribute, as in this HTML code describing a server-side HTML password control:

```
<form id="WebForm1" method="post" runat="server">

<input
type=password>

</form>
```

If you've programmed in HTML, you're familiar with this classic set of HTML controls displayed when you click the HTML tab on VB .NET's Toolbox.

However, the WebControls give you more features than their traditional HTML counterpart (compare the HTML button to the WebControl LinkButton) or are entirely new (such as the Calendar WebControl). Generally speaking, WebControls are far richer — they have many more members (methods, events, and properties) than are available to HTML server-side controls.

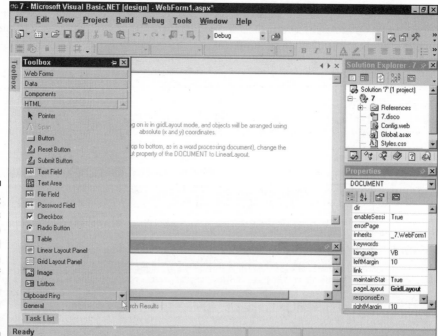

Figure 11-8:
Click this arrow to scroll through the entire list of controls in a Toolbox tab category.

Also, the HTML object model is restrictive. Each HTML control has an attribute collection that the programmer uses to change the attributes of the tag (the control). An attribute is coded using a name/value pair (just as all properties and indeed all variables are structured), but the HTML name/value pair isn't strongly typed.

Following is a typical name/value pair in HTML:

```
type=button
```

Compare that to a WebControl's property specification in HTML source code:

```
BorderColor="blue"
```

HTML controls require that you write source code pretty much the same way you programmed in traditional ASP. If you're uncomfortable with ASP.NET, you can still include HTML controls on your WebForms — and even mix and match WebControls and HTML controls on the same page.

If you decide you want to force a classic HTML control to be a server control, right-click the control in the design window and choose Run as server control. VB .NET automatically changes the underlying HTML code from this:

```
<input type=button value=Button>
```

to this:

```
<input type=button value=Button id=Button1 runat="server">
```

Although WebControls also have an attribute collection, they are far richer than HTML controls. WebControls includes a standard set of properties and boast a consistent and type-safe object model.

WebControls feature high-level abstractions that have no HTML equivalent (see the Calendar control, for instance). WebControls do not map directly to HTML tags, so you can program with a single (but multipurpose) TextBox instead of having individual, distinct tags for various TextBox uses. In other words, whereas HTML has Text column, TextArea, Password column and File column controls, you can transform a single WebForm TextBox into password-style by changing the TextBox's TextMode property to Password.

Also, remember that the HTML code that results when a WebControl is rendered (by your server) must be, after all, HTML. If there is no direct equivalence between your WebControl and an HTML control; something has to give.

Put another way: If you double-click a DataGrid control in the Toolbox and thereby add one to the design window (to your WebForm), you probably think that this object is being injected into the HTML and given a name (an *ID* in HTML). Wrong. Rendered by HTML, the DataGrid becomes an elaborate, lengthy HTML table. VB .NET works feverishly to render your WebControl into HTML. And if you change a property of the WebControl in the Properties window, VB .NET translates that change into HTML for you.

In contrast, HTML controls map one-for-one directly to HTML tags. There is no abstraction.

The WebControl Collection

When translated into HTML, each WebControl contains the `runat="server"` attribute, `asp:` is prepended to the name of the WebControl. This identifies the control as an ASP.NET control:

```
<asp:ListBox id=ListBox1 runat="server"></asp:ListBox>
```

The WebControls offer several significant bonuses to programmers. They can automatically detect which browser they've landed in and respond appropriately. In other words, you don't have to write HTML code to see whether the request for your Web page comes from Netscape instead of Internet Explorer, and then write more code to cope with Netscape's differences. Instead, some WebControls can vary how they are rendered, to optimize their features for either browser.

In addition, WebControls share a number of properties and methods in common and you, the programmer, benefit from this consistency. For example, the code syntax for ToolTip, BackColor, Visible and other members of the ListBox WebControl is identical to the code syntax used for the other WebControls.

So if you understand the syntax and parameters when using the ListBox, you'll have no trouble dealing with all the other WebControls. Microsoft describes the WebControls as *strongly typed* which, in this context, means that the terminology used to manipulate the WebControls has been chosen to be easily recognized and remembered by the user (in this case, the *user* is the *programmer*). A weakly typed line of code would look like this:

```
Table(4).Row(0).Update
```

whereas strongly typed code would look like this:

```
Table("Publishers").Row("Address").Update.
```

Also note that you can now bind *any* property of a WebControl to data in VB .NET. A group of WebControls (on the Data tab of the Toolbox) is available to assist you in binding and accessing data stores.

Buttons for submission

The WebControl button has several properties not available for the HTML button. For example, you can attach a ToolTip explaining the purpose of the button. This tip is displayed to the user each time the mouse hovers over that button, as shown in Figure 11-9.

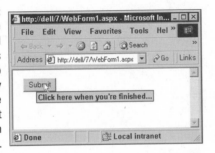

Figure 11-9: The WebControl button's ToolTip property tells the user what the button does.

In a browser, the various button-style controls permit the user to send information to the server. ASP.NET button controls include the ordinary button, a button with a hyperlink, and an ImageButton, which permits you to display a graphic on your button. (You can perk up the looks of a Web page by using something more imaginative than the familiar battleship-gray button). ImageButtons also provide you with an X/Y coordinate showing where the user clicked within the image. This way, you can display, for instance, a picture of two musical instruments and ask users to select the instrument they are interested in. For an example of what you can do by changing the ImageURL property of the ImageButton control, see Figure 11-10.

The LinkButton appears to the user as an ordinary hyperlink on the Web page. If you put a LinkButton WebControl and a Hyperlink WebControl on a Web page, they look the same, as you can see in Figure 11-11.

The difference is that an ordinary hyperlink, when clicked, immediately discards your Web page and takes the user to another Web page specified by the URL of the hyperlink. A LinkButton, by contrast, permits you to intercept, examine, and possibly react — server-side — to the user's click. The LinkButton forces your form to be posted back to the server.

Figure 11-10:
Spice up
your Web
site's
buttons with
the
ImageURL
property
and the
ImageButton
control.

Figure 11-11:
The user
sees no
difference
between a
LinkButton
and a
traditional
hyperlink.

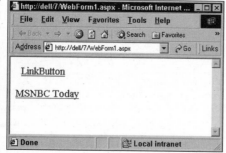

CommandName and CommandArgument properties

Button controls have CommandName and CommandArgument properties
that you can use to pass information back to the server about the purpose of
the control. If you change those properties in the Properties window, the elements are added to your HTML, like this:

```
<asp:Button id="Button1" runat="server" Text="Button"
        style="Z-INDEX: 101; LEFT: 148px; POSITION:
        absolute; TOP: 107px" CommandArgument="Area code"
        CommandName="Sisily"></asp:Button>
```

You can see that the properties are available to the button's events by writing
this code inside the button's click event:

```
Private Sub Button1_Click(ByVal sender As System.Object,
        ByVal e As System.EventArgs) Handles Button1.Click

    Response.Write(Button1.CommandName)
    Response.Write(Button1.CommandArgument)

End Sub
```

Buttons in container controls

You can place ASP.NET Buttons in DataList, DataGrid, and Repeater controls. However, when contained, you don't write code in a `Click` event. Instead, the user clicks the button, and the event message "bubbles up" to the container control, such as the DataList control. Then the DataList's `ItemCommand` event — instead of the button's `Click` event — is triggered. Note that you can use the CommandName and CommandArgument properties of several buttons in a container control as a way of identifying the purpose and identity of each button.

Labeling

The Label control isn't interactive; the user can't modify it. Clicking it has no more effect than pressing your finger on the return address label on an envelope. For read-only data displays, however, the Label works quite well. You can use it as a label by placing it near other controls to explain their function. Or you can use the Label to display rows from a database without permitting the user to make any changes to those rows.

You can, of course, label things by simply typing directly into the design window (with the HTML tab selected). That puts your typed text into the HTML like this:

```
<p>Current Row: </p>
```

However, using the Label control gives you more flexibility and is easier — you get more options, and you can manipulate those options in the Properties window with ease. What's more, you can easily move the Label to different locations on the page.

I don't want to suggest that writing HTML source code is clumsy or inefficient, but if you've been used to the RAD conveniences of writing programs in VB, you might see HTML as a step or two backward in the evolutionary progress of computer languages.

Making text interactive

If you want to permit the user to enter text, the TextBox is often your choice of control. You can display default text, allow the user to edit that text, or allow the user to enter entirely new text of their own.

TextBoxes can be single-line or multi-line; can be password style (****
appears instead of characters when the user types); and can have scrollbars to permit the user to scroll through a document that's too large to view in its entirety in the TextBox window.

You can adjust the properties of a WebControl TextBox in the Properties window (in design mode) or by directly modifying the HTML (in HTML Code view mode). Here are a few example properties:

```
<asp:TextBox id="TextBox1" Text="Data for you" Font-
        size="medium" ForeColor="blue" BackColor="white"
        TextMode="MultiLine" Height="46"
        runat="server"></asp:TextBox>

<asp:TextBox id="Textbox2" Text="Data for you" Font-
        size="Medium" Font-names="Comic Sans MS"
        ForeColor="blue" BackColor="white"
        TextMode="MultiLine" Height="48"
        runat="server"></asp:TextBox>
```

What is this odd choice of names for the Font-size property? Why the hyphen? The hyphen is making its first appearance in mainstream computer languages thanks to HTML's quirky punctuation. And why the especially odd plurality of Font-names when it refers to a single name, not a collection? VB users would expect `FontSize` and `FontName` instead. But who's complaining? In VB .NET, the Visual Basic language blows away many familiar, two-decades-old Basic language conventions. For example, VB .NET employs two punctuation marks never found previously in Basic: the brace and the bracket.

Using CheckBoxes and RadioButtons

CheckBoxes are used for binary input; the user gets to choose yes or no. When checked, the user is saying *yes*. For instance, if you're giving the users a choice between italic or bold text, put a CheckBox on your page and they can choose one, or both, of these styles.

RadioButtons (previously known as *option buttons*) permit you to create a list of choices. But whereas you can choose more than one CheckBoxes, you can choose only one among a group of RadioButtons. When the user clicks one of the RadioButtons in a group of such buttons, whatever button was previously selected is unselected. Only one RadioButton in a group can be chosen at a time. This type of control is useful when you have mutually exclusive options, such as permitting the user to choose among one of three colors for the text in a TextBox, as shown in Figure 11-12.

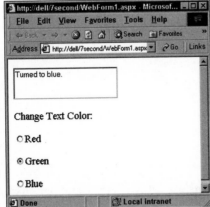

Figure 11-12:
Use Radio
Buttons for
a mutually
exclusive
set of
options.

Each time you add a new RadioButton to your WebForm, VB .NET generates a new and different GroupName property for that RadioButton (RadioButton1, RadioButton2, and so on). However, the purpose of RadioButtons is that when the user clicks one of them, the previously selected one is unselected. So, after you've added all the RadioButtons that you intend to use in a group of mutually exclusive options, hold down the Ctrl key and click each RadioButton that you want to group. Then in the Properties window, type a GroupName property. That name will be shared by all of them, and therefore they will behave as a group. (You can have more than one group of RadioButtons on a single WebForm. Just give each group a new GroupName.)

CheckBoxes and RadioButtons don't require that you add Label controls to describe their function. Instead, just type your description in their Text property.

To display multiple CheckBoxes or RadioButtons, you might want to consider using the new CheckBoxList or RadioButtonList controls. This HTML produces what's displayed in Figure 11-13.

```
<asp:CheckBoxList runat="server" ID=CheckBoxList1>
<asp:ListItem Text="Italics" Value="1" selected="true"/>
<asp:ListItem Text="BoldFace" Value="2" selected="true"/>
</asp:CheckBoxList >

<asp:RadioButtonList runat="server" ID=RadioButtonList1>
<asp:ListItem Text="Red" Value="1" selected="true"/>
<asp:ListItem Text="Green" Value="2"/>
</asp:RadioButtonList >
```

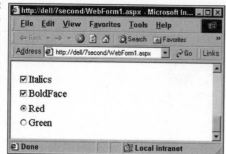

Figure 11-13:
The
CheckBox-
List and
RadioButton
List controls
generate
their own
groups
automat-
ically.

Displaying lists

The ListBox control shows the user a list of choices, and permits the user to scroll through the list and select either one or more items in the list. If you want to permit more than one selection at a time, set the SelectionMode property to Multiple.

In design mode, you can use the Items collection (click it in the Properties window) to describe the selections, as shown in Figure 11-14.

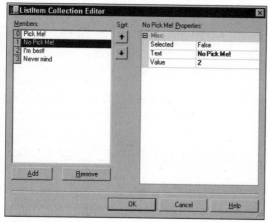

Figure 11-14:
This dialog
box makes it
easy to add
items to
your
ListBoxes
and
DropDown-
ListBoxes.

Or if you want, click the HTML tab on the design window and type the HTML source code, like this:

```
<asp:ListBox id=ListBox1 runat="server" Width="217px"
          Height="167px" font-size="Large">

<asp:ListItem Value="1">Pick Me!</asp:ListItem>
<asp:ListItem Value="2">No Pick Me!</asp:ListItem>
<asp:ListItem Value="3" Selected="True">I'm
          best!</asp:ListItem>
<asp:ListItem Value="4">Never mind</asp:ListItem>

</asp:ListBox>
```

You can also populate a list control by binding it to a database.

The DropDownListBox is similar to the ListBox, but makes more efficient use of screen space. The user doesn't see the entire list because by default only a single item is displayed. See the difference in Figure 11-15.

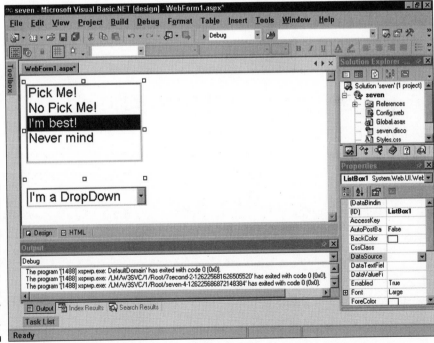

Figure 11-15: A DropDown style ListBox uses up less space in a browser than the ordinary ListBox.

Chapter 12

Active Server Pages: Mixing HTML with VB

In This Chapter

▶ Understanding ASP

▶ Setting up ASP.NET

▶ Writing a standard script

▶ Writing your first ASP script

*B*efore tackling the new features available in Microsoft's latest initiatives — .NET and ASP.NET — you should first understand what ASP itself is and does. You can use Active Server Pages (ASP) to display data in a Web page. With the ASP technology, you basically blend VBScript with HTML, creating a Web page that runs partly in the user's browser and partly on your server.

When a Web page is loaded into a browser, the browser handles the typical HTML codes, such as <H1>, which causes the browser to display text as a large headline. If a Web page contains ASP programming, however, a VBScript engine (or in the new ASP.NET, the full VB .NET language engine) on the server interprets that programming and then sends the result to the user's browser. (You can also use JScript, but in this book, VBScript is, obviously, the preferred language.)

What use is ASP in a real-world situation? Without ASP, Web pages can be mere exercises in publishing — not all that much more useful or advanced than the traditional advertisement. If you own a bookstore, you can print a flyer or take out an ad in a paper. You can do the same kind of thing with your Web site: List titles and display covers.

But adding ASP to your Web pages enables you to let users tap into your databases directly (read-only, of course, unless you specify otherwise). With ASP, you could let a visitor to your bookstore's site see the latest discounts, see all the books you offer, compare prices interactively, and even place orders. In other words, users can do things that used to require a phone call to someone in your office. Think of it this way: The ASP technology — to a great extent — lets users be their own customer service department.

VBScript is similar to VB, but it's designed to run in browsers (as well as servers), so it's missing some commands — notably, commands that may endanger a user's local computer. In other words, VBScript is stripped-down VB. It doesn't have file renaming, file deleting, disk formatting, or similar commands because VBScript can run immediately when a Web page is loaded into a browser. You wouldn't want mindless, nasty people putting the following code in a Web page that you innocently load into your browser while surfing the Web:

```
function BlastIt()
    Format C:\
end function

<body onload="BlastIt">
```

If VBScript included file-formatting commands, that code would fry your C drive. Fortunately, VBScript doesn't include the Format command in its vocabulary nor other commands that could be dangerous in the wrong hands. The full VB .NET language is available when you write ASP.NET code, as you can see in Chapter 13. However, not to worry: ASP.NET programs run exclusively on the server and only the result of their activities (HTML pages) are sent to the user's browser.

This chapter shows you how to get ASP.NET up and working on your machine. Before you do that, however, you find out how to create a "virtual" (simulated) client/server on a standalone machine. In that way, your computer can interact with a "server" that's actually right there in your desktop computer.

Setting Up ASP.NET

In the past couple of years, many people have had problems setting up a *local* ASP testing platform. In other words, you want to use a single desktop machine to write and debug ASP or ASP.NET applications. You need to install Microsoft's "fake" server right there on your local hard drive. This allows you to test your ASP code by "deploying" it to the fake server and then watching how it works on the "client" browser. This same system is used by ASP.NET.

ASP and ASP.NET run on a server (*ASP* means Active *Server* Pages). When a browser requests the Web page on which ASP.NET code resides, ASP.NET composes HTML code out of any VB programming you've included in the page, adds that code to any other HTML in your source code for that page, and then sends the finished page to the visitor's browser. At this point, the results are displayed to the visitor. This behavior (in which the computing is distributed across two machines) would seem to require that you have two computers to test it. One computer acts as a server for the other, client computer.

Recognizing that a two-machine testing system is impractical, Microsoft came up with a way for a single computer to simulate a client/server relationship.

This simulation was called Personal Web Server in Windows 98 and Peer Web Services in NT 4. Now it's being called the *Personal Tier*. (Don't ask.) Personal Tier supports Internet Explorer on Windows 2000, 98, 95, and NT 4.0.

Personal Tier applications run within the Internet Explorer process, so they require a different way of accessing files stored on your computer.

I used Windows 2000 in this book because at the time of this writing it was the only version of Windows that can host Visual Studio .NET — the IDE that you use to create and test ASP.NET. In Windows 2000, the client/server simulator is called Personal Web Manager and is part of IIS, Microsoft's Internet Information Services. However, by default, IIS is not installed when you install Windows 2000. The technical reviewer for this book has also used Windows XP in testing the examples in this book and found no problems.

Follow these steps

To be able to use Visual Basic .NET and test ASP.NET examples in Windows 2000, you should install IIS and Script Debugger. If IIS isn't properly set up on your computer and you try, for instance, to create a new Visual Basic .NET Web application project, you'll get the error message shown in Figure 12-1.

Figure 12-1:
Without IIS installed on your machine, Web server simulation isn't possible, and therefore you can't test ASP.NET code.

Microsoft Development Environment

Unable to create Web project 'WebApplication1'. Could not find a web server at 'DELL' on port 80. Please check to make sure that the web server name is valid and your proxy settings are set correctly. If you are sure that everything is correct, the web server may be temporarily out of service.

OK

Alas, installing a "personal Web" (a Web server and server extensions) is neither automatic nor straightforward. Follow these steps:

1. **On a computer running Windows 2000, choose Start↪Settings↪ Control Panel.**

2. **Double-click the Add/Remove Programs icon in Control Panel.**

   The Add/Remove Programs dialog box appears.

3. **Click the Add/Remove Windows Components icon (on the left side).**

   The Windows Components Wizard opens.

4. **Choose Internet Information Services (IIS) and Script Debugger and then click Next.**

5. **When you're asked to insert the Windows 2000 CD, do so.**

6. **Click OK.**

   The Wizard copies the necessary files from the CD. This can take quite a while. Don't lose heart if nothing seems to be happening.

7. **Click Finish.**

To see what you've accomplished, choose Start⇨Programs⇨Administrative Tools. (In some Windows 2000 configurations, you will *not* see an Administrative Tools option. In that case, choose Start⇨Settings⇨Control Panel and open the Administrative Tools folder in Control Panel.)

You'll see that three new utilities have been added to your Administrative tools:

✔ Internet Services Manager

✔ Personal Web Manager

✔ Server Extensions Administrator

You now have a fake Web and fake server to work with. They do such a good imitation of a real server sitting somewhere out there on the Internet that neither your browser nor ASP.NET will be able to tell the difference.

Creating an ASP.NET test directory

You can mark directories on a Web server executable or not executable (meaning that they do not permit the execution of scripts, objects, or the code they contain). In this section, you see how to create a directory on your hard drive to hold .ASP and .ASP.NET files and test them. This directory will be marked executable.

Follow these steps to create a directory where your .ASPX files can be executed. You will also specify a name, or *alias,* for this directory's path:

1. **After you've followed the steps in the preceding section and installed IIS, choose Start⇨Settings⇨Control Panel⇨Administrative Tools⇨ Personal Web Manager.**

   Or, if you don't see Personal Web Manager, use Start⇨Programs⇨ Administrative Tools⇨Personal Web Manager, as shown in Figure 12-2.

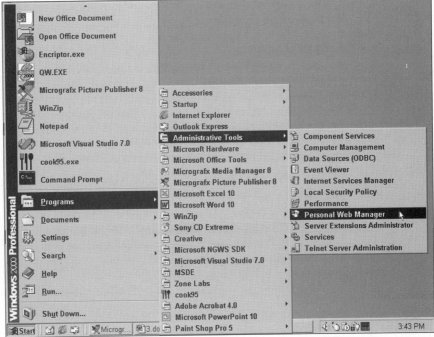

Figure 12-2:
Manage
your
"personal
Web" with
this utility.

When PWM opens, the dialog box in Figure 12-3 appears. My computer is
named DELL, so the screen lists my home page as being available at
`http://dell`. You'll see a different name. This home page is a pretend
Web site that you can use to test ASP, WebForms, and any other Internet
programming you create in VB .NET.

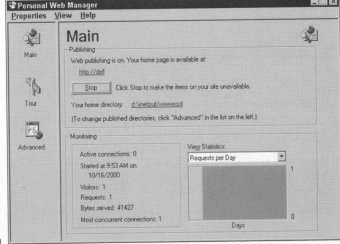

Figure 12-3:
You can
create
virtual
directories
and
otherwise
manage
PWS.

2. **Click the Advanced icon in the left pane.**

   The Advanced Options screen shown in Figure 12-4 appears.

3. **Click Add.**

   The dialog box shown in Figure 12-5 appears. In the middle section, you specify the level of access that visitors are permitted when they get to the directory. Read permission allows an .HTM page to be sent to the visitor's browser. However, you would not select Read permission for directories containing applications or databases that you don't want a visitor to have direct access to. The Write option permits visitors to save files in this directory. The Script option permits .ASP.NET scripts to be executed.

   In the Application Permissions section, you can specify that scripts, or other code (or neither or both) can be executed in this directory.

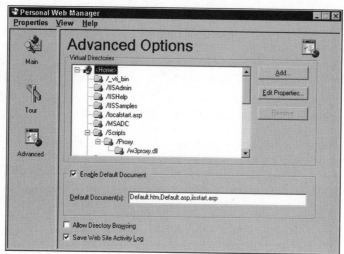

Figure 12-4: Advanced options include editing existing virtual directories and adding new ones.

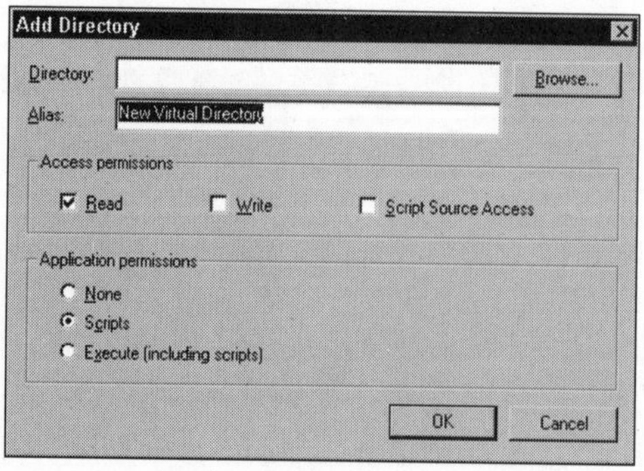

Figure 12-5: Create a new virtual "Web" directory here and also specify that code can be executed in this directory.

4. **Only you will be using this directory, so go hog-wild, throw caution to the wind, and click all three Access Permissions check boxes and the Execute (Including Scripts) option.**

   No need to protect your computer from your own self. Right?

   If you intend to give other users access to this directory, don't give both Execute and Write permissions (someone could upload and then run a nasty virus). Also, if you don't want outsiders reading your scripts or peeking at your programs, don't simultaneously permit Read and Execute.

5. **Type a directory name**

   If you type *C:\ASPNET Test Directory* as your directory name, you can refer to it elsewhere in this book.

6. **Type your alias for this directory (replace the default alias *New Virtual Directory*).**

   Type **tests** as the alias. You can use this nickname as part of the URL that you type into your browser to load and test a page with ASP.NET. (However, in most cases you can simply test ASP.NET by pressing F5 to execute the program, just as you do with ordinary Windows program testing in VB .NET. See the Warning following this numbered list.)

   You can use the alias to save yourself the trouble of typing in the full directory path to an ASP.NET file. Here's an example URL using the alias tests, to execute the ASP.NET file named trial1:

   ```
   http://dell/tests/trial1.aspx
   ```

7. **Click OK in the Add Directory dialog box.**

   A warning message tells you that you're playing with fire by permitting both the Write and Execute options.

8. **Click Yes, admitting that you're a wild one all right and are willing to take this risk.**

   A new message asks whether you want to create this new directory.

9. **Click Yes to create the new directory.**

   Your new virtual directory's alias, tests, now appears in the list on the Advanced Options page, as shown in Figure 12-6.

10. **Close the dialog box.**

ASP and ASP.NET provide a way for a client browser (located on the Internet) to ask for information from your database located on your server. Here's the scenario: Someone (anywhere) loads your Web page. That person's browser interprets the page's HTML code and displays the page. The person clicks a button or otherwise causes a message to be sent back (this is called postback) to your computer. Your computer (the server) interprets the page's ASP.NET code (the code is written mostly in VB .NET, with perhaps some HTML), runs the code, and then sends the results back to the user's browser as standard HTML. In other words, the user can employ any browser, even Netscape's Navigator, because the client side of this operation doesn't need any special Microsoft components. All the user's browser sees is ordinary HTML.

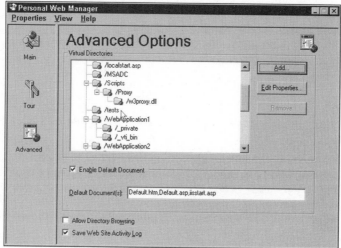

Figure 12-6:
There it is,
tests, your
newly
created
"server"
directory.
Put your
.ASPX files
in this
directory

Remember that you can't just double-click an .ASPX file to automatically load it into Internet Explorer and thereby execute it. (You *can* do this to load and execute an ordinary .HTM file.) To run an .ASPX file, you must type its URL in the address field in Internet Explorer, and then click the Go button to the right of the address field. VB .NET automatically creates .ASPX files when you create a WebForm project in the IDE. And you can also just press F5 to execute that project (using the virtual directory technology). Nonetheless, it's useful to understand how to work with virtual directories and how to test .ASPX files outside the IDE.

Writing Your First ASP Script

Now for some fun! In this section, I show you how to write a simple ASP script. The HTML code that is generated by this script will be downloaded to a browser ("downloaded" to your browser for this test example). Remember that in this example, you're working with ASP, not ASP.NET.

With VBScript in ASP, or more likely VB .NET in ASP.NET, you can make calculations, something HTML cannot do. HTML can't even add 2 + 2; it's a page description language that tells the browser how large to make text, what color to display it in, whether it's italic, and so on.

So, when you write ASP, you're able to calculate — add sales tax, check data entry, and so on. Wait a minute. Can't you just insert some VBScript right into HTML and have it execute client-side, in the visitor's browser, without going to the trouble of executing it on the server-side? Yes, but I can think of at least two big reasons why a client-side scripting solution is less than ideal:

✔ Not all browsers (translation: Netscape Navigator) can execute VBScript.

✔ Executing a script on the server enables you to access a database on the server. This means the information you show the user can be up-to-the-minute accurate.

Writing a standard (not ASP) script

In this example, you use VBScript, but the script you write isn't an ASP script. Instead, it runs in the client's browser (not on your server). This example sets the stage for understanding the differences between standard scripting, ASP scripting, and ASP.NET. To see how to run a standard script, follow these steps:

1. **Choose Start⇨Programs⇨Accessories⇨Notepad.**

2. **Type this HTML page into Notepad:**

```
<HTML>
<HEAD>

<SCRIPT LANGUAGE=vbscript>
a = 2 + 2
msgbox a
</SCRIPT>

</HEAD>

<BODY>
The result of 2 + 2.

</BODY>
</HTML>
```

When you include a <SCRIPT> section in your HTML page like this, it executes as soon as the page is loaded into Internet Explorer. (In Navigator, you see the script code instead.)

3. **Choose File⇨Save As.**

The Save As dialog box appears.

4. **Browse your hard drive until you locate the special directory that you created in the section "Creating an ASP.NET test directory," earlier in this chapter.**

If you followed along with the example, the directory is named `C:\ASPNET Test Directory`.

5. **In the File Name box in the dialog box, type** SCRIPT.HTM.

6. **Click the Save button.**

Your file, SCRIPT.HTM, is saved to your special test directory.

7. **Run Windows Explorer (choose Start➪Programs➪Windows Explorer).**

8. **Browse with Explorer until you locate the directory where you stored SCRIPT.HTM.**

9. **Double-click SCRIPT.HTM.**

Assuming that you have Internet Explorer as your default browser, IE runs and it loads SCRIPT.HTM. As soon as your script is loaded into Internet Explorer, you see the message box shown in Figure 12-7.

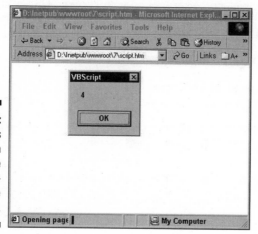

Figure 12-7:
This calculation was made with client-side scripting.

Writing the script in ASP

The process of translating the VBScript from the previous example into an ASP page is relatively straightforward. Just remember these points:

✔ If you're writing HTML, you use the ordinary HTML tags, such as <BODY> or <H1>.

✔ When you want to signal to the server that some code needs to run on the server (called *server-side*), you use the percent (%) symbol.

To see how to write an ASP page, follow these steps:

1. **Choose Start⇨Programs⇨Accessories⇨Notepad.**

2. **Type the following ASP code into a blank page in Notepad:**

```
<HTML>
<HEAD>
</HEAD>

<BODY>

AN ASP EXAMPLE
<BR>

<%
a = 2+2
response.write " The result of 2 + 2: "
response.write(a) %>

</BODY>

</HTML>
```

   Notice that the VBScript code is located between the <% and %> symbols. Everything outside those symbols is HTML code.

3. **Choose File⇨Save As.**

   The Save As dialog box appears.

4. **Browse your hard drive until you locate the special test directory that you created in the section "Creating an ASP.NET test directory," earlier in this chapter.**

5. **In the File Name box, type** TEST1.ASP **and then click Save.**

   Your file, TEST1.ASP, is saved to the test directory.

6. **Run Internet Explorer.**

7. **In the Address box, type the URL for this .ASP file.**

   Instead of including the drive and directory, substitute the alias that you gave this hard drive location in the "Creating an ASP.NET test directory" section, earlier in this chapter. If you followed along with the example, you named the alias tests. The URL you type in Internet Explorer would look like this:

```
http://computername/tests/test1.asp
```

   where *computername* is the name of your computer. If you don't know the name, follow the instructions in "Finding your computer's name" sidebar.

8. **While in Internet Explorer, press F5 or click the Go button.**

   Assuming that you typed the correct URL path in Step 7, your TEST1.ASP page is loaded and the ASP code is executed, as shown in Figure 12-8.

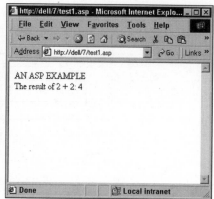

Figure 12-8:
Your first
ASP job
executes
perfectly,
displaying
the results
of server-
side
calculations.

When testing .ASP files, you must remember two things:

✔ Save the file with an .ASP, *not* an .HTM, extension. Without the .ASP, the browser will not execute any ASP code in the page.

✔ You must type the URL in Internet Explorer's Address field. This URL is the location of the .ASP file on your hard drive, but instead of using the full path, you must use the alias you defined for this drive and directory. In other words, you can't autoload an .ASP file into Internet Explorer by double-clicking its filename in Windows Explorer.

If you made an error typing your ASP code in Notepad, Internet Explorer displays a message like this:

```
The page cannot be displayed
There is a problem with the page you are trying to reach and
          it cannot be displayed.
---------------------------------------------------------------
          --------------------
Please try the following:

Click the Refresh button, or try again later.

Open the dell home page, and then look for links to the
          information you want.
HTTP 500.100 - Internal Server Error - ASP error
Internet Information Services
---------------------------------------------------------------
          --------------------
Technical Information (for support personnel)

Error Type:
Microsoft VBScript compilation (0x800A0408)
Invalid character
/tests/test1.asp, line 12, column 15
```

```
response.write " The result of 2 + 2: "
--------------^
Browser Type:
Mozilla/4.0 (compatible; MSIE 6.0b; Windows NT 5.0; .NET CLR
        1.0.2914)
Page:
GET /tests/test1.asp
Time:
Saturday, July 14, 2001, 10:36:34 AM
More information:
Microsoft Support
```

Don't be dismayed. Just look down far enough in the message to locate the Error Type and see whether you can figure out what you did wrong.

Now that you've seen the difference between client-side and server-side (ASP) scripting, you might want to move up to the big time: ASP.NET. That's the topic of Chapter 13.

Finding your computer's name

When you test an .ASP Web page, you need to type your computer's name as part of the URL you type in Internet Explorer's Address field. The computer name is used as the "server name" by PWS.

If you don't know your computer's name, follow these steps:

1. **Right-click the My Computer icon on the desktop and choose Properties.**

   The Properties dialog box appears.

2. **Click the Network Identification tab.**

3. **On the Network Identification page, look for the Full Computer Name.**

   That's your computer's name.

Chapter 13

ASP.NET: Mixing HTML, XML, and VB .NET

$\boldsymbol{1}$n this chapter, you see ASP.NET in action. You find out how to get past firewalls, save the contents of variables, and make ASP.NET jump through some other hoops.

Verifying Your Virtual Server

This first example verifies that you have your "personal Web" virtual directory up and running correctly (see Chapter 12). You can create ASP.NET programs within the Visual Studio .NET IDE, but you can also write them in something as humble as the Windows Notepad, as you'll see. Follow these steps:

1. **Run Windows Notepad.**

2. **Then type the following into Notepad:**

```
<html>
<head>
</head>
<body>
<script language="VB" runat="server">
```

```
dim firstnum as integer, secondnum as integer, totalnum
        as integer

Sub DoAdd(necessary as Object, alsonecessary as
        EventArgs)

   firstnum = cint(txtFirst.Value)
   secondnum = cint(txtSecond.value)

totalnum = firstnum + secondnum

Answer.text = "The sum is: " & totalnum & "<br/>" & _
"The current time is: " & format(Now, "h:mm")

End Sub
</script>

<form runat="server">
<p />



        Enter first number:
        <input type="text" id="txtfirst" runat="server">
        <p />
        Enter second number:
        <input type="text" id="txtsecond" runat="server">
        <p />

        <input type="submit" value="Click here to add..."
                runat="server" onserverclick="DoAdd">
<p />
<p />
<asp:Label id="Answer" runat = "server" />
</form>
</body>
</html>
```

3. **Save this source code from Notepad (choose File⇨Save As).**

4. **Name the file and save it in the directory you created in Chapter 12.**

   To follow along with the examples, name the file FirstTest.ASPX and save it in `C:\ASPNET Test Directory`. The directory uses the alias *tests*.

If you prefer to create this example (and test it) in the VB .NET editor, it's simple. Just run VB .NET, choose Create a New Project (or choose File⇨ New⇨Project). Then double-click the ASP.NET Web Application icon in the New Project dialog box. You'll see the design window for your project. Click the HTML tab at the bottom of the design window. Delete the default code and then type the preceding source code, just as if you were typing it into Notepad. When you are ready to test the program, press F5 and your program will be loaded into Internet Explorer automatically.

Among the many changes you'll find in VB .NET, the traditional VB commands DATE and TIME have been replaced by TODAY and TIMEOFDAY, respectively. You can, however, still use the NOW command, so I used it in the example in this chapter:

```
format(Now, "h:mm")
```

This change and all the other changed syntax in VB .NET are described in the appendix at this book's Web site, which is located at http://www.dummies.com/extras/VBNetDataProg/.

Testing the program

To test the ASP.NET application you just created, follow these steps:

1. **Start Internet Explorer (IE).**

2. **If you don't see the IE address field, choose View⇨Toolbars in IE and click Address Bar to select it.**

3. **Type this into the IE address field:**

   http://*computername*/tests/FirstTest.aspx

   replacing *computername* with the name of your computer. (If you don't know your computer's name, see Step 3 in the sidebar titled "Finding your computer's name" in Chapter 12.)

4. **Run the FirstTest.ASPX program by clicking the Go icon on the address bar.**

   You should see a result that looks like Figure 13-1.

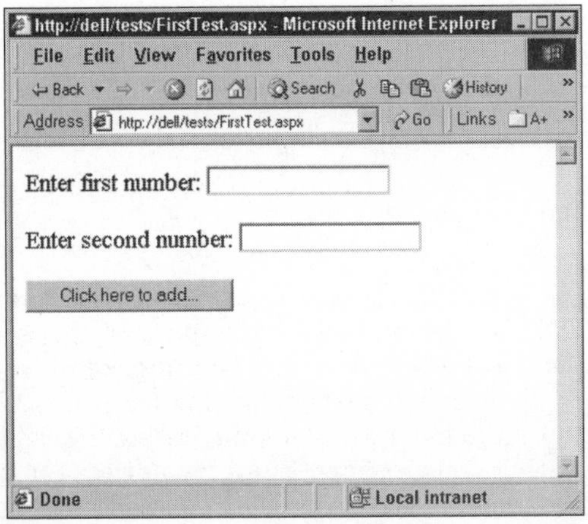

Figure 13-1:
The HTML code on this page was generated on the server using ASP.NET and then sent to the user's browser.

If things are not working

If you don't see the result shown in Figure 13-1, perhaps you're not using Internet Explorer Version 5.5 or later. Choose Help⇨About Internet Explorer and see whether you have Version 5.5. If not, download it from here:

```
http://www.microsoft.com/windows/ie/downloads/default.asp
```

Or possibly you've typed the source code incorrectly. If so, you'll see a compiler error message, like the one shown in Figure 13-2. Check the source code in your .ASPX file to find your mistake. Or, if you prefer not to do all the typing, simply download the correct source code for this book from the appendix at this book's Web site, which is located at `http://www.dummies.com/extras/VBNetDataProg/`.

Figure 13-2:
An error
message
similar to
this is
displayed in
IE if you
have bad
ASP.NET
source
code.

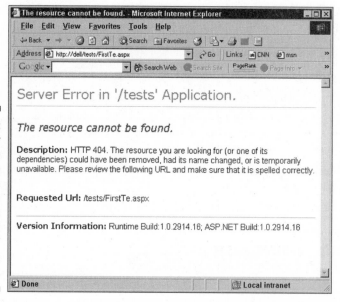

Perhaps you've mistyped the name of the source code file, or some other part of the URL is incorrect. If so, IE displays an error message like this:

```
Server Error in '/tests' Application.

The resource cannot be found.
Description: HTTP 404. The resource you are looking for (or
            one of its dependencies) could have been removed,
            had its name changed, or is temporarily
            unavailable. Please review the following URL and
            make sure that it is spelled correctly.
Requested Url: /tests/FirstTe.aspx
```

This error message is quite helpful. It shows you that the URL includes `FirstTe`, when the URL should be: `http://dell/tests/FirstTest.aspx`.

If your problem isn't a misspelled URL, check that the source code .ASPX file is located in the correct directory (`C:\ASPNET Test Directory`) and that the filename is spelled correctly (FirstTest.aspx).

Taking Your ASP.NET Program for a Spin

After your Web page has successfully reached your browser (as shown in Figure 13-1), it's time to type two numbers into the Web page shown in Figure 13-1. To do that, click the button labeled Click here to add. You should see the result shown in Figure 13-3.

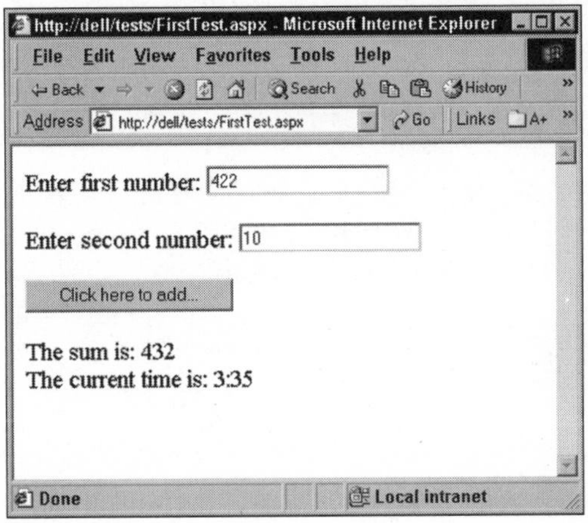

Figure 13-3:
If all goes
well, you'll
see this
result.

If you see the results shown in Figure 13-3, your computer is properly set up. Skip down to the section titled "Understanding ASP.NET Source Code."

However, if you don't see the expected results — you clicked the button but you don't get the result of the addition, or the current time, or both — you've either turned off the "server" or you don't have the ASP.NET engine or support tools properly installed.

Similarly, if all you see is your server-side source code displayed in the browser, you have the same problem (the server-side processing isn't installed correctly, so the server merely reads the source code and sends it off to Internet Explorer as pure text). This section shows you how to cure these problems.

Dealing with firewalls

Many people are using firewall software these days. When you go onto the Internet, you subject your computer (and expose your quivering little hard drive) to all kinds of intrusion. You can prevent your hard drive from acting as a server to other people on the Internet by installing a firewall. One excellent firewall that is free to private users is from ZoneAlarm at `www.zonelabs.com`.

If you do use a firewall and have set its security high, when you reboot you'll be asked whether you want to permit IIS to act as a server (answer Yes so you can work with ASP.NET). Similarly, when you run Visual Basic .NET (Visual Studio .NET), the firewall will detect the built in "server" feature and query you. Again, agree that the IDE (Integrated Design Editor — the Visual Studio .NET program) can pose as a server. After you instruct the firewall about these two "servers," it won't ask you again. These internal "servers" do not expose themselves to Internet traffic — they merely provide a way to test Internet pages on your local computer.

Ensuring proper support

You can get the proper tools you need to write, test, and debug ASP.NET and Visual Basic .NET applications in two ways. The first is to install the .NET SDK. You can find the NGWS SDK (all 86MB of it) for free downloading at

```
http://msdn.microsoft.com/code/sample.asp?url=/msdn-
        files/027/000/976/msdncompositedoc.xml
```

At the current time, this SDK does not include Visual Studio .NET or Visual J++.

Before installing the SDK, ensure that you have Windows 2000 or a later version (and Internet Explorer 5.5 or a later version and IIS) up and running. Then install the Microsoft Data Access Components (MDAC) Version 2.6. Get the MDAC at

```
http://www.microsoft.com/data/download_260rtm.htm
```

This package includes SQL Server, Oracle OLE DB provider and ODBC drivers.

Finally, after installing MDAC, install the SDK.

If you remove IIS for some reason or otherwise change the necessary support platform for ASP.NET, you might need to reinstall the SDK before you can test ASP.NET applications. (If you try to run an ASP.NET application and it simply does nothing, you don't have the "server" working correctly, so you can't test the application.) To cure this, you can try reinstalling the following items in this order: IIS, IE, MDAC, and SDK. In other words, use Control Panel to *uninstall* each of these items — then reinstall them in the order listed here.

Understanding ASP.NET Source Code

In this section, you find out more about ASP.NET by looking at the source code of the ASP.NET application you created earlier in this chapter.

Looking at the browser-side code

When you use ASP.NET, you can specify that ordinary HTML controls are to be used as server-side controls. To do this, you use the `runat="server"` command. When ASP.NET sees this command, it automatically adds a name and a value attribute to your source code. ASP.NET also forces the value of server-side controls to be posted (sent) back to the page. This is a great feature — it preserves the state of the controls and shows the values that the user entered. Note that ASP.NET does this for you automatically.

When users fill in a form on your Web site, they don't want to come back to that form later and find that they have to fill it in a second time! They expect stability and efficiency. They expect the *state* to be preserved. How does ASP.NET manage to preserve state and values (the data the user enters)? It makes some changes to your source code when you specify server-side controls.

With the example program loaded in Internet Explorer (see Figure 13-3), view the changes to your source code by choosing View⇨Source in IE. You'll see some surprises. ASP.NET has been a busy little bunny. It looked at your source code, made some additions and adjustments, and then created the following HTML to send to IE:

```
<html>
<head>
</head>
<body>
<form name="ctrl0" method="post" action="FirstTest.aspx"
        id="ctrl0">

<input type="hidden" name="__VIEWSTATE"
        value="dDwtNjE3Njg2NzIxOzs+" />


<p />

    Enter first number:
    <input name="txtfirst" id="txtfirst" type="text" />
    <p />
    Enter second number:
    <input name="txtsecond" id="txtsecond" type="text" />
    <p />
```

```
        <input name="ctrl1" type="submit" value="Click here to
              add..." />
<p />
<p />
<span id="Answer"></span>
</form>
</body>
</html>
```

First, notice that all *your* Visual Basic source code has been stripped out. That code runs on the server and is never sent to the user's browser. Only pure HTML is sent to the user. (Well, you can also send DHTML and other items, but VB source code is never sent — the user's browser has no VB .NET interpreter or compiler sitting there, ready to execute code).

Using ID to access controls

In the ASP.NET source code, you specified the following:

```
<form runat="server">
```

and ASP.NET translated this into its own source code:

```
<form name="ctrl0" method="post" action="FirstTest.aspx"
            id="ctrl0">
```

ASP.NET gave the form a name and an ID. Every server control is given a unique ID. If you don't supply one yourself, ASP.NET will. Unique IDs allow you to write programming for every server control. You identify a control by its ID; perhaps using that ID as the name of an event, such as ctrl0_Click.

In the following example, you add code to react if the user enters a larger number than you want in the TextBox, which is given the ID txtfirst. Note that the source code is in boldface:

```
Sub DoAdd(necessary as Object, alsonecessary as EventArgs)

if cint(txtFirst.value) > 999 then
answer.text = "You must provide a number lower than 1000."
exit sub
end if
    firstnum = cint(txtFirst.Value)
```

You use the ID of the TextBox (txtfirst) to examine the value the user entered. If the value is unacceptable, you use the ID of the label (answer) to display a warning to the user.

Preserving information

Notice that ASP.NET adds a hidden control to the page (the user never sees it):

```
<input type="hidden" name="__VIEWSTATE"
         value="dDwtNjE3Njg2NzIxOzs+" />
```

This stealth control stores information about the Web page (such as the text size of a control's caption). If you or the user should specify a different size for that caption, or a different color, or some other property adjustment, the change will be preserved. But what exactly does *preserved* mean?

If you've programmed in Windows, perhaps you've stored a user's custom settings in an .INI file or, more recently, in the Registry. If you permit the user to adjust aspects of your program — preferences such as color, text size, or background graphics — you must somehow *preserve* the user's specifications. That way, when the user runs the application later, those preferences will still be in effect and the user won't have to re-enter them.

In a traditional Windows program, user preferences are read from the Registry each time the application is started. This is practical because Windows is a closed system: The state must be preserved only from one execution of the application to the next. A Windows application isn't run, and rerun, minute to minute — you use it for an hour or two, and then maybe use it again next week.

Not so for Web pages. Their specifications must be preserved much more frequently because Web pages are requested fairly often. For example, the user might click a hyperlink in your page, but later click the Back button to return to your page — generating a new request. This is like starting, then shutting down, and then rerunning a Windows program all in a matter of minutes.

To provide one example, information such as the text color of a control's caption on a Web page is not automatically communicated between server and browser each time a page is requested. The hidden VIEWSTATE control automatically saves the state of any changed properties on the page and its components.

New Visual Basic .NET techniques

The example you've worked with so far in this chapter illustrates several elements of VB .NET. Notice in the source code that you first defined a subroutine. It's a typical VB event subroutine, and you must include two arguments: `necessary as Object` and `alsonecessary as EventArgs`. You don't often *use* these arguments in your programming, but they must be listed anyway.

In addition, ASP script language code is delimited (enclosed by) <% and %> symbols, but ASP.NET code is delimited the <script> and </script> tags.

Also note that this subroutine is called when the user clicks the Click here to add button:

```
<input type="submit" value="Click here to add..."
     runat="server" onserverclick="DoAdd">
```

You can use a variety of events to trigger VB routines. The runat="server" command makes this input control a server-side control, so you can use it in your ASP.NET programming. The onclick event is processed server side. Without that runat="server" command, the click event would be handled client side (in the event handler of the visitor's browser).

You also had to force (coerce) the characters that the user entered in the TextBox (which are string data types by default) to change them to integer data types. (This kind of data type conversion is sometimes called *converting* or *casting*.) Visual Basic, which has long had the capability to guess which data type is required in a particular context, did the casting for you. If you put 4 into a TextBox, for example, VB made that 4 a string data type. But if you later did something like this:

```
TextBox1.Value = TextBox1.Value + 7
```

VB would notice the + command and know that it had to temporarily change the string digit in TextBox1 to a regular number (an integer data type) to add it to the 7. Then VB would change the result of the addition back to a string to display the result in TextBox1.

This feature, called the *variant* variable type, has been stripped from VB .NET. You, the programmer, must coerce (or *convert*, or *cast*, whatever you prefer) data types into whatever the programming context demands at the time. That's why you must use the Cint command (*C*oerce into an *int*eger):

```
firstnum = cint(txtFirst.Value)
secondnum = cint(txtSecond.value)
```

If you try to assign the value of the txtFirst TextBox directly, without first changing the data from string to integer, you run into trouble. Try replacing the preceding code with this traditional VB programming:

```
firstnum = txtFirst.Value
```

Save the changes to the source code to the FirstTest.ASPX file and then try to load this page into IE.

TIP

Painless testing

When you use Notepad and IE to write ASP.NET, the testing cycle can be relatively painless if you remember the following:

1. **In Notepad, make your changes to the source code.**

2. **Press Alt+F, S to save (replace) the changes.**

3. **Press Alt+Tab to switch back to IE.**

4. **Press F5 to reload the page.**

   You might get the following warning: The page cannot be refreshed without resending the information. Click Retry to send the information again, or click Cancel to return to the page that you were trying to view.

5. **If you get the warning mentioned in Step 4, click the Retry button, or alternatively click**

Cancel and then click the Back icon in IE (or press the Backspace key) to get to the earlier version of the page. Then press F5 to load it.

Remember that the ASP.NET code is executed on the server side, so you want to be at the first instance of your page in the browser.

6. **Press F5 to reload the page and test it.**

I said that testing can be *relatively painless* because many of the error messages generated by the compiler are excellent. However, recall that I mentioned in an earlier tip that you can create ASP.NET in the Visual Studio .NET IDE (Integrated Design Environment). And you can test it there, too. You'll get the same error messages in the browser, but VB .NET's IDE has additional debugging tools.

When you rerun the example with `firstnum = txtFirst.Value` in the source code, you get this error message:

```
ASP.NET Error

Unhandled Execution Error
Description: An unhandled exception occurred at runtime
            during the execution of the current web request.
            Common sources of these errors include (but are
            not limited to):

Attempts to access a method or property on an uninitialized
            object reference
Attempts to load a class that has not been deployed within
            the web application's "bin" directory
Attempts to assign/cast a variable to an object reference not
            compatible with its type
```

```
Attempts to access a file that does not exist on the file
          system
Please review the stack trace below to get a better
          understanding of what the error is and where it
          originated from in the code.

          Important Note: Runtime errors often occur only
          when certain conditions/scenarios are met (for
          example: a null-reference error may only happen
          when a user leaves a text field on a form empty).
          Consider using a debugger to more accurately
          walkthrough the specific steps/conditions that
          caused a failure to occur.

          Exception Details: System.InvalidCastException:

          Stack Trace:
```

You need not look at the stack trace, which consists of the machine language instructions that few programmers understand.

The error message is correct: This is an invalid cast. In other words, you didn't convert the string type to a numeric type as you should have. (This error is referred to as an InvalidCastException. *Exception* means *error*. Why they don't use the word *error* is beyond me. Error handlers, for example, are called *exception handlers*. Send me an e-mail message if you know why this strange usage — with roots in C and C++ — has been adopted in VB .NET.)

Whew! I got a bit worked up there for a minute. But I've cooled down now. Take a look at these next lines of VB code:

```
Answer.text = "The sum is: " & totalnum & "<br/>" & _
"The current time is: " & format(Now, "h:mm")
```

Traditionally, you would create a line break in VB in this way:

```
Break = Chr(13) & Chr(10)
```

But those old printer codes don't impress HTML. When HTML sees something like that Break definition, it ignores it. (Unlike other languages, HTML doesn't collapse, halt the program, or shut everything down when an error occurs; it simply does whatever it can to display the page as best as possible; there are no HTML exceptions. What it doesn't understand, it blithely ignores.)

Try to be flexible

When writing VB .NET in an ASP.NET page, you combine HTML and VB by adding the HTML line-break tag <br/> to your VB code. This is just one of the several dozen new tricks you have to know if you want to transfer your VB programming skills to the brave new .NET world.

If you've been used to the sophisticated capabilities of Visual Basic (the world's highest-level computer language and by far the most popular language), you must learn to be patient with the several compromises that are now necessary. True, we're regressing in some ways. Programming for the Internet page rather than a Windows application requires various steps backward — at least for a time. We're losing some debugging efficiency. We're losing some of the freedom that Visual Basic 6 offered us (default properties, automatic variable data type conversion, automatic support library invocation, implicit variable declaration, and other features. See the appendix at this book's Web site, which is located at `http://www.dummies.com/extras/VBNetDataProg/`, for an explanation of the differences between VB 6 and VB .NET.

Programming for Internet Web pages is fundamentally different than programming for the Windows operating system. And the languages that work with the Internet paradigm are less sophisticated than those designed to create traditional Windows applications. Languages that work with Windows have been improving and evolving for 20 years. Way back when in 1981, a word processor demanded that you insert rudimentary delimiter tags such as <ITAL> and </ITAL> around text you wanted to italicize. This approach quickly changed to one in which you simply highlighted text and clicked the Italic button. But now, after all these years, we've regressed to the old delimiter tagging around HTML elements. One can hope that we'll quickly move beyond this unsophisticated way of communicating with our computer.

A Peek Beneath

If you've been assuming that ASP.NET is a busy beaver beneath the surface, you're right. The source code you write — and the HTML that ASP.NET translates it into — is merely the visible 30% of the iceberg. When you look at the HTML that ASP.NET produced from the example in this chapter, you can see a few adjustments it made to your source code: changing the label to a SPAN; stripping the VB code; providing names, IDs and other elements if you left them out of the source code; adding the hidden VIEWSTATE; and inserting values (the numbers the user enters as well as the sum and time of day).

If you want to see more of ASP.NET's activities, try another experiment. Remove the arguments from the subroutine (using the code you wrote in Notepad earlier in this chapter). Change:

```
Sub DoAdd (necessary as Object, alsonecessary as EventArgs)
```

to:

```
Sub DoAdd
```

Press Alt+F, S in Notepad to replace your source code with the new version, and then reload the .ASPX file into IE. You should now see the ASP.NET error message page. Scroll down until you see the two hyperlinks at the bottom of the page. The first link, Show Detailed Compiler Output, tells you that there's a problem with the subroutine call. Click the second hyperlink, Show Complete Compilation Source.

Now you'll see a huge listing, illustrating how much ASP.NET compilation blossoms from the few, simple lines of your original source code. Take a brief look at it.

You can see the new `IMPORTS` command, specifying all the code library name-spaces that are (or may be) needed to create the object. Notice that your little program is a class (it can produce an object). In addition to *importing,* it also *inherits* and *implements.* Moving down a little way in the code, you'll find your `Sub DoAdd`. You'll also see a group of `Public Subs` that create controls (components).

ASP.NET is an exciting new technology — in some ways easier to create, test, and manage than ASP.

Part VI

Hands-On Programming

The 5th Wave

By Rich Tennant

IT WAS THE LAST TIME EMILY SERVED ALPHABET SOUP TO HER WORD PUZZLE PLAYING HUSBAND.

ADO.NET...
XML...
DAO...

Obsessive...
fanatical...
fixated...Ooo-
compulsive...

In this part . . .

*O*nly programmers allowed. Well, everyone is welcome — at least, all programmers who want to get some hands-on database programming. Sure, other parts of this book have lots of programming too, but Part VI is the fun zone for writing and testing database application source code without relying too much on assistants, such as wizards and components. Sometimes, if you want something done right, you've just got to do it yourself.

The chapters in this part explain the best, tested database programming strategies. You also discover how to cross the bridge from the older (but sturdy and time-proven) ADO technology to the new, exciting ADO.NET strategies. When you try the examples in these chapters, you'll get a good idea of what's best for each database programming job you're doing.

At the end of this part, Chapter 17 gives you a list of the more common (and more mystifying) database programming errors. Read this chapter to avoid puzzling over some real head-scratchers. You also see how to use the new VB .NET `Try-Catch-Finally-End Try` structure to trap errors the modern, structured way. You want to be modern, don't you?

Chapter 14

Migrating to ADO.NET

- -

In This Chapter

▶ Making the transition from ADO to ADO.NET

▶ Creating DataSets programmatically

▶ Understanding DataSets

▶ Translating VB 6 ADO

▶ Quick syntax

- -

*I*n this chapter, you find out about the basics of managing data and databases in the .NET environment. ADO was the name of Microsoft's database technology before the .NET initiative, so what do you suppose Microsoft calls ADO's successor technology? Right: ADO.NET.

ADO.NET is what Microsoft describes as an "evolutionary improvement" over ADO, its older database technology. One improvement is evident when you need to divide a job between two servers. Microsoft says that because ADO.NET uses an XML scheme to transmit data sets between controls and because the data sets are easily detached from their source database, it's easier to ramp up the scale of an operation. (XML stands for Extensible Markup Language — an HTML-like communication scheme now becoming popular as a way to send messages over the Internet, among other uses.)

This is what's known as *scalability*.

Suppose that you create a database-driven Web site that becomes more popular than you expected. Happy you! But you soon notice that response time is sometimes sluggish. The solution: Divide the user-interface processing and the business-logic processing between two or more servers rather than relying on the original single server. When users log on and visit various pages in your site, they are working with one of the servers. Other users are working with the other server as they check order status, submit new orders, and so on. (See the tip later in this chapter on *n-tier* programming.) This major adjustment is made less difficult because of the modular, detached technology of the ADO.NET DataSet and the XML communication system used by ADO.NET.

Another advantage of ADO.NET is that XML is designed in a way that permits many kinds of controls to receive and process a data set sent as an XML file. If you've used ADO, you'll recall that it featured disconnected recordsets, but they could be sent only to a COM control. And COM causes a performance hit. Microsoft says that the ADO.NET DataSet provides superior performance because no COM-based data type conversion is necessary (as required by the ADO recordset).

The Data Set and the DataSet

The primary technology you'll use in ADO.NET is the data set. A *data set* is a copy of data (containing as many data tables as you want) that is held in memory. A data set does not require any active connection to the database(s) from which it was derived.

You can transmit a data set between controls, as an XML file. As you probably guessed, you manage a data set with a *DataSet object*. This object offers all the expected properties and methods: DataTable objects (a collection) with their rows (the actual data), columns (the names of categories of data, or the *schema*), and relationships.

Further, there are two data set commands that you use: the SqlCommand object and the OleDbCommand object. The SQL object is used to assist with communication between a table in a data set and a table or view in an SQL Server (7.0 or later) database. The OleDb object does the same, but for an OLE DB provider.

Moving from ADO to ADO.NET

If you've used ADO, you'll want to understand how the syntax of ADO.NET differs. But before exploring the changes, be aware that you *can* use ADO in a VB .NET program if you want. Instead of making ADO.NET itself backward compatible with ADO, Microsoft has chosen to make ASP.NET embrace ADO for those who can't or won't make the move to ADO.NET. (This is similar to the capability of using ASP and ASP.NET simultaneously, in parallel, on the same server.)

Rest assured that the entire ADO object model (set of objects, and their properties and methods) is still available. Now, though, you also have available an additional set of classes particular to the .NET framework. This new set is collectively referred to as ADO.NET.

When you connect to a database using ASP.NET, you can use the native SQL provider or the ADO.NET provider. If you're accessing a data source such as

Access, Excel, a simple comma-delimited file, or some other straightforward variety, you must use the ADO.NET provider. (*Delimited* means *separated by* — the individual fields in a comma-delimited database source are separated by commas.)

If your database is Microsoft SQL Server, you can use the somewhat faster SQL provider. The ADO.NET provider also works with an SQL Server database, but it's a bit slower.

ADO.NET has XML at its core and also offers n-tier development. ADO.NET is divided into two primary categories of classes: the DataSet object (which is disconnected) and Managed Providers (which are connected). In the rest of this chapter, you explore these primary elements of ADO.NET.

In math, the letter *n* can stand for "any number." In computing, a *tier* refers to a self-sufficient application (or portion of an application) running on an individual computer. An *n-tier application* is a single solution (program) divided into three or more pieces — with each piece running on a different computer. This speeds things up because a job can be subdivided and can have the services of three multiprocessors. In a typical 3-tier application, the user-interface portion of the application resides in the user's computer, the business logic resides in a server somewhere, and the data itself is in yet another server dedicated to database storage and maintenance.

Why ADO.NET?

ADO expects a tightly coupled (always connected) environment, but ADO.NET embraces the emerging programming model: a loosely coupled (the connection is frequently interrupted and then reestablished as necessary), XML-based, Internet programming environment. ADO.NET is designed to work well with the special demands of Web programming.

An *n-tier* program is also known as a *distributed* program. This is yet another way of referring to a disconnected, loosely coupled application: The application is divided into pieces that run on different computers, though they do communicate with each other and share a common goal.

One often-mentioned special demand of distributed programming is that you must maintain the state (global variables and so on) during HTTP transmissions between the tiers. *State* refers to information that a program needs to store and recall. (For instance, if users fill in an address form, your Web site should retain that information — users don't want to have to go back at another time and fill in their address again!) Contrast this problem to the older, tightly coupled client/server environment, where the line of communication was deliberately maintained as long as an application was running, thereby avoiding the need to explicitly maintain state.

Is OLE DB dead?

Even though you now have Managed Providers, should you assume that OLE DB is no longer useful or relevant for the ADO programmer? Microsoft suggests that you choose the technology that suits your job. Use OLE DB when appropriate, right alongside the new, far simpler Managed Provider technology for different (less "rich") jobs.

OLE DB exposes data stores in a "rich" way. *Rich* is one of Microsoft's favorite words. By *rich,* they generally mean loaded with features.

Although Managed Providers are not exactly rich, they are easier to use. Managed Providers use a simple interface that sacrifices some functionality in the service of simplicity and efficiency. (They run fast.) Microsoft suggests that you now encode data as simple XML when possible, and then use Managed Providers to expose that data. However, if you require a true rich store, go ahead and make an OLE DB provider for it. Either way, you can choose the tool that fits your job.

ADO did evolve to include RDS (Remote Data Services). This gave rise to the invention of the *disconnected recordset.* However, the result was cobbled together — though not embarrassingly Frankensteinian. Disconnected datasets in ADO.NET are considerably improved compared to their earlier implementation in ADO.

Microsoft wanted all elements of the .NET world to conform: using the same diction, the same data types, and the same way of identifying classes and members. This means that ASP (VB .NET, C#, or other languages used for server-side programming), ADO.NET, and all other tools in the .NET framework should march to the same drummer. This makes sense — it simplifies things if your database programming can share a basic philosophy and grammar with your server, Windows, and other programming.

We all hope that when this great merger takes place — when all the languages share so many qualities — that *internal consistency* will be enforced as well. For example, if collections can have 1 as a lower boundary, why can't arrays?

Another problem with ADO was that it was based on the relational database model (which, a few years ago, was the "great new thing" that refused to consider the concept of ordered lists of data — a database had no such thing as a "first" record, "second" record, "last" record, and so on). But XML-based data systems require hierarchical data that is, in two words, *not relational.*

The ADO.NET Managed Provider

The first two elements of the ADO.NET Managed Provider are much the same as they were in ADO. First you create a *connection* to a particular data source and then you execute a *command* that describes the subset of data you want out of the connection.

The most common type of command is an SQL statement. It might, for example, request all data from the author-last-name and author-first-name columns. The ADO.NET DataReader class, however, is only somewhat similar to the ADO read-only, forward-only recordset. The DataReader carries out the command.

The third and final element of the Managed Provider is the DataSetCommand. It acts as a bridge between the Managed Provider and the DataSet. (The DataSet is discussed later in the chapter.)

Creating a DataSet Programmatically

To see how to create a connection, create a command, and then carry out that command to pump data into a DataSet, follow these steps:

1. **Start a new VB .NET Windows-style application by choosing File⇨ New⇨Project.**

2. **Give the application a name.**

3. **Double-click the Windows Application icon.**

4. **Put a DataGrid (from the Windows Forms tab on the Toolbox) onto Form1.**

   Get ready to type some code. But first, you need to import a few namespaces.

5. **Double-click the form to open the code window. At the top, above the first line (above** `Public Class Form1`**), type these five lines:**

   ```
   Imports System.Data
   Imports System.Data.OleDb
   Imports System.Data.SqlTypes
   Imports System.Data.SqlDbType
   Imports System.Data.SqlClient
   ```

6. **Locate the** `Form_Load` **event.**

   This is where initialization — things you want to do before displaying a form to the user — usually takes place.

7. **Just above the** `Form_Load` **event, type this:**

   ```
   Dim ds As DataSet = New DataSet()
   ```

   This makes `ds` a global variable, usable by all procedures in the form. This isn't strictly necessary in this example, but I generally like to make the DataSet variable global to a form because I often need to use it in several procedures.

8. In the `Form_Load` **event, type the following:**

```
Private Sub Form1_Load(ByVal sender As System.Object, _
        ByVal e As System.EventArgs) Handles MyBase.Load

Dim nwindConn As OleDbConnection = New _
        OleDbConnection("Provider=SQLOLEDB;Data _
        Source=localhost;Integrated Security=SSPI;Initial _
        Catalog=northwind")

Dim selectCMD As OleDbCommand = New OleDbCommand("SELECT _
        * FROM Customers", nwindConn)

selectCMD.CommandTimeout = 30

Dim dataAdapter As OleDbDataAdapter = New _
        OleDbDataAdapter()
  dataAdapter.SelectCommand = selectCMD

  nwindConn.Open()

  dataAdapter.Fill(ds, "Customers")

  nwindConn.Close()

  DataGrid1.DataSource = ds

End Sub
```

9. Type this entire next line — starting with `Dim` **and ending with** `north-`
`wind")` **—** *on a single line* **in the code window:**

```
Dim nwindConn As OleDbConnection = New _
        OleDbConnection("Provider=SQLOLEDB;Data _
        Source=localhost;Integrated Security=SSPI;Initial _
        Catalog=northwind")
```

10. Press F5 to run this program.

11. Click the + button in the grid, and then click Customers.

Your DataGrid fills with loads of data from the Northwind sample database that comes with VB .NET, as shown in Figure 14-1.

Note that the `Imports` statements in Step 5 are not strictly necessary. You *could* omit them, but then you'd have to specify the namespaces (`System.Data`, `System.Data.OleDb`, and the rest of the items following the `Imports` command are all namespaces) for each class that required these libraries (such as using the longer, fully-qualified version, `System.Data.OleDb.OleDbConnection`, rather than the simpler form, `OleDbConnection`). After you import a namespace, you can leave its name off any references in your code to objects within that namespace.

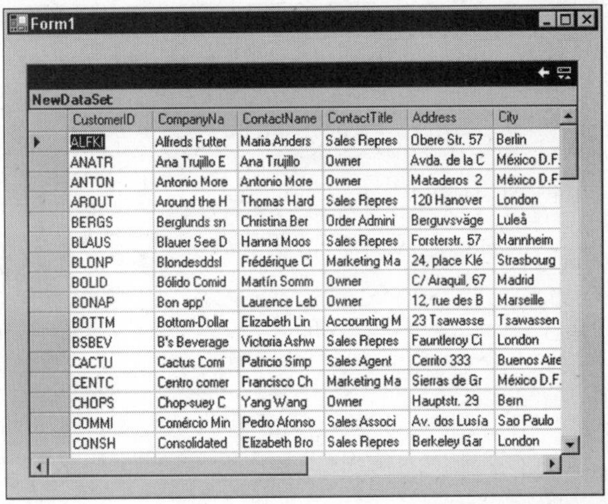

Figure 14-1:
This grid
fills with
columns of
data without
the help of
a wizard.

Few people, including myself, are privy to the secret reason why you need *five* `System.Data Imports` statements. Few people know why they can't be combined into a single big `System.Data` library. It must have something to do with the way the people who wrote ADO.NET wanted to organize things. They have their containers and their idea of the proper granularity, so that's what we get. One little problem for us: It's impossible to memorize all the locations of the items we need — which namespaces hold which functions. So there will be lots of trial-and-error work for programmers, deciding which namespaces to import and how to "qualify" functions we need to use. (*Qualify* here means which namespaces must be spelled out to specify a particular language element in our programming code and which can be left out.)

To avoid this problem, I suggest that whenever you work with data, just add all five namespaces and don't worry about it. In the example you're building right now, for instance, only two namespaces are necessary:

```
Imports System.Data
Imports System.Data.OleDb
```

But go ahead and include them all. Why worry?

If you have problems

In the preceding example, you attempt to connect to the database with the following code:

```
Dim nwindConn As OleDbConnection = New
        OleDbConnection("Provider=SQLOLEDB;Data
        Source=localhost;Integrated Security=SSPI;Initial
        Catalog=northwind")
```

More about namespaces

Namespaces are a new feature of VB .NET. They are designed to prevent confusion if two classes (in two different namespaces) share the same name.

For example, suppose you have a `StrBreak` function in MyNameSpace1 and a `StrBreak` function in MyNameSpace2, a different namespace. You import both of these namespaces into the same project:

```
Imports MyNameSpace1
Imports MyNameSpace2
```

Now suppose that somewhere lower in the code you try to use the `StrBreak` function.

Which of the two `StrBreak` functions is selected?

Fortunately, Microsoft has thought through this problem. If you try to use an ambiguous command — such as `StrBreak` in the preceding example — the VB .NET editor will underline `StrBreak` in your programming code, indicating that it is a problem. VB .NET will also list the problem in your Task List window, informing you that you need to "fully qualify" which namespace should be used. In other words, you would have to add the namespace's name to the function name, like this:

```
MyNameSpace2.StrBreak
```

If you haven't installed the examples for Visual Studio .NET, which include the Northwind sample database, you won't be able to test this example. (You use another sample database named pubs in this book as well.) If you need to, go back to the VS .NET CD and reinstall this stuff. Follow these steps:

1. **Choose Start⇨Settings⇨Control Panel.**

2. **Double-click the Add/Remove Programs icon.**

3. **In the list of currently installed programs, select Microsoft Visual Studio .NET.**

4. **Click the Change/Remove button.**

5. **Follow the instructions to install all samples and examples.**

If that doesn't do the trick, re-install the .NET SDK. The nwind.mdb sample database is installed when you install VB .NET.

Understanding the code

In this section, you look at the rest of the source code in the example to see what's happening. After the OLE DB connection is made, an SQL query is defined in this line:

```
Dim selectCMD As OleDbCommand = New OleDbCommand("SELECT *
        FROM Customers", nwindConn)
```

This line says to get all data from the Customers table in the Northwind database, defined in the `nwindConn` connection. * means *all* in SQL, the query language often used to get subsets — DataSets — of information from data sources.

Then you tell this command to spend no more than 30 seconds trying to get its DataSet. Next you define a `dataAdapter`. Finally, the connection is opened to the database and the `dataAdapter` is used to fill `ds`, the previously defined global DataSet variable, with the Customers table.

Note that you can use an alternative line to fill the DataSet:

```
dataAdapter.Fill(ds)
```

But if you do, when the DataGrid is displayed, the + node (the icon you click to reveal the data) reads *Table* rather than the more informative *Customers*.

After closing the connection, you fill the DataGrid with the contents of your DataSet:

```
nwindConn.Close()
DataGrid1.DataSource = ds
```

The ADO.NET code in the preceding example shouldn't seem alien if you've used ADO. But you must get accustomed to a few changes. The `Set` command isn't used *anywhere* in VB .NET! For a comprehensive tutorial on the changes made to the VB language between VB 6 and VB .NET, see the appendix on this book's Web site at `http://www.dummies.com/extras/VBNetDataProg/`.

ADO's version is

```
Set myRecordset = myCommand.Execute
```

In ADO.NET, this becomes:

```
dataAdapter.SelectCommand = selectCMD
```

The DataSet

The ADO.NET DataSet is like a local cache of tables — disconnected from the database that was the source of those tables. You can think of a DataSet as a collection of recordsets, but the ADO.NET disconnected DataSet is more powerful and more flexible (*richer* if you prefer) than its ancestor, the ADO disconnected recordset. The disconnected recordset was no more capable than the connected recordset, featuring only four elementary methods: `MoveFirst`, `MovePrevious`, `MoveNext`, and `MoveLast`.

MoveFirst, MovePrevious, MoveNext, and MoveLast have been removed from ADO.NET. The following ADO version of a loop that could extract all the data from a column (field):

```
Do While (Not myRecordset.EOF)
  t = myRecordset("au_fname")
  MyRecordset.MoveNext
```

becomes the following in ADO.NET:

```
While (drDataReader.Read)
t = CStr(drDataReader("au_fname"))
```

Microsoft discovered that many ADO programmers used the MoveNext command at the *start* of their Do-While loop (thereby starting with the "second" record by mistake). MoveNext should be at the end of a loop (as illustrated here). So, to prevent future incidents, the ADO.NET DataReader object now *requires* you to specifically invoke its Read method, which, by design, positions you at the first record of the DataSet. No worries about where to put a MoveNext command — it's no longer needed. And, thus, MoveNext, MovePrevious, MoveFirst, and MoveLast are all gone from the ADO.NET language.

A DataSet is comprised of several types of object collections: Tables, Columns (fields), Relations, Constraints, and Rows (records). The first four object types make up the DataSet's relational schema (its structure), and the Rows (records) hold the data itself. Given that these are collections of objects, more than one object can be in each collection — more than a single table, for instance, in the Tables collection.

A set of Columns, Constraints, and Rows collections are contained *within* each table object collection (the table object is also known as a DataTable). A DataTable remembers its original state, as well as the modifications made to it.

Beyond Disconnected Recordsets

ADO permitted disconnected recordsets, and perhaps you used them in some of your applications. This next example shows you how to translate VB 6 ADO code that creates and manipulates a disconnected recordset so that it will work in VB .NET.

ADO offered VB programmers something new. You could detach recordsets from their database to work on them locally, and then insert the result back to the database by updating the database. This approach conserves resources and takes a load off the server's processor. It also promotes the new distributed computing paradigm upon which XML, not to mention .NET, rests.

What's more, you could create a recordset independently and use it as a way to store temporary data without involving a database at all! Suppose that you want to use data binding, attaching a control such as a TextBox to a data-related control such as the ADODataSetView control. Normally, you attach the TextBox to a data-related control that is, itself, connected to a database. In VB 6, however, it became possible to use ADO to just create a new independent recordset. To do that, you define the fields you want in the recordset and then use the Open command. You can quite easily use an ADO.NET DataSet independently from any database, saving the results to your hard drive. For a simple application, this works just fine. (A DataSet can contain multiple tables.)

Here's code that, *in VB 6, using ADO,* creates a disconnected recordset. If you want to try this out in VB6, just start a new project and add a ListBox to Form1. Then type the following source code (remember that you can run VB6 and VB .NET simultaneously without any side effects, so if you have VB .NET up and running, don't feel that you have to shut it down just to play around with VB 6). However, if you *install* VB 6 after having already installed VB .NET, all bets are off. I've tried it; it destabilizes VB .NET. Perhaps, though, that won't be a problem by the time you're reading this book.

Here's the VB 6 code:

```
Private Sub Form_Load()

Dim rs As New ADODB.Recordset
rs.CursorLocation = adUseClient

'Here you define three new fields, then open the recordset
    rs.Fields.Append "key", adInteger
    rs.Fields.Append "Name", adVarChar, 40, adFldIsNullable
    rs.Fields.Append "Address", adVarChar, 40,
            adFldIsNullable

    rs.Open , , adOpenStatic, adLockBatchOptimistic

'Fill in some records

rs.AddNew Array("key", "Name", "Address"), Array(1,
            "Rec1Name", "Rec1Address")
rs.AddNew Array("key", "Name", "Address"), Array(2,
            "Rec2Name", "Rec2Address")

rs.MoveFirst

List1.AddItem "Key     Name        Address"
List1.AddItem " "

' Show the original records
While rs.EOF <> True
```

```
List1.AddItem rs!Key & "          " & rs!Name & "      " &
          rs!Address
rs.MoveNext
Wend

'"save" the records
rs.UpdateBatch adAffectAll


'Edit the first record
rs.MoveFirst
rs!Name = "New Name"
rs.MoveFirst

List1.AddItem " "
List1.AddItem " "

'Show the new, and previous, contents of both records
While rs.EOF <> True
List1.AddItem " "
List1.AddItem rs!Key & "         " & rs!Name & "     " &
          rs!Address
List1.AddItem rs!Key.OriginalValue & "         " &
          rs!Name.OriginalValue & "       " &
          rs!Address.OriginalValue
rs.MoveNext
Wend

End Sub
```

Translating VB 6 and ADO to VB .NET and ADO.NET

Now it's time to translate the preceding VB 6 code so that it works in the VB .NET world. If you simply cut and paste this code into VB .NET, it will flag all kinds of errors. For example, the default name for a ListBox in VB 6 is `List`, but in VB .NET it's `ListBox1`. VB .NET and the entire .NET prefer longer and more descriptive naming conventions. For example, what was `Text1.SelText` in VB 6 is now `TextBox1.SelectedText`. In keeping with this trend, the VB 6 `List1.AddItem` method must be translated into VB .NET's `ListBox1.Items.Add`.

But that's only the tip of the translation iceberg. VB 6's `Array` function has been removed from the language in VB .NET. What's more, VB .NET will have no idea what you mean by `ADODB.Recordset` or `CursorLocation` or `adUseClient` in this VB 6 code:

```
Dim rs As New ADODB.Recordset
rs.CursorLocation = adUseClient
```

In fact, the VB 6 code is filled with enums (*enumerations* — what we used to call *constants* such as `adUseClient` or the color `vbBlue`), and none of these enums are recognized by VB .NET. Enums that begin with the letters *ad* are intended to provide a parameter to a property in this case (`adInteger` and `adVarChar` are examples in the previous code).

In VB .NET, you must provide a more specific reference when you use an enum. For example, you must translate the VB 6 version:

```
rs.CursorLocation = adUseClient
```

to this VB .NET version:

```
ds.CursorLocation = CursorLocationEnum.adUseClient
```

Wow! you say. How will I remember the proper names for all these enums? You won't. However, VB .NET can help you figure out the proper syntax in several ways. First, you can just type the source code in the VB .NET IDE and its Intellisense features (statement completion, auto list members, and so on) will kick in and provide you with suggestions in the form of lists that pop out while you type a line of code in the code window.

Intellisense should provide the correct name when the parameter or member has a specific data type, as opposed to just integer or string. Be sure that the Intellisense features are turned on (Tools⇨Options⇨Text Editor⇨All Languages). Then, if you're typing your code and the editor can't tell what the argument requires, type **ADODB.** (including the period) and Intellisense will go to work..

You can figure out how to do things also by using an old standby: Use the Help Search or Index features to locate topics in the vast Help database.

Finding syntax the easy way

Yet another, and sometimes easier, way to get all the proper syntax is to shut down VB .NET and use Windows Explorer to locate Project1.VBP (or whatever name you gave the VB 6 version). Double-click the .VBP file and it will be loaded into VB .NET. VB .NET recognizes it as a VB 6 file, and the Visual Basic Upgrade Wizard starts running. Among other translations of VB 6 into VB .NET, all the right enum syntax is added automatically.

If double-clicking a .VBP file loads it into VB 6 (instead of VB .NET, where you want it), use the VB .NET File⇨Open⇨File feature, and then browse your hard drive and load the .VBP file.

The translator does an impressive job of adjusting many elements of VB 6 code. However, you must still often tweak the code by hand to make it work within VB .NET.

Chapter 15

Acronym Soup: DAO, XML, ODBC, ADO, ADO.NET

· ·

In This Chapter

▶ Sorting out database technologies

▶ Using ODBC

▶ Working with DAO

▶ Working toward Universal Data Access

▶ Understanding ADO

· ·

Chapter 14 gives you a taste of ADO.NET. Chapter 16 examines ADO.NET in detail. In this chapter, you find a bridge between those two chapters — an explanation of what the many database programming terms mean and how they're related. Oh yes, you also look at XML (a technology that, theoretically, will someday permit universal data access), the buried treasure toward which all the other roads — DAO, ODBC, and ADO — supposedly lead. XML packages are supposed to be self-describing, which means that they contain both an explanation of their structure as well as the data that fills that structure. As you may remember, however, when DataSets are translated into XML, they are divided into two files: the schema (structure) and a separate file that holds the data.

Don't run for the exits just because the subject of contemporary database programming has some contradictions and is littered with acronyms. Understanding these variations and acronyms is important. They represent the yesterday, today, and tomorrow of database management — if Microsoft has anything to say about it. And for a while at least, Microsoft will have something to say about it.

Getting a Handle on Database Technologies

You can store data in databases in hundreds of ways. Most useful computer applications store data, but rarely do they store it the same way as other applications. They usually do it in peculiar, proprietary ways. For example, can you use Access — Microsoft's popular database application — to search the e-mail messages in your Microsoft Outlook Express Inbox database? Nope.

But you *should* be able to search those messages. For instance, you should be able to add a subset of those messages to your company's customer-service database if you want. You should be able to store or copy e-mail anywhere, but you can't. Access saves data in files with an .MDB extension; the latest version of Outlook Express stores e-mail in files with a .DBX extension. And the twain does not meet. (Even Outlook Express itself has different database styles — two years ago it stored your e-mail in .MBX files!)

And how about plain .TXT files produced by Notepad or other simple, but often useful, text editors? Why can't a database application retrieve data from these kinds of files? Or from any and all kinds of files?

Data universality is hampered by various current trends, including the increasing importance of distributed computing and client/server computing. A primary trend today involves working harmoniously with applications and data spread across two or more machines. (In other words, the Internet and intranets sometimes extract DataSets from their database application or fracture an application into several parts running on several different computers and cause other divisions.)

Increasingly, businesspeople are realizing that lots of important information remains unused or unintegrated because it's not in the "proper" format. Companies establish sites on the Internet and ask visitors for feedback on their products. More and more, that feedback comes in the form of e-mail. How many companies can make wide use of the information in that email? Can they sort it, search it, and otherwise exploit it in an organized fashion? In other words, can they manage the data and store it for efficient integration into other data? Very few companies could do these things until ADO.NET. And even fewer could make efficient use of HTML-based data such as the Web-based catalogs of their competitors. Companies *do* like to check out competitors' catalogs, you know.

Understanding Open Database Connectivity (ODBC)

ODBC, or Open Database Connectivity, is a Microsoft database standard that is still widely used. ODBC takes on the burden of translating proprietary database formats into formats that database applications can understand.

Simply put, ODBC sits on your machine or a user's computer (the client) and translates any remote (server) relational database into data packages that your client application can handle. On a fundamental level, your application can use SQL to query or modify the data held in a remote database without worrying about the details of the remote database's methods of storing that data (such as punctuation, organization, and labeling).

One useful feature of ODBC is that you can specify ODBC *connections* (technically, they're called *Data Source Names,* or *DSN*). You give these connections a name, and then the next time you want to connect to that database, all the necessary information (password, log-on information, type of database, and so on) is already filled in, and you can just employ the DSN itself.

However, like many other acronyms you've gotten used to over the years, ODBC is now in the twilight of its useful life. Microsoft has announced its successors: OLE DB and, finally, ADO.NET. ODBC enables you to get relational data into a client computer. ADO.NET enables you to get *any* data source's data into a client computer — at least, that's the promise.

These days, a source of data is called a *data store* rather than a *database.* This new term is to help us broaden our definition of where useful data can be stored. It need not be in a proper database file; instead, you can now get data from simple .TXT files, e-mail files, and more.

ADO.NET can access data from many kinds of sources. Potential ADO.NET data stores cover the waterfront, including structured, semistructured, and unstructured data; relational and nonrelational data; SQL-based and non-SQL data. Examples include desktop databases, flat-files, mail stores, directory services, personal information managers (PIMs), multidimensional stores, and even those elusive OLAP cubes (don't ask).

Working with Data Access Objects (DAO)

Only a year or so ago, the most popular database technology was Microsoft's DAO, Data Access Objects. DAO is robust, well tested, and was used by most database programmers until recently. They understood its object model (all its syntax and how to program its methods and properties).

However, DAO had several weaknesses. It is best at single-desktop-computer work database management rather than distributed client/server, Internet, or intranet database management. In addition, DAO doesn't like old database formats (but lots of businesses have stuff stored in legacy formats), and it doesn't like new data formats, such as HTML, DHTML, e-mail, and plain text. It wants relational data — data organized into tables, fields, indices, and relations. You can't blame DAO for these things because it was never designed to do anything other than what it does — and does splendidly. Nevertheless, the time has come to phase out DAO and raise the curtain on the new stars of the database world.

What solution does Microsoft propose for addressing the shortcomings in DAO and other schemes? Universal Data Access through XML. This plan doesn't require that you massage data. You don't have to pour e-mail files, a bunch of old .DBF dBASE files, and Notepad .TXT files through filters until they end up in a new, all-purpose file type.

Tools that support the XML strategy are designed to package data from its current format, provide self-describing, plain-text packages, and then send those packages freely (no firewall blockage) over an intranet or the Internet. When received, the XML data packages can be absorbed into whatever data store the receiving party uses. In theory, this approach will let you, the programmer, send or receive data without worrying about its native format. It doesn't matter whether the comes from or goes into .TXT, .MDB, .DBF, or .DBX files.

XML isn't a product that you can buy. Instead, it's the name of an industry standard that is in the process of being defined. Microsoft supports XML and has built the entire .NET system on XML.

Now, you may be asking, "Isn't this the same promise that we've been offered before?" What about all the previous attempts to resolve the Babylon problem, such as the Symphony application suite offered in the mid-80s as the solution to the confusion of file types and data storage schemes?

Sure, for more than two decades, developers have been playing the universal data access tune. XML is simply the latest attempt to offer everything to everyone in the Web-development crowd.

So, do I believe that XML is a step in the right direction? Yes. And to move toward XML and the .NET technology, you must discover ADO.NET. You may not want to rewrite your existing key database applications or even create important new ones in ADO.NET just yet. One, ADO (without the .NET) is proven, well-established machinery. It works, and works well. Two, ADO.NET (as I write this) isn't finished yet, so stability and feature issues are not at this point fully ironed out.

That said, you should learn how to program ADO.NET. In all likelihood, it will become the technology of choice for database programming during the next year and beyond.

Understanding ADO (ActiveX Data Objects)

With ADO (ActiveX Data Objects), database programming became somewhat simpler to write, and new capabilities pointed the way to true distributed computing.

Consider just a few intriguing features of ADO: building recordsets from scratch (without any database connection) and disconnecting recordsets from the server. When disconnected, they continue to work fine in your workstation (client) computer. Just like a worm chopped in half, they behave normally. And later, you can rejoin these recordsets to their original database or merge them into other databases. This can greatly improve the scalability of an application because lots of people need not maintain ongoing connections to the same database, thereby jamming the traffic on the server. Instead, they all work independently with disconnected recordsets sitting in their own personal machines.

If you know how to use ADO, you can use it to get virtually any kind of data: HTML, e-mail, plain text, as well as traditional relational data and even legacy data sources.

ADO offers all the features of its ancestors (DAO and RDO), but it requires some changes in programming techniques. (See Chapter 16 for migration tips and examples.) For example, ADO is said to flatten the object model of DAO and RDO. *Flattening* means streamlining the model by reducing the number of objects but increasing the number of properties and methods of the objects that remain. Think of it as getting rid of all your appliances and then replacing them with fewer new ones that do more things.

Flattening also generally lessens the emphasis on the object hierarchy. Put simply, you can create objects without having to create other, higher objects. You can create a recordset without first having to create a connection object for it, for example.

The next chapter looks more closely at the technologies that lead up to, and support, ADO.NET. Chapter 16 continues your grand tour of database technologies.

Chapter 16

More about ADO.NET

*T*his chapter takes you deeper into the ADO.NET framework, explaining more about the various ways to manipulate and benefit from the new DataSet concept. You look at ways to map aliases (make one-to-one substitutions) when, for example, you are using a DataSet from Greece and prefer to program with English words for the various columns in the data store.

You also consider the various commands used with DataSets. Next, you see how to create a read-only, sequential DataReader object. Then you find out how to deal with version conflicts (concurrency), which arise when two or more people are working on the same record. You write some programming that decides which contending modified version of the record should be the one that gets saved back to the database.

And because XML is used to store data in a recordset as well as to transmit data between applications, you spend some time fine-tuning your grasp of XML.

Some Advantages of ADO.NET

The ADO.NET technology has been designed to provide you with as much flexibility as you might need — and database programming can require flexibility. Above all, remember that ADO.NET supports disconnected DataSets. The reason is that maintaining a continuously open connection between client and server is not only wasteful of system resources, it's often simply not possible in the world of Internet programming. So many people, so little power and memory in your server.

What's more, the typical database can handle only a few concurrent open connections. That pretty much eliminates old-style connected programming for any but the least popular Web sites. When you program for the Web, you must face the fact that four visitors to your site can suddenly swell to 400 — and many of these visitors might want to view your catalog or place an order at the same time.

Web programming is always essentially disconnected programming. When a server sends an ASP.NET HTML page to a user's browser, it discards its copy of that page. It pays no more attention to the user's browser until another request arrives from the user. It's like the relationship between the president and hundreds of clamoring reporters.

ADO.NET and ASP.NET are based on the premise that you'll often be programming for a disconnected architecture. You permit your application to connect to a database only while fetching data or saving changed data back to the database. Otherwise, you are not connected — and the database can therefore service some other request for data. If your application is designed to work on a single-user, standalone computer, and therefore requires a continual connection, use ADO instead of ADO.NET.

Remember that Microsoft is now using the term *column* to mean what used to be called a *field*. Likewise, they now use the term *row* for what used to be called a *record*. This seemingly endless shifting of terminology . . . well, it's the way things are. Keeps us all on our toes.

After data has been extracted from its data store, the resulting set of data is then translated into XML. If you need to store the DataSet as a file, it's stored in XML format. If you send the DataSet to another application, it is transmitted as an XML file. The translation to and from XML is handled for you automatically by ADO.NET. I have more to say about XML later in this chapter.

In ADO, you were forced to use what is called COM when transmitting a disconnected recordset, but in ADO.NET you use the simpler, cleaner XML stream. Among the benefits of the XML scheme are that no data-type conversions are required. With COM, ADO data types must be converted to COM data types, slowing things down.

Another advantage is that firewalls generally have no problem permitting the transmission of XML (ordinary HTML, which XML resembles, is considered harmless by firewalls). XML is seen as text — probably formatting or simple data — with no capability to spread viruses, inject worms, or otherwise threaten security. A COM transmission, on the other hand, makes a firewall slam shut because the transmission is fundamentally a binary — possibly an executable — form of information.

Finally, the XML technology places no restrictions data types, unlike the limited set offered by the older COM technology.

Of course, there is no perfect technology. XML has its critics, and they point out its flaws. The number-one defect: platform independence has been a frequently sought goal that has so far proved elusive. Already there are an estimated 500-plus proprietary flavors of the supposedly "universal" XML data structure. Also, XML's claims that it is self-documenting are doubtful. We don't have artificial intelligence yet, so the notion that a file could arrive at a server and explain itself to a receiving application seems a bit far fetched. There are other criticisms, too, including XML's famous verbosity.

Here are some reasons for you to consider switching from ADO to ADO.NET, particularly for distributed applications. Although ADO did introduce the concept of the disconnected recordset, ADO is nonetheless optimized for connected programming. ADO fundamentally assumes a continuous connection between the database and the application using it. ADO.NET, on the other hand, is optimized for the opposite: connect-on-demand programming.

 In ADO.NET, your application communicates with a database using the DataSetCommand object, which in turn sends messages through an OLE DB provider. *You* have the ability to customize code in a DataSetCommand object to, for example, validate changes to data or improve the efficiency of updating the database. In ADO, you were forced to communicate with the database through the OLE DB provider alone.

Think of an ADO recordset as essentially a single table, and if you want data from more than one database table, you have to use a JOIN query. The ADO. NET DataSet is a collection of one or more tables (DataTable objects). So data extracted from more than one table in a database is represented in the DataSet as more than one DataTable object. This is easier to visualize because there is essentially a one-to-one relationship between the structures in the database and the DataTable objects in the DataSet.

Working with the DataSet Object

Like objects everywhere, the DataSet class offers collections and properties. You'll want to understand the structure of the DataSet object.

Collections within collections

The DataSet has two primary collections: tables and relations. Lower in the hierarchy are several collections within the DataTable object: rows, columns, keys, childrelations, and parentrelations. The DataRow class includes a RowState property indicating whether, and how, the row (record) has been modified since its DataTable was first loaded from the database. The RowState property can be set to modified, new, deleted, and unchanged.

Substituting names (mapping)

When you first load the data from a database into a DataSet, the names of the tables and columns in the DataSet are the same as those used in the database. If you prefer to use different names while working with the DataSet, just create your new names in the DataSet command, and then *map* your names to the ones used in the original database. Both the OleDbCommand and SqlCommand use their TableMappings collections to map custom names to database names. When you return the data to the database, all will be well — any edited data will flow into the correct columns and tables as named originally in their database.

Why would you want to map, or rename, tables and columns? Perhaps the database is written in a foreign language and you find it easier to work with mapped aliases rather than foreign words. Or maybe you have an in-house naming scheme for your databases but are working with DataSets from some other organization. You want to maintain the custom naming scheme in your programming. So map.

Read-Only Sequential

If your application merely needs a read-only version of a DataSet, create an OleDbDataReader (or SqlDataReader). These objects have properties and methods that can assist you in scanning the query result. Also, they retrieve data faster than a DataSet. You get such methods as `NextResult` (the equivalent of the ADO `MoveNext` command), and instead of ADO's EOF (end-of-file) delimiter, you get the ADO.NET HasMoreRows property to see whether you've reached the last of the records.

EOF is an ancient command, used for more than 20 years to indicate that a file or recordset has reached its end:

```
Do While (Not myRecordset.EOF)
```

However, those in charge of naming things (or should I say *renaming* things) at Microsoft have decided that you can use the new Read property in VB .NET to detect the end of a set of data:

```
While (drDataReader.Read)
```

Suppose that you want to instantiate an OleDbDataReader or SqlDataReader object. In the following example, I assume that you have added an SqlConnection object named SqlConnection1 from the Toolbox to your form, and that you have right-clicked the SqlConnection1 icon, chosen Properties, then selected pubs.dbo as the ConnectionString property in the Properties window.

Type this at the top of your code window:

```
Imports System.Data.SqlClient
```

Then type this into the `Form_Load` event:

```
Private Sub Form1_Load(ByVal sender As System.Object, ByVal e
        As System.EventArgs) Handles MyBase.Load


    Dim dReader As SqlDataReader
    Dim dQuery As String = "SELECT Au_LName, Au_FName FROM
        Authors"
    Dim dCommand As New SqlCommand(dQuery, SqlConnection1)

    SqlConnection1.Open()

    dReader = dCommand.ExecuteReader

    While dReader.Read()
        Debug.WriteLine((dReader.GetString(0) & ", " &
            dReader.GetString(1)))
    End While

    dReader.Close()
    SqlConnection1.Close()

End Sub
```

Notice that after the usual set of `Dim` statements, you must invoke the
`ExecuteReader` method of the SqlDataReader object before you start reading
the data from the database. The results, as always when printed with
`Debug.WriteLine` or `Console.WriteLine`, appear in the VB .NET Output
window after you press F5. To see the Output window, where the results of running the preceding code will appear, choose View⇨Other Windows⇨Output or
Press Ctrl+Alt+O. (I generally use the Output window in this fashion quite often
while debugging a VB .NET project. I right-click the Output window's title bar
and choose Auto Hide so that the Output window is always available when I
want to see some results after a project is test-executed with F5.)

Sometimes an existing connection — one that's listed as a ConnectionString
property in the Properties window — will fail. You chose pubs.dbo as your
ConnectionString in this example. Nevertheless, it's possible that VB .NET
will halt on this line when you press F5

```
    SqlConnection1.Open()
```

and display an error message saying that it `cannot open a connection`
`without specifying a data source or server`. If that happens to you,
choose the New Connection option as SqlConnection1's ConnectionString in
the Properties window. Then follow the instructions described in Chapter 5
in the section titled "Using a connection control."

What If Someone Else Modifies the Database in the Meantime?

While your DataSet has been disconnected from its database, someone *else* might have also been working with some or all of that data in his or her separate DataSet. Maybe the person modified some of that same data and updated the database by restoring the DataSet's contents to the database. What if the person edited a record that you also edited? Should you overwrite the other person's changes with your changes? Or vice versa?

Unfortunately, the ADO.NET DataSet commands cannot handle this problem automatically. These commands are not artificially intelligent, after all. ADO.NET will not automatically lock a record in the database and warn others that the record is being edited and they must wait.

What's more, it's up to you to write programming to solve a potential problem when new versions of a record conflict. If this is a possible problem for the database you're working with, you have to find a solution and write the source code for that solution yourself. What's more, if the database you're working with could have a problem with conflicting records, you have to find a solution and write the source code for that solution yourself.

The problem of two or more users in conflict during their attempts to flush back disconnected data into a database is called the *problem of concurrency*. When two or more users try to update a given record, should the changes made by the last person to update that record win?

Optimism versus pessimism

You can approach the concurrency problem in two fundamental ways: pessimistic concurrency and optimistic concurrency. *Optimistic concurrency* prevents outsiders from changing a record (row) only while another person is updating that record. The updating usually takes very little time, so the lockout is brief.

Pessimistic concurrency, by contrast, locks out others for a longer time. The lock starts when one user accesses a record (which that user might potentially edit or delete) and is in effect until the original user sends the record back to the database. (This is similar to the older style of database programming that maintained an open connection between an application and a database.)

Pessimism

Pessimistic concurrency is useful if you need to freeze a record while, for example, making arrangements for a customer. For example, if an Amtrak agent is talking to someone about booking a sleeping car room on the train for a popular holiday, pessimistic locking will prevent two agents in two different stations from contending for the same room — thereby angering a customer. In that type of situation, you'd want to lock the record for that room until the first customer makes up his or her mind and either reserves that room or not.

The problem is that when you're using a DataSet, you can't use pessimistic concurrency. It's not practical in a disconnected architecture, and it's not scalable for the same reason that maintaining an open connection between an application and a DataSet isn't scalable.

Optimism

Optimistic concurrency locks a record only briefly, during the save to a hard drive. This prevents a nasty collision if two different records are simultaneously sent to the same record location in a database.

When a user attempts to update a record under optimistic concurrency, the updated data is compared to the existing record in the database. If there is any difference between them, the update is rejected. An exception is raised (an error message is generated). *You, the programmer,* must handle such errors in ADO.NET. You must write programming that responds to this type of error (using the `Try-Catch` error handling system in VB .NET) and decides what to do about the changed record. Do you accept it? Or do you have some criteria that can reconcile a data clash?

One version of optimistic concurrency is known as "last-in wins." This version doesn't compare the updated record to the original record. It merely lets each new update replace the previous version of the record. The last-in wins approach is the most scalable approach you can employ.

Comparing versions with optimistic concurrency

When deciding which record gets saved, classic optimistic concurrency compares versions by checking their version number (or, in some cases, their time and date stamps) or by saving all the values (all the data in the DataSet is saved when the data is initially read).

If the version number approach is used, each record must have a version number (or datestamp) column. This special column is saved on the client computer when the record is first read. Then if that client has modified a record, the database is checked to see whether the stored version number matches the version number currently in the database. If they match, it proves that no other person has modified that record since it was "checked out" for use by the client. Therefore, it is safe to update the record with the client's edited version. You can use an SQL statement like the following to conduct this test:

```
UPDATE myTable SET Field1 = ChangedValue1, Field2 =
         ChangedValue2
WHERE ClientStoredStamp = OriginalStampInDatabase
```

If this SQL is attempted, but the ClientStoredStamp doesn't equal the OriginalStampInDatabase, an error is returned and you can write programming to make a decision about what to do. (You could store the client's editing and thereby replace the current record, extract the current record to compare it to the client's edited record, or save both versions and ask a human to make the decision.) It's also your responsibility to write the programming that updates the version or datetime column whenever a record is modified.

The other primary approach to managing optimistic concurrency is to save a copy of a record when it is first read. This means your DataSet will have two copies of any record that is read: the one from the database and the one the user modified. Using this approach, when the user attempts to update a record, the original version that came from the database is compared to whatever is now in that database. If they match, there's no problem. It proves that no one has messed with the record while it's been "checked out" of your DataSet, so you can go ahead and save the updated version (containing the user's modifications) to the database without worrying about overwriting someone else's work.

Every DataSet command includes four parameter collections, one for each of the four commands: Select, Update, Insert, Delete. Each parameter corresponds to a placeholder (? in an SQL statement) in the command text. The properties of a parameter specify both the column the parameter is associated with and whether or not the parameter represents the edited version or the original version. These parameter collections make it possible for the DataSet command to generate dynamic SQL (or provide parameters to a stored procedure).

Building optimistic concurrency parameters

Fortunately, VB .NET will build the necessary DataSet parameters for you to implement optimistic concurrency using the SQL or stored procedure approach. Here's how:

1. **Create a VB .NET project that includes a data connection using an SqlDataAdapter object (see " Using SqlDataAdapter" in Chapter 3).**

2. **In the design window tray, right-click the SqlDataAdapter icon and choose Configure DataAdapter.**

   The Data Adapter Configuration Wizard opens.

3. **Click Next.**

4. **In the Which Data Connection list, choose the *computername*.pubs.dbo data connection, and then click Next.**

   Substitute your computer's name for *computername*. If the pubs.dbo connection is not listed, follow the steps in the "Connecting to SQL Server" section of Chapter 3.

5. **Choose the Use SQL Statements option, and then click Next.**

6. **Click the Query Builder button.**

7. **If the Add Table dialog box appears automatically, go to Step 9.**

8. **If the Add Table dialog box does not appear, right-click the background in the top pane of the Query Builder dialog box and choose Add Table.**

9. **In the Add Table dialog box, choose Authors, and then click the Add button.**

10. **Click Close to close the Add Table dialog box.**

11. **In the Authors table, choose the All Columns option, and then click OK.**

    This SQL statement is accepted and displayed.

12. **Click the Advanced Options button.**

13. **Choose the Use Optimistic Concurrency option, and then click OK.**

14. **Click Finish**

    The Wizard closes.

Now look at the code in the editor. You need to write some programming for the `RowUpdated` event, to ensure that the records that were supposed to be updated were, in fact, updated. (*Updated* means that records were changed in the database.)

Verify your work as follows. Clicking the SqlDataAdapter1 icon in the design window. In the Properties window, locate the UpdateCommand object, and then the Parameters collection under that. Click the ellipsis (...) button next to the Parameters collection to see the SqlParameter Collection Editor, as shown in Figure 16-1.

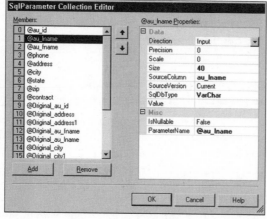

Figure 16-1:
You can manipulate the parameters collection for any command object.

A Brief Look at XML

This book is not the place to dive into XML theory and practice. Just be aware that VB .NET automatically creates XML for you when your program builds a DataSet. XML also underlies other VB .NET elements, but it's mostly accomplished behind the scenes and you need not write the code, nor even understand it.

In this section, you briefly consider the underpinning structure — the data storage and message-sending format used by ADO.NET. When you create a DataSet in VB .NET, it's translated into XML. For example, if you create a DataSet based on the Authors table in the Pubs sample database, you can then look over in the VB .NET Solution Explorer window and find an .XSD (XML schema) file. *You* didn't create this schema; VB .NET built it when you created your DataSet. Here's an example of an XML schema file that describes the structure of a DataSet:

```
<xsd:schema id="dsAuthors"
          targetNamespace="http://www.tempuri.org/dsAuthors.
          xsd" xmlns="http://www.tempuri.org/dsAuthors.xsd"
          xmlns:xsd="http://www.w3.org/1999/XMLSchema"
          xmlns:msdata="urn:schemas-microsoft-com:xml-
          msdata">
  <xsd:element name="authors">
    <xsd:complexType content="elementOnly">
      <xsd:all>
        <xsd:element name="au_id" type="xsd:string"/>
        <xsd:element name="au_lname" type="xsd:string"/>
        <xsd:element name="au_fname" type="xsd:string"/>
        <xsd:element name="phone" type="xsd:string"/>
        <xsd:element name="address" minOccurs="0"
          type="xsd:string"/>
```

```
            <xsd:element name="city" minOccurs="0"
                type="xsd:string"/>
            <xsd:element name="state" minOccurs="0"
                type="xsd:string"/>
            <xsd:element name="zip" minOccurs="0"
                type="xsd:string"/>
            <xsd:element name="contract" type="xsd:boolean"/>
        </xsd:all>
      </xsd:complexType>
      <xsd:key name="Constraint1" msdata:PrimaryKey="True">
        <xsd:selector>.</xsd:selector>
        <xsd:field>au_id</xsd:field>
      </xsd:key>
    </xsd:element>
    <xsd:element name="dsAuthors" msdata:IsDataSet="True">
      <xsd:complexType>
        <xsd:choice maxOccurs="unbounded">
          <xsd:element ref="authors"/>
        </xsd:choice>
      </xsd:complexType>
    </xsd:element>
</xsd:schema>
```

As you can see, XML is often rather verbose and redundant. Let's just shudder, and move on.

Using XML Designer

You *can* go the other way, too. Instead of coding a DataSet and then watching VB .NET turn it into XML for you, you can do the opposite. You can first create an XML schema, and then let VB .NET's XML Designer translate it into a DataSet. In this section, you see how to get the XML Designer up and running and how to use the Designer to build a DataSet from an XML schema.

You begin your exploration of XML Designer by adding an XML schema to an existing ASP.NET project. Start a VB .NET Web project or open an existing one. Choose Project⇨Add New Item. In the Add New Item dialog box, shown in Figure 16-2, double-click XML Schema.

As soon as you choose the XML Schema icon, you're shown the Design view of the new file, which is named XSDSchema1.XSD (XSD stands for XML Schema Definition). There's nothing to see yet in the Design view, but a message tells you to create a schema by dragging objects from Server Explorer or the Toolbox. If you want, you can also right-click the Designer window and choose an option to do some lower-level schema designing.

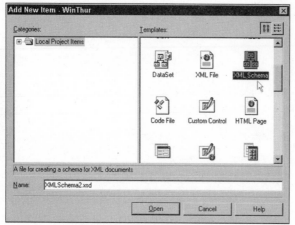

Figure 16-2:
The XML
Schema
icon is your
gateway to
designing
XML
structures.

Before going any further, take a look at the default schema template. Click the XML tab at the bottom of the Designer window. You see the framework code that is required in any schema file:

```
<?xml version="1.0" encoding="utf-8" ?>

<xsd:schema id="XMLSchema1"
 targetNamespace="http://tempuri.org/XMLSchema1.xsd"
 elementFormDefault="qualified"
 xmlns="http://tempuri.org/XMLSchema1.xsd"
          xmlns:xsd="http://www.w3.org/2001/XMLSchema">
</xsd:schema>
```

The code specifies two local namespaces and the standard XSD namespace located at the World Wide Web Consortium (W3C), which contains such schema metadata as definitions of permitted data types and element attributes such as order. W3C is attempting to standardize XML. More power to them.

Creating types

Now you're ready to build a schema for an XML type. Click the Schema tab at the bottom of the Designer window, and then open the Toolbox. There they are! Metadata items you can add to your schema, as shown in Figure 16-3. Don't ask me what an XML type or metadata are: You'll find out soon enough.

The two kinds of XML schema types are the *simple* type, which contains only text content, and the *complex* type, which can contain other schema types, attributes, or both. A complex type can be mapped to a relational table in a database. If you do that, the simple types (the contained subtypes in the complex type) are equivalent to the columns in a database's table.

Figure 16-3:
Your set of
tools when
creating
XML
schema.
(Ignore the
pointer.)

First let's create a simple type (called ZipCode). Your schema will specify that
each item of data must not be larger than five characters. (You use this type
later as a subtype by placing it in a complex type called Voter.) Follow these
steps:

1. **In the Toolbox, double-click the simpleType icon.**

   It's placed in the Design window.

2. **Click the TextBox containing simpleType1 and replace the default
   name (simpleType1) with ZipCode.**

3. **Click the ComboBox list and select xsd:string as your variable type, as
   shown in Figure 16-4.**

   This is the default anyway.

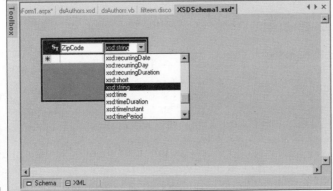

Figure 16-4:
Many XSD
variable
types are
available.

4. **Click the XML tab at the bottom of the Designer window.**

   You can see that the following line has been added to the schema

   ```
   <xsd:simpleType name="ZipCode" base="xsd:string"/>
   ```

5. **Click the Schema tab.**

6. **Just below ZipCode, click to reveal a hidden list of attributes for your type and select xsd:length, as shown in Figure 16-5.**

Figure 16-5:
Each cell you click reveals another drop-down list.

7. **In the cell right next to xsd:length, type 5 and press Enter.**

   That value is added to the underlying XML. If you check the XML, you'll see this code:

   ```
   <xsd:simpleType name="ZipCode" base="xsd:string">
       <xsd:length value="5"/>
   </xsd:simpleType>
   ```

8. **Click the next cell below the xsd:length cell.**

   Each cell that contributes to making up a simple type in the Designer contains the list of attributes, as shown in Figure 16-6. However, you don't want any further attributes, so ignore the cell below the xsd:length cell.

Figure 16-6:
Each cell can be defined using its own list of attributes.

If you want to get rid of an unwanted type, right-click it and the menu in Figure 16-7 is displayed.

Watch out, the Delete option removes the entire type, not just a cell within it.

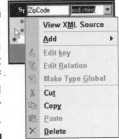

Figure 16-7:
Use this menu to get rid of unwanted elements or types.

To delete, cut, or otherwise modify a specific cell, first click that cell's name to highlight it. Then right-click the cell's name and you'll see a cell-specific menu, which differs from the larger type menu in Figure 16-7. Note that even if you merely want to rename a cell, you must still go through this process and delete the cell's name using the menu before renaming it.

Adding a complex type

Now it's time to add a complex type that, among other things, will contain the simple ZipCode type you just defined.

The complex type will be named Voter and will include several other types. A complex type defines a structure, a hierarchical diagram that specifies relationships between the elements of data it contains. Your Voter type will include the following subtypes: FirstName, LastName, VoterID, and the simple type you defined previously named ZipCode. Follow these steps:

1. **With the Schema tab selected in the Designer, double-click the ComplexType icon in the Toolbox to add it to the Designer window.**

2. **Rename the icon from the default complexType1 to** Voter.

3. **Click the first cell on the left under Voter, click the down-arrow to drop-down the list, select Attribute, and then type** FirstName.

4. **Add additional cells for LastName and VoterID.**

   Both have the default string data type.

5. **Add a cell for Zip. Set its data type by clicking the cell to the right of Zip, and then selecting ZipCode from the list.**

Now that you've created a complex type, peek at the XML that the Designer has built for you:

```
<?xml version="1.0" encoding="utf-8"?>
<xsd:schema id="XSDSchema1"
          targetNamespace="http://tempuri.org/XSDSchema1.xsd
          " xmlns="http://tempuri.org/XSDSchema1.xsd"
          xmlns:xsd="http://www.w3.org/1999/XMLSchema">
     <xsd:simpleType name="ZipCode" base="xsd:string">
         <xsd:length value="5"/>
     </xsd:simpleType>

     <xsd:complexType name="Voter">

         <xsd:sequence/>
         <xsd:attribute name="FirstName" type="xsd:string"/>
         <xsd:attribute name="LastName" type="xsd:string"/>
         <xsd:attribute name="VoterID" type="xsd:string"/>
         <xsd:attribute name="Zip" type="ZipCode"/>

     </xsd:complexType>

</xsd:schema>
```

The parser identifies problems

XML Designer has a built-in *parser*, which is a utility that reads XML source code and notifies you about any flaws and badly formed XML it finds. To see the parser do its thing, you need a bad line. Working with the preceding code, type the following boldface line directly into your XML source code, which will give the parser problems:

```
<xsd:element name="Zip" type="ZipCode" />

</xsd:Woof Woof>

</xsd:sequence>
```

Now click the Schema tab in Designer. Instead of a diagram of your schema, you see the following message from the parser:

```
The XML Designer encountered the following error while
          reading this file:
The 'xsd:complexType' start tag on line '6' doesn't match the
          end tag of 'xsd:Woof' - line 12, column 18
Please return to source view and correct these errors.
```

This is pretty good, specific information. (The parser often relies on the inherent tag/end tag symmetry to discover anomalies in XML source code.)

One little annoyance is that like several features in computer programming languages (arrays, for instance), the parser considers the first line to be line 0. So when you try to locate line 6, you actually count up from line 1 to line 7.

Remove the offending `Woof Woof` line in the source code and return to Schema view. You see the diagram again, but no error message.

Building relational tables

You might have noticed that the simple and complex types you've created are similar to HTML or XML elements. A type has the same, somewhat ambiguous and fragile relationship to an element that a class has to an object that can be instantiated from it. It's similar to the distinctions — and these too are fragile distinctions — between design-time and run-time programming, between class and object, or between property and method. All too often, they are distinctions without differences.

But note that a schema is supposed to be metadata (data about data), a design or structure that will later be actualized (brought into existence) when elements are created containing data. This is like the relationship between a database's columns (which have names for each type of data, such as PhoneNumber) and records (which contain the data, such as someone's phone number).

So, aren't you surprised to see an icon representing an *element* in the schema Toolbox? An element "object" is just a complex type or, put another way, a relational table. You create tables with XML Designer, and then create one-to-many relationships between those tables. In this way, you design what eventually becomes a new DataSet.

XML Designer builds a table by first creating an element containing a complex type. Within that type, it places subelements corresponding to the columns in the table. Each subelement contains attributes defining the column's name and data type and the frequency of occurrence of that column.

XSD doesn't contain an attribute for every feature in an ADO.NET DataSet. So, if an attribute isn't part of XSD's vocabulary, such as read-only, an *annotation* is used to note that feature. Annotations look like this:

```
<annotation>
    <appinfo>
        <msdata:readonly="True" />
    </appinfo>
</annotation>
```

A primary key can be specified using XSD. It's indicated with code like this:

```
<key name=" MyKey" msdata:primarykey="True">
    <selector>.</selector>
    <field>VoterRegNum</field>
</key>
```

Adding an element

Continuing with the example schema you've been building in this chapter, double-click the element icon in the Toolbox to add it to Designer. This is now an unnamed complex type:

```
<xsd:element name="element1">
      <xsd:complexType>
          <xsd:sequence/>
      </xsd:complexType>
</xsd:element>
```

That means it's the basis of a relational table. You can now add more elements to specify the columns.

You can also add unnamed complex types *within* this relational table, thereby nesting a new relation inside the original, container relation. Follow these steps:

1. **Change the name of the new element from element1 to** VoterStats.

   When you change the name, the variable type (the cell to the right of the name cell) automatically fills with a variable type of the same name (VoterStats). You can leave this variable type name as-is.

2. **Click the first cell in the first row (right below the E symbol).**

   An arrow appears.

3. **In the drop-down list, select element, named Element1 by default.**

   (All items you enter in the first column become elements automatically, so you don't have to select Element from the list. I just wanted you to see the list so you would know that there are alternative types you can choose.)

4. **Change the name of the element from Element1 to Frequency.**

5. **Add two elements named Registration and Party.**

   Leave all these elements set to the default data type, string.

6. **Double-click the element icon in the Toolbox to add a second relational table framework. Name it** Verification **and add two subelements: Vcode and BackCodes. Leave both data types set to string.**

7. **Drag a Key icon from the Toolbox and drop it on the Verification element.**

   The Edit Key dialog box appears, as shown in Figure 16-8.

8. **In the Fields list, click the first cell to select VCode.**

9. **Choose the DataSet primary Key option, as shown in Figure 16-8.**

10. **Click OK to close the box.**

    A key symbol is added to the VCode cell in the Verification element box in the diagram.

Defining a relation

To define a relation, continue as follows:

1. **Drag the Relation icon from the Toolbox and drop it in the VoterStats element box (not just anywhere on the Designer window).**

   The Edit Relation dialog box appears, as shown in Figure 16-9.

2. **In the Foreign Key Fields list, choose BackCodes, as shown in Figure 16-9.**

3. **Click the New button to choose a new key.**

4. **In the Parent Fields list, choose Registration, and then click OK.**

5. **Choose the Create Foreign Key Constraint Only option, and then click OK.**

   In the Designer, you see a diagrammatic representation of the relation between these two tables, as shown in Figure 16-10.

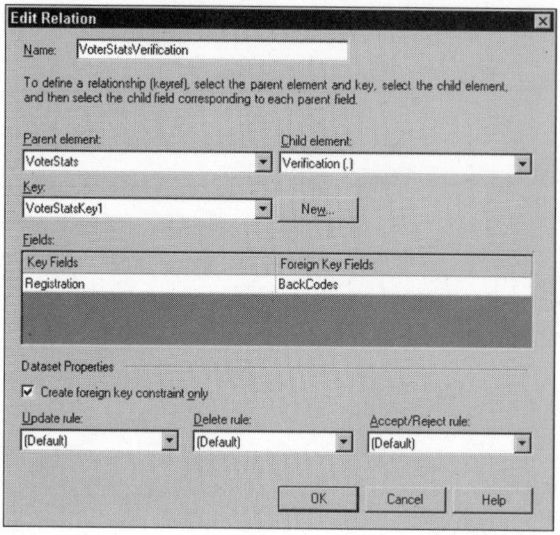

Figure 16-9:
Here's
where you
specify the
features of a
relation.

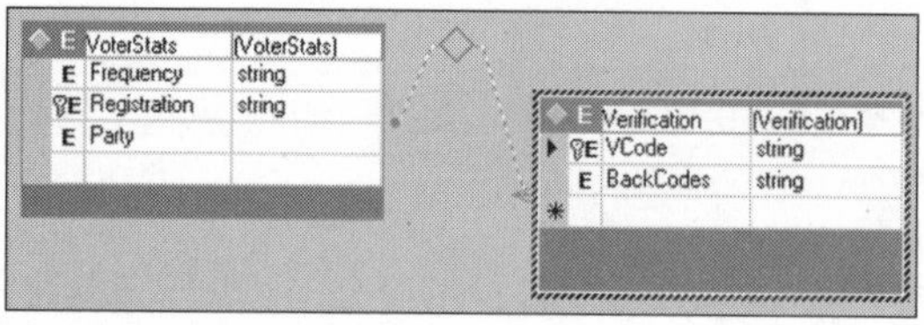

Figure 16-10:
Notice the
new key
symbol
next to
Registration
and the
dashed lines
illustrating
the relation.

6. **Click the XML tab to see the complete set of table and attribute definitions that XML Designer has created for you:**

```
<?xml version="1.0" encoding="utf-8" ?>
<xsd:schema id="XMLSchema1" targetNamespace="http://tem-
     puri.org/XMLSchema1.xsd"
     elementFormDefault="qualified" xmlns="http://tem-
     puri.org/XMLSchema1.xsd"
     xmlns:xsd="http://www.w3.org/2001/XMLSchema"
     xmlns:msdata="urn:schemas-microsoft-com:xml-
     msdata">
  <xsd:simpleType name="ZipCode">
    <xsd:restriction base="xsd:string">
      <xsd:length value="5" />
    </xsd:restriction>
```

```
        </xsd:simpleType>
        <xsd:complexType name="Voter">
            <xsd:sequence>
                <xsd:element name="FirstName" type="xsd:string"
                />
                <xsd:element name="LastName" type="xsd:string"
                />
                <xsd:element name="VoterID" type="xsd:string" />
                <xsd:element name="Zip" type="ZipCode" />
            </xsd:sequence>
        </xsd:complexType>
        <xsd:element name="VoterStats">
            <xsd:complexType>
                <xsd:sequence>
                    <xsd:element name="Frequency"
                type="xsd:string" />
                    <xsd:element name="Registration"
                type="xsd:string" />
                    <xsd:element name="Party" />
                </xsd:sequence>
            </xsd:complexType>
            <xsd:key name="VoterStatsKey1">
                <xsd:selector xpath="." />
                <xsd:field xpath="Registration" />
            </xsd:key>
        </xsd:element>
        <xsd:element name="Verification">
            <xsd:complexType>
                <xsd:sequence>
                    <xsd:element name="VCode" type="xsd:string"
                    />
                    <xsd:element name="BackCodes"
                type="xsd:string" />
                </xsd:sequence>
            </xsd:complexType>
            <xsd:key name="VerificationKey1"
                msdata:PrimaryKey="true">
                <xsd:selector xpath="." />
                <xsd:field xpath="VCode" />
            </xsd:key>
            <xsd:keyref name="VoterStatsVerification"
                refer="VoterStatsKey1"
                msdata:ConstraintOnly="true">
                <xsd:selector xpath="." />
                <xsd:field xpath="BackCodes" />
            </xsd:keyref>
        </xsd:element>
    </xsd:schema>
```

7. **If you want, you can edit this schema. When you've finished editing, click the Schema tab to see whether the parser finds any errors to report.**

Word has it that in a future version of VB .NET, the code window for an XML schema will flag errors with a sawtooth red line under the problem, and you can also move the mouse pointer on top of the error to see the error message.

Although the new official name for fields is now *columns*, you'll still see the term *fields* used, as in the preceding XML lines. For example:

```
<xsd:field xpath="BackCodes" />
```

Generating your DataSet

Now for the good part: actually creating your DataSet. Follow these steps:

1. **Click the Schema tab.**

2. **Right-click the *background* of the Designer window (don't click one of the boxes in the diagram) and choose Generate DataSet, as shown in Figure 16-11.**

   After some grinding and toiling behind the scenes, the new DataSet is constructed. Now it's time to see it.

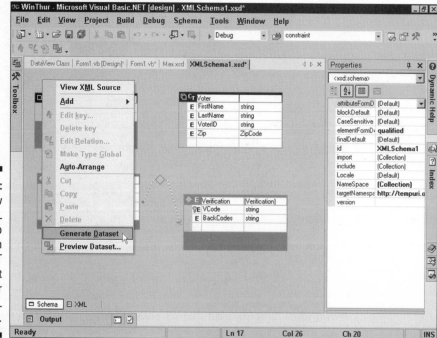

Figure 16-11: Here's how you tell XML Designer to build an ADO.NET DataSet from your XML schema.

3. **In the title bar of Solution Explorer, click the Show All Files icon.**

   Note that by default, Solution Explorer hides some files. To see these files, click the name of your project (the line in boldface in Solution Explorer) to reveal the icons in the Solution Explorer toolbar. Then click the Show All Files icon. Now click the + symbols in Solution Explorer to reveal the hidden files.

4. **In Solution Explorer, locate the XSDSchema1.XSD file, and click the + symbol next to that .XSD file to reveal the DataSet file that has been constructed.**

   It's named XSDSchema1.VB.

5. **Right-click XSDSchema1.VB and choose View Code to see the source code that defines your new DataSet in VB .NET format.**

Here's a brief sample of the first lines of that source code file (the entire file is 1,246 lines long!):

```
'------------------------------------------------------------
                   ------------------
' <autogenerated>
'      This code was generated by a tool.
'      Runtime Version: 1.0.2914.16
'
'      Changes to this file may cause incorrect behavior and
'              will be lost if
'      the code is regenerated.
' </autogenerated>
'------------------------------------------------------------
                   ------------------

Option Strict Off
Option Explicit On

Imports System
Imports System.Data
Imports System.Runtime.Serialization
Imports System.Xml


<Serializable(), _
  System.ComponentModel.DesignerCategoryAttribute("code")> _
Public Class XMLSchema1
    Inherits System.Data.DataSet

    Private tableVoterStats As VoterStatsDataTable

    Private tableVerification As VerificationDataTable

    Public Sub New()
        MyBase.New
        Me.InitClass
```

```
End Sub

Private Sub New(ByVal info As SerializationInfo, ByVal
        context As StreamingContext)
    MyBase.New
    Me.InitClass
    Me.GetSerializationData(info, context)
End Sub

<System.ComponentModel.Browsable(false), _

        System.ComponentModel.DesignerSerializationVisibil
        ityAttribute(System.ComponentModel.DesignerSeriali
        zationVisibility.Content)> _
Public ReadOnly Property VoterStats As
        VoterStatsDataTable
    Get
        Return Me.tableVoterStats
    End Get
End Property

<System.ComponentModel.Browsable(false), _

        System.ComponentModel.DesignerSerializationVisibil
        ityAttribute(System.ComponentModel.DesignerSeriali
        zationVisibility.Content)> _
Public ReadOnly Property Verification As
        VerificationDataTable
    Get
        Return Me.tableVerification
    End Get
End Property

Protected Overrides Function ShouldSerializeTables() As
        Boolean
    Return false
End Function

Protected Overrides Function ShouldSerializeRelations()
        As Boolean
    Return false
End Function

Protected Overrides Sub ReadXmlSerializable(ByVal reader
        As XmlReader)
    Me.ReadXml(reader, XmlReadMode.IgnoreSchema)
End Sub

Protected Overrides Function GetSchemaSerializable() As
        System.Xml.Schema.XmlSchema
    Dim stream As System.IO.MemoryStream = New
        System.IO.MemoryStream
    Me.WriteXmlSchema(New XmlTextWriter(stream, Nothing))
```

```
        stream.Position = 0
        Return System.Xml.Schema.XmlSchema.Read(New
            XmlTextReader(stream), Nothing)
    End Function

    Private Sub InitClass()
        Me.DataSetName = "XMLSchema1"
        Me.Namespace = "http://tempuri.org/XMLSchema1.xsd"
        Me.tableVoterStats = New VoterStatsDataTable
        Me.Tables.Add(Me.tableVoterStats)
        Me.tableVerification = New VerificationDataTable
        Me.Tables.Add(Me.tableVerification)
    End Sub
```

This is a typed DataSet class, which inherits from the ADO.NET DataSet class and then adds its own properties. These properties permit direct access to the tables and columns in the schema. Because the typed DataSet class is inherited from the ADO.NET class, it also gets all the properties and methods of the ADO.NET DataSet class.

ADO.NET offers access to the data in a DataSet through what is called *strong typing*. Strong typing avoids vague or ambiguous diction. Instead of Items(2), you use more meaningful names such as VotersDataSet.Voters("Joan Loude"). You can access tables and columns by name rather than dealing with collections. However, to offer this feature, a great deal of VB .NET code must be written by the autogenerator, as in:

```
'       This code was generated by a tool.
```

Strong typing creates more readable code. For instance, in ADO, you might use this less efficient code (it changes some data in a recordset):

```
AdoRecordSet.Find("VoterId = 'Deloria'")
AdoRecordSet.Fields("VoterId").Value = "Z22"
```

But now you can streamline this job in ADO.NET with this strongly typed line of code:

```
VotersDataSet.Voters("Deloria").VoterID = "Z22"
```

This is a simpler, more intuitive approach. I'll let you decide whether or not it is worth requiring 1,246 lines of VB .NET code to describe the structure of a simple DataSet.

In addition to its greater readability, this ADO.NET approach is easier on the programmer in another way — it makes possible what Microsoft calls the Intellisense feature in the editor. *Intellisense* can fill in the remainder of your line of code as you type in the beginning of that line. In our brave new world of thousands of objects, with thousands of methods, the auto-completion feature of Intellisense is essential. Gone are the days when we programmers could remember all the statements and functions in a computer language, much less the arguments and parameters that each of them can take.

This gazillion-possible-functions effect is even worse now that VB .NET *overloads* so many functions, providing, for example, 18 possible argument lists for the simple `Console.Writeline` function. Try this example. In the VB .NET code window, type this line:

```
console.WriteLine(
```

As soon as you type the parenthesis symbol, a box pops out suggesting one *of* eighteen possible argument lists you can give this function. Press your up or down arrow keys to see them all.

Fortunately, Intellisense is implemented for the VB .NET editor in the VS .NET IDE. At the time of this writing, however, the XML Designer window does not yet support Intellisense, though it is expected to in the future.

Another advantage of the ADO.NET strongly typed DataSet (over the ADO weakly typed recordset) is that errors involving types trigger an error message during compilation rather than at runtime. For example, if you attempt to store a floating-point variable in a record designated integer, ADO.NET flags that error when you try to compile your code. If constant compilation is included in the final version of ADO.NET, you may even see the error flagged as soon as you type it.

Dropping a table into XML Designer

In addition to its capability to generate DataSets, XML Designer can also accept tables directly from a database. It then translates that table's structure into an XML schema for you. It also displays the table in the Designer window, along with any XSD controls you've added from the Toolbox.

To try this feature, follow these steps:

1. **Click the XMLSchema1.xsd tab at the top of the code/design window.**

2. **Open VB .NET Server Explorer (press Ctrl+Alt+S).**

3. **Locate the *computername*.pubs database, where *computername* is the name of your computer.**

4. **In the design window, click the Schema tab.**

   Recall that you can't add controls or other items unless you're in Design or Schema view.

5. **Delete all the elements and types you created previously in this Schema window.**

6. **In Server Explorer, under the Pubs database, locate the Tables entry, and then locate the Publishers table. Drag Publishers from the Server Explorer window and drop it into XML Designer.**

   It's diagramed, as shown in Figure 16-12.

The table has been translated into this XML in the schema:

```xml
<?xml version="1.0" encoding="utf-8" ?>
<xsd:schema id="XMLSchema1"
            targetNamespace="http://tempuri.org/XMLSchema1.xsd
            " elementFormDefault="qualified"
            xmlns="http://tempuri.org/XMLSchema1.xsd"
            xmlns:xsd="http://www.w3.org/2001/XMLSchema"
            xmlns:msdata="urn:schemas-microsoft-com:xml-
            msdata">
    <xsd:element name="Document">
      <xsd:complexType>
        <xsd:choice maxOccurs="unbounded">
          <xsd:element name="publishers">
            <xsd:complexType>
              <xsd:sequence>
            <xsd:element name="pub_id" type="xsd:string"
          />
          <xsd:element name="pub_name" type="xsd:string"
            minOccurs="0" />
          <xsd:element name="city" type="xsd:string"
            minOccurs="0" />
          <xsd:element name="state" type="xsd:string"
            minOccurs="0" />
          <xsd:element name="country" type="xsd:string"
            minOccurs="0" />
              </xsd:sequence>
            </xsd:complexType>
          </xsd:element>
        </xsd:choice>
      </xsd:complexType>
      <xsd:unique name="DocumentKey1"
          msdata:PrimaryKey="true">
        <xsd:selector xpath=".//publishers" />
        <xsd:field xpath="pub_id" />
      </xsd:unique>
    </xsd:element>
</xsd:schema>
```

The XML Designer can also work with files having the following extensions: .TDL (Template Description Language), .WEB, .RESX, and .XSLT.

In addition to the Toolbox, Server Explorer, and right-clicking the background of the Designer window, you can manage the XML Designer also by using the Schema menu and the Schema Toolbar (shown in Figure 16-13).

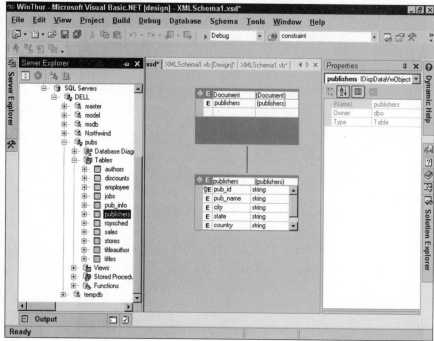

Figure 16-12:
XML
Designer
accepts
ordinary
database
tables, as
well as XML
controls.

Figure 16-13:
The Schema
Toolbar
offers you
only a few
of the
options
available in
the Schema
menu or
Toolbox.

Here's a summary of the important controls and objects you can add to XML Designer when it's in Schema view if you right-click the background of the Designer window and choose Add:

✔ **New element:** Inserts a new element type in your document.

✔ **New attribute:** Inserts a new attribute type in your document.

✔ **New simpleType:** Declares a new simple type.

✔ **New Any:** Declares a generic new type.

✔ **New AnyAttribute:** Inserts a new attribute of any type into your document.

✔ **New key:** Displays the Key Editor so you can specify the primary column by which two relations will be joined.

✔ **New relation:** Displays the Relation KeyRef Editor so you can build parent-child relationships between two complex elements.

✔ **New complexType**: Declares a new type that can include elements and attributes.

✔ **New Group:** Adds a new container type that you can use to set attributes for multiple objects at once.

✔ **New attributeGroup:** Allows you to group attributes together, provide a name for this attribute group, and then reference the attribute group in an element.

Which of these options are enabled or disabled depends on where you click, in the Designer window. If you click the background, you see the options displayed in Figure 16-14.

Figure 16-14: Click the background in the Designer and you can add the choices shown in boldface.

If you click the title bar (the top, dark-gray area in one of the diagram boxes, as shown by the mouse pointer in Figure 16-15), you get a different set of items you can add to the diagram (the table or XML Schema control).

You also have the choice of using the following features in XML Designer (from the Schema menu, the Schema toolbar, or by right-clicking the background of XML Designer):

✔ **Edit a key:** Displays the Key Editor so you can make changes to the key in a complex element.

✔ **Edit a relation:** Displays the Relation KeyRef Editor so you can make changes to specifications about the relationship between two complex elements.

✔ **Make Type Global:** Promotes a complexType to a global type. If this element was contained by another element, the container becomes an instance of the new global type.

✔ **Generate a DataSet:** Creates an ADO.NET DataSet based on the schema file.

✔ **Generate Instance:** Instantiates an object.

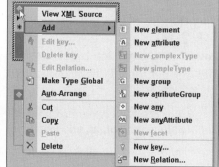

Figure 16-15:
These are
the items
you can add
to a table or
control.

Using Data view

XML Designer isn't limited to XML schema. It can also provide you with a nice tool for visualizing and manipulating an .XML file (a data file, not just any .XML).

To see how this works, follow these steps:

1. **Choose Project⇨Add New Item.**

2. **In the Add New Item dialog box, double-click the XML File icon.**

3. **Type the following in the new XML file:**

```
<XML ID="Movies">
<films>
   <film copyrightnumber="133117">
     <name>Annie Hall</name>
     <director>Woody Allen</director>
     <star>Diane Keeton</star>
   </film>
</films>
</XML>
```

XML Designer now displays two tabs on the bottom of its window, XML and Data (this is not a schema .XSD file, so there is no Schema tab).

4. **Click the Data tab to see the result shown in Figure 16-16.**

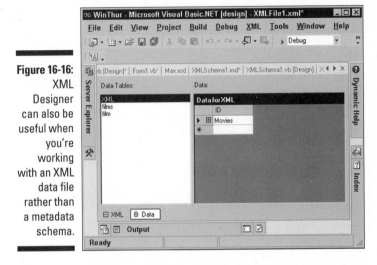

The Data view offers two views, selected by clicking the items in the left
column (in this example, you can choose between films, the table, and film,
one of the records in that table). The Data tab appears when you add an XML
data file to your project. In the DataTables column, each relation in the XML
is displayed in nesting order from highest to lowest. Click a table and data is
displayed in the Data zone of the Designer window.

Note that a new Data menu and toolbar have been added to the IDE. Also, a
new context menu is available. Let's look at that context menu. Right-click the
background of the Designer and choose Create Schema. Then double-click
XMLFile1.XSD. (I'm assuming that the XML file you've been working with was
named XMLFile1.XML, the default name when you add the first XML file to a
project.)

XML Designer generates the following schema out of your XML data file (no
one ever claimed that XML was not a *verbose* language):

```
d:schema id="XML"
          targetNamespace="http://tempuri.org/XMLFile1.xsd"
          xmlns="http://tempuri.org/XMLFile1.xsd"
          xmlns:xsd="http://www.w3.org/1999/XMLSchema"
          xmlns:msdata="urn:schemas-microsoft-com:xml-
          msdata">
  <xsd:element name="films">
    <xsd:complexType content="elementOnly">
      <xsd:all>
        <xsd:element name="film">
          <xsd:complexType content="elementOnly">
```

```
      <xsd:all>
        <xsd:element name="name" minOccurs="0"
  type="xsd:string"/>
        <xsd:element name="director" minOccurs="0"
  type="xsd:string"/>
        <xsd:element name="star" minOccurs="0"
  type="xsd:string"/>
      </xsd:all>
      <xsd:attribute name="copyrightnumber"
      type="xsd:string"/>
    </xsd:complexType>
  </xsd:element>
 </xsd:all>
 </xsd:complexType>
</xsd:element>
<xsd:element name="XML" msdata:IsDataSet="True">
  <xsd:complexType>
    <xsd:choice maxOccurs="unbounded">
     <xsd:element ref="films"/>
    </xsd:choice>
  </xsd:complexType>
</xsd:element>
</xsd:schema>
```

To summarize, while in the Data view, you can

✔ Edit existing records by clicking any cell

✔ Add new records by double-clicking the lowest record (row of cells) in the Designer's Data view

✔ Right-click the background of the Designer window to generate a schema based on the table (as you did previously in this chapter)

✔ View the XML schema

Chapter 17

Killing Bugs

. . . .

. . . .

*N*o programming project of any significance simply comes to life error free. You always have to test your application and then track down the inevitable problems that are revealed only during the testing phase. Then you must correct them.

Bugs usually aren't a result of negligence. It's just that any sizable application is like a large office: There are an enormous number of interacting behaviors. Without a Department of Problem Solving, the situation will begin to degenerate into mob rule or random noise.

Database programmers face some additional debugging challenges. For one thing, when you're working with databases, errors can be generated in the database engine, in your VB .NET application, or in some cases, in code residing on a client or server in another part of the building or another part of the world. Increasingly, database applications and other types of applications are being broken up into parts: *distributed* among more than one hard drive. Perhaps the user interface is displayed in a browser in Bangkok, the business logic (the part that accepts the user's input, interprets it, and provides responses) resides on a hard drive in your main offices in San Diego, and the database used by the program sits in a computer in Tulsa.

Gone are the days when you could count on everything — all the programming and all the data — to be sitting right there on your personal hard drive in your self-contained personal computer.

Also consider how the Web browser — most often Internet Explorer — is increasingly replacing the standard, traditional window model as the host for applications. This is not to say that browsers are full-fledged operating systems (not yet, anyway). But VB .NET code, VB-created components, and VBScript code can be mixed in with HTML browser code. And you may work with such hybrid environments as Active Server Pages .NET or even DHTML. (DHTML, or dynamic HTML, is a client-side Microsoft standard that was never really agreed to by Netscape, so it's used primarily with intranets rather than Internet programming.)

The old days, when you only had to worry about errors generated in the comfy world of the VB .NET editor and the Windows operating system, are pretty much history. Today, errors can jump up at you from several interacting locations: UserControls, HTML, browser script, ASP code, server-side classes, remote databases, and many other components and objects, some of them even running on (relatively) alien engines such as Java.

This chapter explores the more common types of errors you're likely to encounter and the VB .NET tools and techniques you can use to overcome them. Some of these techniques will perhaps be familiar to you, but others are sure to be new. Have you heard of Try-Throw-Catch?

What's a Poor Debugger to Do?

VB .NET offers an unquestionably excellent, powerful suite of debugging tools. What do you do when you get an error message? You can sit around and mope, or you can take steps. I suggest taking steps.

Recall that in VB .NET — unlike earlier versions of VB — you must declare (Dim) all variables. (This is the default VB .NET behavior, though you can turn it off, as I describe shortly.) *Explicit declaration* means that you must declare variables. You must declare X, for example, using Dim X as Integer or Dim X As Object or whatever As data type you want, before you can use the X variable. If you want to avoid the necessity of declaring each variable, put the following line at the top of your programming code window (above any procedures):

```
Option Explicit Off
```

Option Explicit is on by default in VB .NET and it's the option that demands that each variable be explicitly declared.

A second option is off by default in VB .NET: `Option Strict` works with `Option Explicit`, but the `Strict` option prevents implicit conversion of data. For example, with `Option Strict On`, this following example (which forces the `A` variable to be converted to a string data type) would fail to run:

```
Dim A as Integer
A = 1
TextBox1.Text = A
```

Although `Option Strict` is off by default, you can turn it on by typing the following line at the top of your code window:

```
Option Strict On
```

I suggest that you leave VB .NET's default `Option Explicit` turned on. That way, you'll force yourself to get used to programming the new VB .NET way, in which you must *declare all variables*. This will help you decrease the number of bugs you have to track down. As for `Option Strict`, the jury is still out. It forces you to use `.ToString` often to convert numeric variable types into text (string) types before you can display them in TextBoxes or message boxes. You also might have to resort to such programming commands as `CType`, `CInt`, and others. Nonetheless, obscure bugs and mathematical imprecision can result if you leave `Option Strict` turned off. My advice? While you're learning the basics of VB .NET, leave it turned off. You'll have to worry less about variable types. But when you start to work on more sophisticated programs, consider turning `Option Strict` on.

Now let's see how to deal with bugs that get into your source code in spite of all your best efforts.

Using VB .NET's Excellent Facilities

Often, you can handle errors with the famous VB debugging facilities: the Command window (formerly the Immediate window), watches, the Locals window, breakpoints, single stepping, and other debugging features.

Start testing a VB .NET program by pressing F5 to execute your program. Then, to begin debugging, you can pause (break) the program by choosing Debug➪Break All or by pressing Ctrl+Break. You then enter break mode. In break mode, you can test the contents of variables by typing their names directly in the Command window, as you see later in this chapter. However, I want to warn you of some naming confusion regarding this window. In all previous versions of VB, it was called the Immediate window. In VB .NET's Debug➪Windows menu, it is also called the Immediate window. When the window is opened (as well as in some VB .NET documentation), however, it is called Command Window — Immediate.

Start by finding out where the error happened

Debugging starts by finding out where the bug is located: which line or lines of source code are causing the problem. Alas, this isn't always a straightforward process, particularly when you're dealing with errors that occur outside traditional VB code, such as a database refusing to accept a DataSet that you are trying to Update into the database.

You begin your tour of the VB .NET debugging suite by looking at ways that VB .NET can help you locate a typical error. Type this function in the VB .NET code window:

```
Function Trythis As Integer

    Zum = Nara

End Function
```

As soon as you enter the Zum=Nara line of code, VB .NET does not like it. To demonstrate its displeasure, it underlines both Zum and Nara.

VB .NET's Auto Syntax Check feature watches as you type each line of code. As soon as you finish a line, it checks the line to see whether you mistyped anything or made some other kind of error such as leaving out something necessary. (VB knows you're finished with a line when you press the Enter key or click the mouse pointer on another line.)

If the syntax checker has a problem with the line, it underlines the error or errors with a sawtooth blue line (blue by default, anyway). In the preceding code example, you typed a few variable names, neither of which you declared. VB .NET requires that all variables be declared (unless you add Option Explicit Off up at the top of your source code).

So you get jagged lines, under each of the undeclared variable names. Figure 17-1 shows what happened when I pressed the Enter key after making these two errors.

Figure 17-1:
VB .NET
helpfully
flags errors
in your
source
code.

```
Function Trythis() As Integer

    Zum = Nara

End Function
```

Move your mouse pointer on top of one of the sawtoothed words in your code, and VB .NET provides an explanation of the error. Don't click, just slide the arrow onto the bad part, as shown in Figure 17-2.

```
Function Trythis() As Integer

      Zum = Nara
                    The name 'Nara' is not declared.
End Function
```

The Auto Syntax Check feature is similar to Microsoft Word's Check Spelling as You Type feature. With this feature turned on, as soon as you type each word in a Word document, that word is spell checked. And if the word is misspelled, it is underlined with a sawtooth red line. This drives me crazy. I don't want to worry about spelling while I'm writing; I'll spellcheck when I'm finished. Fortunately, you can turn off the constant spellcheck in Word. Unfortunately, you can't turn off Auto Syntax Check — at least you can't in the current beta of VB .NET. (In previous versions of VB, you could.) Although Auto Syntax Check doesn't bother me, it might bother some programmers. Perhaps it will be made optional at some future time.

To make the jagged blue lines go away, declare the two variable names, like this:

```
Dim zum As String
Dim nara As String
```

If you turn off Auto Syntax Check (assuming you *can*), you'll still be warned about such errors when you press F5 to test and run your code. Press F5 and a message appears, telling you that there were build errors and asking whether you want to continue. If you choose No, you can look in the Task List window and see the errors described, as shown in Figure 17-3.

Double-click one of the errors in the Task List window and you'll be taken to the line in the code window where the error occurred. What's more, the specific command that caused the problem is highlighted.

Figure 17-3:
The Task
List window
lists errors
in your
code.

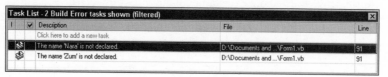

If an error occurs outside traditional VB .NET code (if the error is generated server-side in script, for example), you often have to resort to inelegant methods for tracking it down. One of the more popular of these inelegant methods involves planting message box commands here and there in your source code, displaying the current state of variables. Then, periodically, the code halts and displays the message box.

You can use the `msgbox` command in script and in objects embedded in a Web page. If a message box appears before the error is generated, the line that contains the error is likely to follow the line with the message box in the source code, and vice versa. Note, however, that the `msgbox` technique is often undesirable. It stops execution each time, and it can be used in only user services. Server-side components, more often than not, are compiled for unattended execution, which means message boxes won't be displayed at all.

Making Use of the Try-Catch-End Try Structure

Some errors occur only during runtime. Your code is valid, but something unexpected happens when the program is running. This is often a problem related to contacting a peripheral, such as a hard drive. For example, suppose that the user has no file named xxxxx on drive C:\ and your program executes this code trying to open that file:

```
Private Sub Form1_Load(ByVal sender As System.Object, ByVal e
        As System.EventArgs) Handles MyBase.Load

    Try

        Dim sr As New System.IO.StreamReader("c:\xxxxx")

        Catch er As system.IO.FileNotFoundException

        MsgBox(er.ToString)

    End Try

End Sub
```

The error message shown in Figure 17-4 is displayed. You need to prevent, or at least gracefully handle, runtime errors. It's no good having a smoothly running program that suddenly halts if the user, say, forgets to put a disk in drive A or fails to close the drive door. Don't give your user the hair-raising message shown in Figure 17-4.

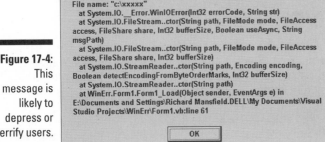

Figure 17-4: This message is likely to depress or terrify users.

```
WinErr                                               X
System.IO.FileNotFoundException: Could not find file "c:\xxxxx".
File name: "c:\xxxxx"
   at System.IO.__Error.WinIOError(Int32 errorCode, String str)
   at System.IO.FileStream..ctor(String path, FileMode mode, FileAccess
access, FileShare share, Int32 bufferSize, Boolean useAsync, String
msgPath)
   at System.IO.FileStream..ctor(String path, FileMode mode, FileAccess
access, FileShare share, Int32 bufferSize)
   at System.IO.StreamReader..ctor(String path, Encoding encoding,
Boolean detectEncodingFromByteOrderMarks, Int32 bufferSize)
   at System.IO.StreamReader..ctor(String path)
   at WinErr.Form1.Form1_Load(Object sender, EventArgs e) in
E:\Documents and Settings\Richard Mansfield.DELL\My Documents\Visual
Studio Projects\WinErr\Form1.vb:line 61

                        [   OK   ]
```

How runtime errors occur

Runtime errors include unexpected situations that can come up when the program is running. While you're writing a program, you can't know a number of things about the user's system. For example, how large is the disk drive? Is it already so full that when your program tries to save a file, there won't be enough room? Are you creating an array so large that it exceeds the computer's available memory? Is the printer turned off, but the user tries to print anyway?

Whenever your program is attempting to interact with an entity outside the program — such as the user's input, disk drives, Clipboard, RAM — you need to take precautions by using the Try-End Try structure. This structure enables your program to deal effectively with the unexpected while it runs.

Unfortunately, your program can't correct many runtime errors. For instance, you can only let the user know that his or her disk is nearly full. The user will have to remedy this kind of problem; you can't correct it with your code.

Runtime errors can also occur because of such unexpected problems as numeric overflow (a variable grows too large for its variable type) or array boundary violations (an attempt is made to access an item from an array index outside the range of the array). Other runtime errors result from attempts to use remote objects' methods or properties incorrectly (such as when accessing a database, an API, or a COM object). Remote objects return error messages, error codes (numbers that you must then look up in an error code list), or a combination of the two.

Sometimes the error message is returned within an object or directly by a function. When you use a function that is supposed to provide you with the length of some text but it returns -1, that's an error flag. In all these cases, you must read the documentation that describes both how error messages are returned to your project and what those messages mean. Often, however, VB .NET intercepts incoming error messages from remote classes and signals them to your project as a VB .NET-style runtime error.

Understanding Try

If you suspect that a particular location in your source code may be responsible for a runtime error, use the Try command to trap the error. It's always better to attempt to set things right by handling the error if possible within your project, rather than shifting the burden off to the user.

If you don't use Try and solve the problem in your VB .NET source code, Visual Basic displays an error message to the user. You might want to provide your own runtime error messages (you see how in a moment). To users, the kind of message displayed in Figure 17-4 can be obscure, confusing, and sometimes, frightening. VB .NET error messages are generally intended for you, the programmer, not for ordinary users who will likely find them frightening and confusing.

Instead of displaying a forbidding system message, you might want to substitute your own, custom, user-friendly error message, like the one shown in Figure 17-5.

Figure 17-5:
You can provide a custom error message, in plain English.

Here's the code:

```
Protected Sub Button1_Click(ByVal sender As Object, ByVal e
        As System.EventArgs)


    Try
```

```
        Dim sr As New System.IO.StreamReader("c:\xxxxx")

        Catch er As system.IO.FileNotFoundException

        MsgBox("No file named xxxxx was found on Drive C:")

    End Try

End Sub
```

Notice that you put the Try-End Try structure around possible error-triggering code. Here's how the Try-End Try structure works:

```
Try
'watch the line(s) of code here for any problems
Catch a type of error
' insert line(s) of code here to handle that particular error
Catch another type of error
' insert line(s) of code here to handle that second error
Finally
'insert optional line(s) of code here that you want executed
            within the Try structure
End Try
```

It's pretty easy to understand the relationship between Try and Catch. It's similar to the following:

```
 ' Start of Try structure
If there was an error Then 'Catch
React in some way to this error
End If 'End of Catch code block
If there was a different error Then 'Catch
React in some way to this error
End If 'End of Catch code block
' End of Try structure
```

The purpose of that Finally zone in the Try-End Try block is mysterious at first. Why do you need it? Couldn't you just put the code *after* the End Try? I explain the Finally command shortly.

The term *exception* is used in C-like languages (and now in VB .NET) to mean *error*. Code between the Try and End Try commands is watched for errors. You can use the generic exception or merely trap a specific exception such as the following

```
Catch er As DivideByZeroException
```

To see a list of specific exceptions, choose Debug⇨Windows⇨Exceptions and then expand the Common Language Runtime exceptions. You may have to do a bit of hunting. For instance, the `FileNotFound` error is located two expansions down in the hierarchy: Common Language Runtime Exceptions⇨SystemIO. So you have to expand both (click the + next to each) to finally find `FileNotFoundException`. However, the Exceptions window does include a Find button that should help you locate the precise exception you're after. (Find is not working at the time of this writing.) Also notice in the Exceptions window that you can make the program ignore any of the exceptions (click the Continue option in the Exceptions window). This is the equivalent of `On Error Resume Next` in VB 6.

Here is a list of some errors you can trap in VB .NET. In the System namespace:

```
ApplicationException
ArgumentException
ArgumentNullException
ArgumentOutOfRangeException
ArithmeticException
ArrayTypeMismatchException
BadImageFormatException
DivideByZeroException
DllNotFoundException
FormatException
IndexOutOfRangeException
InvalidCastException
InvalidOperationException
InvalidProgramException
MethodAccessException
MissingFieldException
MissingMemberException
MissingMethodException
NotFiniteNumberException
NotImplementedException
NotSupportedException
NullReferenceException
OutOfMemoryException
OverflowException
SystemException
UnauthorizedAccessException
```

And in the SystemIO category:

```
DirectoryNotFoundException
EndOfStreamException
FileNotFoundException
InternalBufferOverflowException
IOException
PathTooLongException
```

You can include in your source code as many `Catch` phrases as you want, and respond individually to each of them. You can respond by notifying the user (as in the preceding example) or by quietly correcting the error in the source code following the `Catch`. You can also provide a brief error message:

```
er.Message
```

Or, as you did in the preceding example, you can provide a fully qualified (meaning "all the adjectives") error message:

```
er.ToString
```

The official syntax

Here's the full, official `Try-Catch-Finally` structure's syntax:

```
Try
    tryStatements
[Catch₁ [exception [As type]] [When expression]
    catchStatements₁
[Exit Try]
Catch₂ [exception [As type]] [When expression]
    catchStatements₂
[Exit Try]
...
Catchₙ [exception [As type]] [When expression]
    catchStatementsₙ]
[Exit Try]
[Finally
    finallyStatements]
End Try
```

Following the `Try` block, you list one or more `Catch` statements. A `Catch` statement requires a variable name and an `As` clause defining the type of exception (`er As Exception`). One Exception type is generic and therefore traps all exceptions, not just a specific one such as `FileNotFound`.

For example, here's how to trap *all* exceptions:

```
Try

    Dim sr As New System.IO.StreamReader("c:\xxxxx")

Catch er As Exception

    'Respond to any kind of error.

End Try
```

An optional `Exit Try` statement causes program flow to leap out of the `Try` structure and continue execution with whatever follows the `End Try` statement — if code is in the `Finally` block, however, it is executed.

Understanding Finally

The `Finally` statement contains any code that you want executed after error processing has been completed. Any code in `Finally` is *always* executed, whether or not any `Catch` blocks were executed. This is the primary reason you would use the `Finally` block: Your source code that follows the `End Try` line *may never execute*, depending on how things go in the `Try` structure.

Perhaps there was a major disaster, so you used the `Exit Sub` or `Exit Function` command to leap out of your block or procedure. In either case, any code in that procedure that follows `End Try` is not executed. By contrast, code in the `Finally` block executes no matter what. The most common use for the `Finally` section is to free up resources that were acquired in the `Try` block, to close opened files, and the like. Note that if you use the `Exit Try` command to get out of a `Try` block prematurely (before executing other `Catch` blocks or other nested `Try` blocks), the code in the `Finally` block will nonetheless execute.

For example, if you were to acquire a Mutex lock (don't ask!) in your `Try` block, you would want to release that lock when you were finished with it, regardless of whether or not the `Try` block exited with a successful completion or an exception (error). It's typical to find this type of code in the `Finally` block:

```
        objMainKey.Close()
        objFileRead.Close()
        objFilename.Close()
'close a file
' close an object reference
'delete a bad file
'tie up other loose ends
```

Throwing exceptions

You can use a `Throw` command to generate your own error flags and attach error messages. This is how you inform outside code that is using one of your methods or procedures that there was an error.

Either of these syntaxes work:

```
Dim e As Exception
e = New Exception("F problem")
Throw e
```

or, more simply:

```
Throw New Exception("Problem in the Addition function")
```

I repeat: When you `Throw` an exception, you're telling an outsider (source code that tried to execute your procedure) that there was a problem.

Here's an example. Suppose that you write a function that wants to always get the name *Bob* sent to it. If the outsider tries to send some other name, you throw back an exception. The `Form_Load` event in this example is the outsider that will call the `IsItBob` procedure:

```
Private Sub Form1_Load(ByVal sender As System.Object, ByVal e
           As System.EventArgs) Handles MyBase.Load

    Try
        IsItBob("Chris") 'call the procedure
    Catch er As Exception 'find out if there was an error
             thrown back at us
        MsgBox(er.ToString) 'if there was an error thrown,
            display it
    End Try

End Sub


    Sub IsItBob(ByVal s As String)
        Dim er As Exception

If s <> "Bob" Then 'they sent the wrong name!
        er = New Exception("This Function needs the name Bob")
             'create an exception variable
        Throw er 'throw it back to the caller
End If

End Sub
```

Here are a few points to remember about the VB .NET's `Try-End Try` approach to error handling:

- ✔ If you want, you can nest `Try-End Try` blocks in other `End-Try` blocks.

- ✔ The new `Try-End Try` technique was written from scratch with .NET in mind. As a happy result, the `Catch` command can catch all errors that can happen in the .NET framework (in any method or property of all the zillions of objects in that framework).

- ✔ Some programmers might be tempted to enclose their entire project in a huge `Try-End Try` block, thereby ensuring that any and every possible runtime error will be caught. This would slow execution somewhat, but it is the safest approach. You could do this by running the entire project from the `Form_Load` event of Form1 or by using a `Sub Main...End Sub` structure.

Tracking Down Logic Errors

Logic errors — the third major category of programming bugs — are usually the most difficult of all to find and correct. Some can be so sinister, so well concealed, that you think you will be driven mad trying to find the source of the problem in your code. VB sensibly devotes the majority of its debugging features and resources to assisting you in locating logic errors.

A logic error occurs even though you have followed all the rules of syntax, made no typos, and otherwise satisfied VB .NET that your commands can be successfully carried out. You and VB think everything is ship-shape. When you run the program, however, things go wrong. Perhaps the entire screen turns black, or every time the user enters $10, your program changes it into $1,000.

VB .NET's set of debugging tools help you track down the problem. As with almost all programming errors, the key to correcting logic errors is finding out where in your program the problem is located. Which line of code (or multiple lines interacting) causes the problem?

Some computer languages have an elaborate debugging apparatus that sometimes even includes the use of two computer monitors: one shows the application just as the user sees it, and the other shows the lines of programming that match the running program. Using two computers is a good approach because when you are debugging logic errors, you often want to see the code that's currently causing the effects in the application.

It's not that you don't notice the symptoms: Every time the user enters a number, the results are way, way off. You know that somewhere your program is mangling the numbers, but until you X-ray the program, you often can't find out where the problem is located.

The voyeur technique

Many logic errors are best tracked down by watching the contents of a variable (or variables). You want to find out just where the variable's value changes and goes bad.

Four of VB .NET's best debugging tools help you keep an eye on the status of variables. You look at them in the following examples. Put a Button on your VB .NET form, double-click the Button, and then type this simple code:

```
Private Sub Button1_Click(ByVal sender As System.Object,
        ByVal e As System.EventArgs) Handles Button1.Click
    Dim a As Double, b As Double
```

```
    a = 112

    b = a / 2

    b = b + 6

End Sub
```

Click the gray margin to the left of the code window to add a red dot (a break-point) to the line a = 112.

Press F5 and then click the button. You are now in break mode, and many debugging features are at your command. Make four of the debugging windows visible by choosing Debug➪Windows and selecting the Locals window. Do the same to select the Watch, Autos, and Command windows.

Look at the Autos window. It displays the contents of all variables that have been declared in your project. Look at the Locals window, which displays the variables that have been declared in the currently executing procedure (as well as the parameters passed to this procedure and its object derivation.

Watch the variables in the Locals window change as you press F8 to execute each line in the example code, as shown in Figure 17-6.

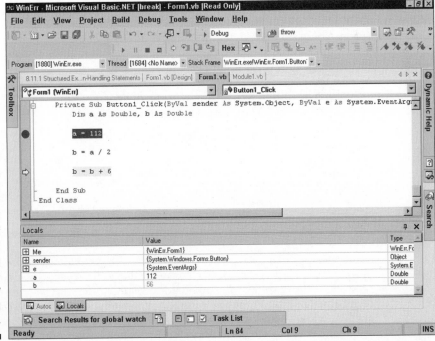

Figure 17-6:
The Locals window displays the contents of all local variables in the currently executing procedure.

Also look at the Command window. In this window, you can directly query or modify variables or expressions. To find out the value in variable b, for instance, just type the following in the Command window and then press Enter:

```
? b
```

The answer — whatever value b currently holds — is displayed (printed) in the Command window. (The ? command is shorthand for the Print command.)

If you want to experiment and actually change the value in a variable during break mode, delete the number in the value column in the Locals or Watch window, and then type your new value.

You can also launch and test procedures (events, subs, or functions) by typing their names and pressing the Enter key. VB executes the procedure and then halts again. This is a good way to feed variables to a suspect procedure and watch it (and it alone) absorb those variables to see whether things are going awry in that procedure.

Using Debug.WriteLine

Some programmers like to insert Debug.WriteLine (formerly Debug.Print) commands at different locations in their code to display the value of a variable. The Debug.WriteLine command displays its results in the Output window.

Try inserting some Debug.Write (MyVariableName) lines here and there in your source code, and then run the program and watch the results appear in the Output window. For example:

```
Private Sub Button1_Click(ByVal sender As System.Object,
        ByVal e As System.EventArgs) Handles Button1.Click

    Dim a As Double

    a = 112
    Debug.WriteLine("Variable a now equals: " & a)

End Sub
```

This displays Variable a now equals: 112 in the Output window

Using several Debug.WriteLine commands is a good idea if you want to quickly see a series of variable values and also write some explanatory message about these values. You could do the same thing with a series of MsgBox commands, but for a group of variables, it's annoying to have to keep clicking each individual MsgBox to close it before you can see the next MsgBox. With Debug.WriteLine, no clicking is involved; when the program runs, all the messages appear in the Output window.

The Command window responds

You can type in the Command window any executable commands that can be expressed on a single line and watch their effect. Note that you do this while the VB program is halted during a run — you can test conditions from within the program while it's in break (pause) mode. You can get into break mode in several ways: by inserting a Stop command into your code, by setting a breakpoint (discussed later in this chapter) in the code, by single-stepping (F8), by choosing Break in the Run menu (or the Toolbar), or by pressing Ctrl+Break.

The watch technique

The Locals window is fine for local variables, but what about form-wide or project-wide variables that are available to a larger scope of your source code? They don't show up in the Locals window.

In previous versions of VB, the Watch window permitted some highly useful debugging techniques: conditionally halting the program, throwing it into break mode so you could examine variable values, see where the break occurred, and examine surrounding conditions. You could break when a condition became true and other tests. In VB .NET, the capability to break conditionally is part of the Breakpoint debugging feature and is discussed in the "Setting Conditional Breakpoints" section later in this chapter.

An alternative way to use the Watch window is to keep an eye on the watches you've defined as you single-step through your code. The Watch window displays the value of all active watches.

Another tool in the Debug menu is the Quick Watch option. If you highlight (select) an expression or variable in the code window, and then choose Debug⇨Quick Watch (or press Shift+F9), VB shows you the current contents or status of the highlighted expression or variable. VB also gives you the option of adding the item to the watched items in the Watch window.

Setting breakpoints

Sometimes you'll have a strong suspicion about which form or module in your application contains an error. Or you might even think you know the specific procedure where the error can be found.

So instead of single stepping through the entire code, press F5 to execute the program at normal speed but then stop when execution enters the dubious form or procedure. After halting the program in a suspect region, you can slow down and press F8 to single-step.

Breakpoints can be one of the most useful debugging aids. As you know, you can press Ctrl+Break and stop a running program in its tracks. But what if it's moving too fast to stop just where you want to look and check on things? What if it's rapidly alphabetizing a large list, for example, and you can't see what's happening?

You can specify one or more breakpoints in your program. While running, the program stops at a breakpoint just as if you had pressed Ctrl+Break. The code window pops up, showing you where the break occurred, so you can see or change the code, single-step, or look at the Watch window to see the values in variables.

You set a breakpoint in the code window by clicking the gray margin to the left of the line where you want the break. A red dot appears in the gray margin. The red dot alerts you that a line of code is a breakpoint. Execution will halt on this line, and VB .NET will enter break mode. Click the red dot a second time to turn it off. You can set as many breakpoints as you want.

Another use for breakpoints is when you suspect that the program is never even running some lines of code. Sometimes a logic error is caused because you think a subroutine, function, or event is getting executed but, in fact, for some reason the program never reaches that procedure. Whatever condition is supposed to activate that area of the program never occurs.

To find out whether a particular event is never executing, set a breakpoint on the first line of code in that procedure. Then, when you run your program, if the breakpoint never halts execution, you will have proven that the procedure is never called.

Sometimes you set several breakpoints here and there in your code but then want to delete all of them. If you've set a lot of breakpoints, the Clear All Breakpoints (Ctrl+Shift+F9) feature allows you to get rid of all of them at once, without having to hunt them down and toggle them off individually by clicking their red dot.

Setting conditional breakpoints

Remember the example in which $10 grew to $1,000 for no good reason? To find out where that happened in your code, you could add breakpoints to stop the program when $10 grows larger than, say, $200 (that's your *condition*). Then, while the program is running and $10 is transformed into $1,000 — your logic error — VB will halt the program and show you exactly where the problem is located.

Type this code:

```
Private Sub Button1_Click(ByVal sender As System.Object,
           ByVal e As System.EventArgs) Handles Button1.Click
```

```
Static moneyvariable = 55

moneyvariable = moneyvariable + 44

End Sub
```

To set a conditional breakpoint, follow these steps:

1. **Click the gray area to the left of the line of code where** `moneyvariable` **is increased by 44 (the second line).**

   (Or click somewhere in the line of code to put your insertion cursor there, and then press F9.) The red dot appears and the line is changed to a red color as well.

2. **Right-click the red part of the line (not the red dot) and choose Breakpoint Properties.**

   The Breakpoint Properties dialog box appears.

3. **Click the Condition button.**

   The Breakpoint Condition dialog box appears.

4. **Type** moneyvariable > 200**, as shown in Figure 17-7, and then click OK.**

   The break is triggered when this variable goes above 200.

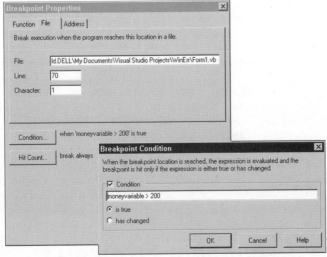

Figure 17-7:
Here's
where
you can
specify a
conditional
breakpoint.

5. **Press F5, and then click your button five times.**

   Your variable exceeds the conditional value and the editor enters break mode.

You can specify any kind of condition by using the Is True, Has Changed, or Hit Count options in the Breakpoint Properties dialog box and its Breakpoint Condition dialog box.

Note that this technique requires that you use the VB .NET Find (Edit⇨Find) utility to locate all places in your code where `moneyvariable` is located, and then set up a conditional breakpoint on each of these lines of code.

Global watches missing

The traditional VB Add Watch feature permitted you to create a *global* (project-wide) condition. You didn't have to set multiple conditional breakpoints; you simply set up a Watch condition that was project-wide in scope. (If `moneyvariable > 200` for the entire project, not a specific procedure or procedures.) Then, as soon as `moneyvariable` exceeded 200 anywhere in the project, VB went into break mode and showed you the line where this happened. I hope this useful (I think *essential*) debugging technique will be made available to VB .NET.

In the code window, right-click a variable name and choose New Breakpoint. Click the Data tab. This is where C programmers — and only C programmers — can specify a break condition that is project-wide in scope (will break and display the line *wherever* in the source code this condition becomes true). At the time of this writing, if a VB .NET (or C#) programmer attempts to set a condition in this tab and then clicks OK, an error message informs you that Basic does not support data breakpoints.

The only substitute — and it's not a complete substitute — is to set a *series* of conditional breakpoints here and there in your source code. You set a normal breakpoint by pressing F9 on a line of code. You can then edit the properties of that breakpoint to only break when A > 90, for example (you edit a breakpoint by right-clicking the code with the breakpoint and then choosing Breakpoint Properties). Place a series of these conditional breakpoints in your code. This helps you find the offending line, but in a large project it doesn't help you nearly as much as a global expression watch. I've always found that global expression watches (such as break whenever moneyvariable > 200) are a major debugging tool, so I'm assuming that VB .NET will offer this feature at some point.

Alternative Debugging Strategies

You likely noticed several other tools on the Debug menu. They're not as widely useful as breakpoints, single stepping, or watches, but when you need these lesser tools, you are glad they're available. Here's a brief survey of the minor debuggers.

Step Over (Shift+F10)

Step Over is the same as single stepping (F8), except that if you are about to single-step into a procedure, Step Over executes the procedure all at once, rather than step-by-step. No procedure calls are carried out, but all other commands are executed. So, if you are single-stepping (pressing F8 repeatedly) and you come upon a procedure that you know is not the location of the bug, press Shift+F10 on that line, and you will step over the entire procedure. This option gets you past areas in your program that you know are free of bugs and would take a lot of single stepping to get through.

Step Out (Ctrl+Shift+F8)

The Step Out feature was introduced in VB 5. You must be in break mode for this to work. It executes the remaining lines of the procedure you're currently in but stops on the next line in the program (following the current procedure). Use this to quickly get past a procedure that you don't want to single-step through.

Run to Cursor (Ctrl+F10)

To use the Run to Cursor option, click somewhere else in your code (thereby moving the insertion cursor). VB remembers the original and new locations of the insertion cursor. Press Ctrl+F10, and the code between the original and new locations is executed.

This is a useful trick when you come upon a large For-Next loop. You want to get past the loop quickly rather than waste time completing the loop by pressing F8 over and over. Just click a program line past the loop, and then press Ctrl+F10. VB executes the loop at normal execution speed, and then halts at the code following the loop. You can now resume stepping from there.

Set Next Statement (Ctrl+Shift+F10)

You must be in break mode to use Set Next Statement. With this feature, you can move anywhere in the current procedure and restart execution from there (it's the inverse of the Run To Cursor feature). While the program is in Break mode, go to the new location from which you want to start execution, and then click the new line of code where you want to resume execution. Now, pressing F8 will single-step from that new location forward in the program.

This is the way to skip over a line or lines of code. Suppose that you know that things are fine for several lines, but you suspect other lines farther down. Move down using Set Next Statement and start single stepping again.

Show Next Statement

If you've been moving around in your program, looking in various events, you may have forgotten where in the program the next single-step will take place. Pressing F8 shows you quickly enough, but you might want to get back there without executing the next line. Show Next Statement moves you in the code window to the next line in the program that will be executed but doesn't execute it. You can look at the code before proceeding.

The Call Stack

The Call Stack feature is on the Debug⊏>Windows menu . The Call Stack provides a list of still-active procedures if the running VB program went into Break mode while it was in a procedure that had been called (invoked) by another procedure. Procedures can be nested (one can call on the services of another, which in turn calls yet another). The Call Stack option shows you the name of the procedure that called the current procedure. And if that calling procedure was itself called by yet another procedure, the Call Stack shows you the complete history of what is calling what.

On Error

VB 6 and earlier versions contained a notorious `GOTO` command used with the `Error` and `Err` objects. This error trapping/handling technique is still supported in VB .NET. You can still use

```
On Error Goto HandleThis

HandleThis:
' take care of the error problem here.
```

or

```
On Error Resume Next
```

Nonetheless, there are compelling reasons to adapt to the new, more flexible, VB .NET `Try-End Try` technique, as you've seen in this chapter. Not least of these reasons is that this technique was developed hand-in-hand with the development of VB .NET itself and can trap any VB .NET runtime error.

If you are trying to translate existing VB 6 or earlier projects into VB .NET, however, you might want to permit them to retain their already-tested `On Error` code.

Part VII
Working with Queries

The 5th Wave   By Rich Tennant

AFTER DISCOVERING **THE LAND OF LOST FILES**, BILL AND IRWIN RUN INTO A TRIBE OF SQL INDIANS.

THIS IS GONNA BE TRICKY. THEY PROBABLY ALL SPEAK A DIFFERENT LANGUAGE.

In this part . . .

It's no use having a database if you don't ask it for information. But you probably don't want a dump — a pile of all the information it holds. That would be about as useful as tipping over a bookcase in the library.

Instead, you want to ask intelligent questions of the database and have it return intelligent lists. That's where SQL comes in — the standard database query language. The chapters in Part VII show you how to get nearly any set of records your heart desires. You also work with VB's excellent Query Designer tool to design and test new SQL queries.

Chapter 18

Automatic SQL: Using Query Builder

*W*hen you open a connection to a database, you generally want to get information out of it. But in most cases, you don't want *all* the information in it, just some. That's where queries come into play.

A *query* is a request for a portion of the information in a database, for example, "Show me a list of all accounts that are past due more than three months." When you run that query, you can put the results into a DataSet. The data you get back in a DataSet can be extracted from more than one table, grouped based on specific criteria, and sorted in many useful ways. Narrowing down data by using a query is one option, but you can also simply load complete tables. Nonetheless, queries are frequently used because often you need not a whole table but only a subset of the data in the table. Queries help you to create smaller, faster, more efficient DataSets. There's no reason to download the name of every person living in Iowa City, if all you need is a list of those who owe you money. In that case, write a query that fills a DataSet with only people who have negative balances in your table of customers.

Over the years, SQL (Structured Query Language) has become the standard way of querying databases. Using SQL, you can specify your queries using understandable, English-like phrases. You ask a query such as, "Give me a list of all publishers located in California, and alphabetize the list by the publishers' names." In return, you get a DataSet containing that data, arranged the way you requested. Any publisher whose State column contains anything other than CA is ignored and does not become part of the DataSet.

Here's the SQL query that builds this California-publishers-only DataSet:

```
SELECT * FROM Publishers WHERE State = 'CA' ORDER BY
            'PubName'
```

This chapter explores the uses of Query Builder, a tool that makes it easy to create even complex SQL queries. You work with Query Builder in several other chapters, but here — and in Chapter 19 — you find out how to take full advantage of this valuable tool.

In this chapter, you explore the kind of SQL query that returns a set of data. However, you can use SQL also to change or delete database information and even to create tables. SQL statements that change a database are called *action queries.* For examples of action queries, see the "SQL Action Queries: Changing a Database" section in Chapter 19.

Using Query Builder

Query Builder is part of a wizard that appears when you add an SqlDataAdapter or OleDbDataAdapter control to a Windows project in VB .NET. If you already have one of these controls on a form, you can access Query Builder by right-clicking one of the controls and choosing Configure Data Adapter.

Variously called Query Builder, Query Designer, SQL Builder, and so on, this useful VB .NET tool makes creating and modifying SQL queries easier. I use the term *Query Builder* because it's used more often than the other terms in the Microsoft documentation. Whatever it's called, this tool is the fastest ways to create an SQL query (without having to write it yourself).

If you haven't yet installed IIS or defined a connection to the pubs sample database, follow the instructions in Chapter 3 in the section titled "Connecting to a Database."

To see how to use Query Builder, start a new VB Windows application and attach a database to it, as shown in the following steps:

1. **Start a new project in VB .NET (choose File⇨New⇨Project).**

   The New Project dialog box appears.

2. **Name this project** Queries.

3. **Double-click the Windows Application icon.**

4. **Click the Data tab in the VB .NET Toolbox.**

5. **Double-click the SqlDataAdapter control.**

   The Data Adapter Configuration Wizard appears.

6. **Click Next.**

7. **On the second page of the Wizard, click the down-arrow and choose the** *computername.***pubs.dbo data connection.**

   Note that you should replace *computername* with the name of your computer.

8. **Click Next.**

9. **Click the Use SQL Statements option, and then click Next.**

10. **Click the Query Builder button.**

    The useful Query Builder utility appears.

Any time you want to access Query Builder in a project containing an OleDbCommand or SqlCommand object (you see its icon in the tray below the design window), just right-click that DataSetCommand icon and choose Configure DataSetCommand. Click Next three times in the Wizard, and then click the SQL Builder button.

Building an SQL query

To build an SQL query using VB .NET's Query Builder, follow these steps:

1. **Open Query Builder, as described in the preceding section.**

2. **In the top (gray) area of the Query Builder window, right-click the background and choose Add Table.**

   The Add Table dialog box appears.

3. **Double-click the Publishers table.**

   The Publishers table is added to Query Builder.

4. **Click Close.**

   The Add Table dialog box closes.

5. **In the Publishers table, select the All Columns option.**

   An SQL query is generated automatically for you:

   ```
   SELECT      publishers.*
   FROM        publishers
   ```

   This query returns all five columns from this table. That's what the * symbol does. If you'd only selected the city and state columns, you would see this SQL instead:

   ```
   SELECT      city, state
   FROM        publishers
   ```

It's customary (though not required) to put SQL commands such as SELECT FROM in all caps and the rest of the SQL statement, such as Authors, in initial caps. However, the Query builder, in its wisdom, chooses to lowercase table, column and other data in a statement.

6. **In the Diagram pane (at the top of the Query Builder window), right-click in the gray background and choose Run.**

   Your query, SELECT publishers.*, is executed against the Publishers database. The Results pane at the bottom of the Query Builder window displays the results of the query, as you can see in Figure 18-1. You get a complete list of all publishers in this database.

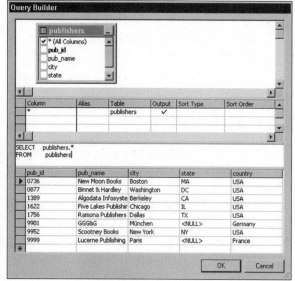

Figure 18-1:
You can view and edit a database's rows using Query Builder.

The four window panes

As shown in Figure 18-2, the Query Builder window has four panes named, from top to bottom, Diagram, Grid, SQL, and Results.

The Diagram pane shows the contents of your data structures (usually tables), as well as any relationships between the structures. The Grid pane enables you to create new relationships and specify a variety of qualities that define your query. In the SQL pane, you can type an SQL query (or just observe an automatically generated SQL query). The Results pane shows you the DataSet that results from executing your query.

Grid   Diagram

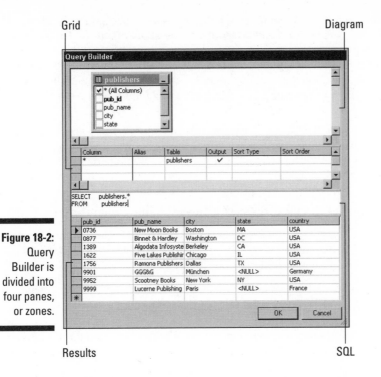

Figure 18-2:
Query
Builder is
divided into
four panes,
or zones.

Results   SQL

Using ORDER BY to Sort Rows

A typical table in a relational database doesn't maintain most of its rows in alphabetical (or any other) order. Notice in Figure 18-1 that the only ordered column is the Pub_id column. This column is always maintained in numeric order because it was designated a key by the database's designer or by a programmer defining the SQL query.

But what if you want the publishers ordered alphabetically by their names? That's probably a more useful order for your DataSet than listing them by an ID number. Remember that unique ID numbers are useful as a primary key in a database — speeding data retrieval (such as your query). But the results of a query, a DataSet, are usually provided for human consumption. And we humans often prefer to have a list alphabetized.

You can adjust the output of a query in many ways by using the Grid pane in Query Builder to specify a sorting order or other kinds of specifications that govern the output. In this section, I show you how to modify the Query Builder's Grid pane to sort your query results alphabetically.

As you can see in Figure 18-1, Query Builder has several columns, including Sort Type and Sort Order. You can modify these elements in the Grid pane:

✔ **Output:** With the Output check boxes, you can specify which columns you want to display in the final result. Each column can contain a particular table. In the examples I describe in this chapter, you're working with only one table: the Publishers table.

   You rarely need to show all columns in your query, but every column with a check mark in its Output check box is shown. If you choose not to display output for a particular column, that column can nevertheless be used as a way of sorting or filtering the data displayed in other columns.

✔ **Table:** The Table column shows which table a column is attached to (so you know which tables' data are displayed in the column).

✔ **Criteria:** These are grouping criteria, including aggregate functions that you use when generating summary reports. The SQL language is extensive and flexible and offers many ways to filter and organize data. You can specify complicated queries, such as. "Find all authors whose first name begins with *L* and who published all their works between 1880 and 1889." For additional details on SQL, see Chapter 19.

After you create some query results (such as the publishers query results in the example described in the preceding section), you can sort the output by following these steps:

1. **In the Grid pane in Query Builder, under the Column heading, click the cell where the * is displayed (see Figure 18-2), and then click the down-arrow button that appears.**

2. **In the list, select pub_name.**

   This is a list of the columns in the publishers table. Your SQL query automatically changes to

   ```
   SELECT      pub_name
   FROM        publishers
   ```

3. **In the Grid pane, click the Sort Type column, and then click the down-arrow button that appears.**

   A list appears, with two options: Ascending and Descending.

4. **Choose Ascending (for an *A* to *Z* rather than a *Z* to *A* ordering).**

   Query Builder automatically adds the appropriate line to your SQL statement (in this case, `ORDER BY pub_id`).

   Note that making this change also turns the list of all columns (except the ID column) in the Results pane from black to gray. The gray color tells you that changes have been made to the query that are not yet shown in the results. The result displayed in gray is an old set that no longer represents the current SQL statement. You have to use the Run command again to create an updated result set if you want to see what the current SQL statement produces.

5. **In the top pane (the Diagram pane) of Query Builder, right-click the gray background and choose Run.**

The results of your current SQL statement are displayed in the Results pane. The list of publishers' names is now displayed alphabetically, as shown in Figure 18-3.

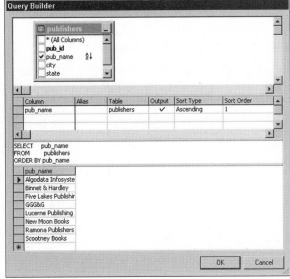

Figure 18-3: Now just the publishers are displayed, and they are alphabetized.

You can sort by multiple columns, too. Why would you do that? Perhaps you want a list of all your contacts sorted first by city, and then in alphabetical order by last name within each city. For an example of sorting by multiple columns, see Chapter 19.

Choosing from 73.2 Million Possible Results, Give or Take a Few

SQL enables you to create requests for information in millions of ways. SQL statements can filter and configure data in highly complicated arrangements. Before you go too far, however, try constructing a few common filters, as described in this section. Note that the following examples build on the example query described in the preceding section.

You try the following filters by adjusting the Criteria column in Query Builder. This way, you'll get a feel for what the Criteria column does. (You might have to stretch the Query Builder window wider to reveal the Criteria column.)

You begin by switching to the authors table, because there are many more authors than there are publishers (believe me, I know):

1. **Right-click the title bar of the Publishers(dbo) box (in the Diagram pane) and choose Remove.**

   This gets rid of the Publishers(dbo) table.

2. **Right-click the Diagram pane and choose Add Table.**

3. **Double-click the Authors table.**

4. **Click Close to close the Add Table dialog box.**

   Notice that the previous DataSet, shown in the Results pane, has turned gray to indicate that it is no longer a valid result of the query now being constructed.

5. **Click au_lname to add the author last name column to your query.**

6. **Type > 'P' in the Criteria cell on the same row that au_lname is listed.**

   This query will display names ranging from *P* to *Z*.

   If anyone has a last name that is simply *P*, *it* will not display. Only records starting with *Pa* and above will display. To include *P*, you would use >= which means *greater than or equal to*.

6. **Right-click the Diagram pane and choose Run.**

   A new line of SQL code is added to the SQL statement in the SQL pane: WHERE (au_lname > 'P'). And in the Results pane at the bottom of Query Builder, the list begins with authors whose names start with *P* and ends with the *Z*s, just as you'd hoped.

How about seeing only Ps and Qs? Change the Criteria cell to **> 'P' AND < 'R'**. The SQL statement changes to WHERE (au_lname > 'P' AND au_lname < 'R'). Choose the Run option and you'll see that only author names beginning with *P* and *Q* are displayed.

If you want to experiment with some of the 73.2 million possible SQL filters, take a look at Chapter 19. The possibilities are not endless, but there are more ways to filter data than you'll ever use in your lifetime, dude.

From Separate Tables: Doing a Join

Sometimes, you want to get data from more than one table at a time. In the pubs sample database that you've been using in this book, for instance, the

Authors table includes all the names of the authors, but to see the titles of these authors' books, you have to look in a different table named Titles. What if you want to retrieve both the names and the book titles into a DataSet? You create a join. (The term *join* is also known as a relationship — hence the term *relational database.*)

To join two tables, they must have a key in common. In the pubs database, the key in the Authors table is named au_id, but the key in the Titles table is named title_id. So these tables do not have a key in common! What to do? Fortunately (actually, this was intentional on the part of the database designer), a *third* table includes both au_id and title_id. This table can serve as a way to link the Authors table to the Titles table.

If that third table did not exist, the person who designed this database would have to add it. You are not likely to be given a database to work with that has the fatal structural flaw of floating tables that should be joinable, but are not.

To see how to create a join, follow these steps:

1. **Open Query Builder and add the Authors table to Query Builder.**

   Follow the steps in the "Building an SQL Query" section, earlier in this chapter.

2. **Right-click the Diagram pane and choose Add Table.**

3. **Double-click the TitleAuthor table.**

   Two things happened when you dropped that second table into Query Builder. First, a symbol that looks like hydraulic piping with a key joins the two tables. Notice that the pipe attaches at the location of the key columns they have in common (in this example, Au_ID). Second, Query Builder automatically modifies the SQL statement to specify the joined columns.

4. **Now add a third table, Titles, to Query Builder.**

   A second join symbol appears, connecting the title_id key column that these two tables have in common, as shown in Figure 18-4.

5. **Click Close to close the Add Table dialog box.**

6. **In the Diagram pane, click the au_lname and title options (as shown in Figure 18-4) next to the two columns you want to display in your query results.**

   To follow my example, you want to display the Author (au_lname) from the Authors table and the title from the Titles table.

7. **Right-click the Diagram pane and choose Run.**

   The author names and the titles of their books are displayed. Now your DataSet displays data from two different, joined tables.

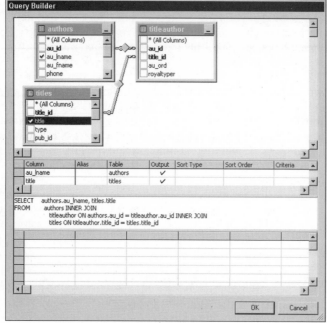

Figure 18-4:
When two
tables have
a key
column in
common,
Query
Builder can
create joins
for you.

Notice that one author name might be repeated several times in this example. That happens if an author has written more than one book. Similarly, if a title is repeated, it means that the book was co-authored. The join requires that the DataSet must include each row in which the key columns (the Au_ID columns) match. Note, though, that the parent key (the primary key) and the foreign key (the key in the second table) are not required to have the same name; they simply need to be defined as a relationship in the database. Even small database applications usually require joins. You need to understand this important feature, particularly how to work with what are called left or right outer joins. You can find that information in Chapter 19.

Dynamic SQL

In the examples in this chapter, you've seen various ways to use SQL queries to create a DataSet. What if you want to permit your user to specify the SQL query?

In the following example, you let the user type a letter or letters, such as *s*, and then use LIKE to show the user all the names that begin with *s*. (You find out more about the important LIKE command in Chapter 19.) Begin by following these steps:

1. **For each of the three tables used in the preceding example, right-click them and choose Remove.**

2. **Click OK to close the Query Builder window.**

3. **Click Cancel to close the Data Adapter Configuration Wizard that hosts Query Builder.**

   You're going to abandon Query Builder in this example; it's a programmer's tool.

You're going to allow the user to type a letter or letters, and then you'll display a list of authors (lastname, firstname) that match the user's input. Here's the SQL statement you'll embed in your source code to match the user's request:

```
"Select * from authors WHERE au_lname LIKE '" & n & "%'"
```

The LIKE operator lets you specify a pattern that must be matched. The % symbol means "and anything else." For instance, 'S%' means "retrieve all records that begin with S and end with anything in addition to that character." In this SQL statement, if the user types *s*, your DataSet will be filled with the rows of any author with a last name beginning with *S*. Follow these steps:

1. **Click the (Form1.vb Design) tab at the top of the VB .NET design window to display your form.**

2. **From the Toolbox's Windows Forms tab, add a Button, a ListBox, and a TextBox to your form.**

3. **At the top of the code window, add this Imports statement:**

   ```
   Imports System.Data.SqlClient
   ```

   You need this namespace so that you can simplify your source code (you can, for example, leave out System.Data.SqlClient when referring to the SqlDataReader.)

4. **Double-click the button to get to its Click event in the code window, and then type this in the event:**

   ```
   Private Sub Button1_Click(ByVal sender As System.Object,
           ByVal e As System.EventArgs) Handles
           Button1.Click

       ListBox1.Items.Clear()

       Dim dReader As SqlDataReader
   ```

```
Dim n As String
n = TextBox1.Text

Dim dQuery As String = "Select * from authors WHERE
    au_lname LIKE '" & n & "%'"

Dim dCommand As New SqlCommand(dQuery, SqlConnection1)

SqlConnection1.Open()

dReader = dCommand.ExecuteReader

Dim t As String
While dReader.Read()
    t = dReader.GetString(1) & ", " &
    dReader.GetString(2)
    ListBox1.Items.Add(t)
End While

dReader.Close()
SqlConnection1.Close()
Exit Sub

End Sub
```

5. Press F5 to run the program, and then type the letter s.

You should see three hits displayed in the ListBox, as shown in Figure 18-5.

Figure 18-5:
The user
gets to
specify the
SQL query
in this
example.

The heart of this program is the line in the code where you specify your query:

```
Dim dQuery As String = "Select * from authors WHERE au_lname
    LIKE '" & n & "%'"
```

Note that when you use the LIKE command, the variable data (the variable n in this code) must be enclosed in single quotes. This forces you to use double quotes around single quotes:

```
'" & n & "%'"
```

(Recall that the % symbol means "plus anything else." For instance, 'La%' means "show all rows that begin with *La* and end with anything in addition to those characters.") When this program runs, if the user types *s* in the TextBox, the SQL query will look like the following in VB .NET:

```
Select * from authors WHERE au_lname LIKE 's%'
```

Notice the single quotes surrounding the variables in this SQL query example from earlier in this chapter:

```
SELECT * FROM Publishers WHERE State LIKE 'CA' ORDER BY
          'PubName'
```

In this example, you used a DataReader object. It is faster than creating a full (modifiable) DataSet. For details about using the DataReader object, see the "Read-Only Sequential" section in Chapter 16.

Chapter 19

A Brief Dictionary of SQL

*U*se this chapter as a quick reference when you want to know how to extract particular data from a database. Each heading in the chapter names an SQL term and describes its purpose, so you can quickly scan these heads to find just the technique you need.

You can experiment with the SQL clauses in this chapter by using the Run command in Query Builder (Chapter 18 describes this handy utility) and seeing what data comes out of the database. (An *SQL clause* is a combination of SQL terms such as SELECT and LIKE, along with database-specific terms such as table and column names.) The examples in this chapter are all SQL clauses.

I feel that I must repeat this warning. Recall that Microsoft has decided to change two key database-related words: *record* and *field*. Some players in computer programming (notably IBM) have long used the term *row* to represent an individual record of data and the term *column* to represent a structural category in a table (such as a `Social Security Number` column). In the past, Microsoft and others have used the term *record* rather than *row* and the term *field* instead of *column*. In this book, I have adopted the new terminology: *row* and *column*.

In this chapter, I illustrate most of the SQL examples by using the Authors table in the pubs sample database, which is used throughout this book. See Chapter 3 if you have not yet installed the necessary support and created a connection to the pubs database.

Note that many flavors of SQL exist (standard ANSI SQL, Microsoft SQL Server's Transact SQL, Oracle's PL/SQL, ODBC SQL, and the version I explain here: Access SQL). Fortunately, these flavors of SQL are similar. However, because there are some differences between them, this chapter is not generic; it demonstrates Microsoft's Access SQL because it remains the most widely used variant in the world.

The commands in the SQL language are referred to as *clauses* (such as `ORDER BY`), *keywords* (such as `TOP`), or *operators* (such as `LIKE` or `BETWEEN`). Some people find these distinctions — an attempt at a primitive grammar — less than useful. For example, in English grammar a clause means a group of words containing a subject and verb. The term clause is used similarly in SQL (`SELECT Author`, for example, is a valid clause in both English and SQL). Unfortunately, though, the single word `SELECT` is also sometimes called a clause in SQL.

In spite of these weaknesses in the terminology, when I refer to the words used in the SQL language (such as `SELECT` or `ORDER BY`), I use clause, keyword, function, and operator because these terms are, by now, the conventions. I also follow the convention of capitalizing SQL commands, which helps to distinguish them from arguments (such as tables and columns).

One additional point: Some might quibble that SQL isn't a full computer language like VB. True enough. SQL lacks important features of a "real" computer language (SQL cannot by itself open a file, for example), and you must use SQL with another, host language. But even though it's small and specialized, SQL is a set of words that, collectively, tell the computer what to do. It can be considered a language. What else would you call it? Some settle this debate by calling it a *query language*. Whatever.

SELECT: The Main SQL Clause to Retrieve Data

The `SELECT` clause, which is undoubtedly one of the more important SQL clauses, appears at the start of each SQL statement that retrieves data from a database.

You can also use SQL to edit, delete, and otherwise manipulate the contents of a database.

Here's the required format for `SELECT`:

```
SELECT column(s) FROM table(s)
```

And here's an example:

```
SELECT      au_lname
FROM        dbo.authors
```

If you want to retrieve all columns from a table, use the * command, as in this example:

```
SELECT      dbo.authors.*
FROM        dbo.authors
```

The following example demonstrates the correct syntax for specifying two columns:

```
SELECT      phone, address
FROM        dbo.authors
```

SQL includes the following optional clauses for use in a `SELECT` clause (I further explain each of these clauses in its own section, later in the chapter):

- ✔ `JOIN`: Specifies the key columns used to connect two tables when getting data from those tables.

- ✔ `GROUP BY`: Specifies the column you want to use to combine rows (records) with the same values when you're summarizing using aggregate functions. For example, if you want a list of total sales by region, so you use `GROUP BY Region`. The new DataSet lists each region only once and includes the tally of the number of sales in each region. The tally (which uses the `SUM` function described later in this chapter) is called an aggregate function.

✔ HAVING: Part of an aggregate function that enables you to specify criteria, such as "Show me only those results in which the name of the region
begins with the letter C." The HAVING clause must be used with GROUPS,
described later in this chapter. It is not identical with the WHERE clause,
which is not used with GROUPS.

✔ ORDER BY: Specifies how to sort the DataSet.

This example alphabetizes the results, based on the data in the Author
column:

```
SELECT      au_lname
FROM        dbo.authors
ORDER BY    au_lname
```

This example sorts on two columns, alphabetizing the last names. And if
rows have identical last names, those rows are ordered alphabetically by the
first name:

```
SELECT      au_lname, au_fname, phone
FROM        dbo.authors
ORDER BY    au_lname, au_fname
```

WHERE: Narrowing the Field

After you specify the column(s) and table(s) by using the SELECT clause and
its required partner, the FROM clause, you may want to further limit the data.
You use the WHERE clause to provide criteria that limits, or filters, data, just
as in English you might say, "Show me only the magazine subscriptions that
cost less than $12 a year."

Here's the required format for WHERE:

```
WHERE column operator criteria
```

This example shows how you use the WHERE clause:

```
SELECT      au_lname
FROM        dbo.authors
WHERE       (Au_lname LIKE 'S%')
```

In this example, the LIKE operator enables you to specify a pattern that must
be matched. The % symbol says, "and anything else." For instance, 'S%'
means "Show all rows that begin with S and end with anything in addition to
that character."

When you use the WHERE clause, you can use various operators to specify a
relationship. Table 19-1 describes the meaning of each operator.

Table 19-1	Operators You Can Use with WHERE
Operator	*Meaning*
<	Less than. For example, the following shows all authors whose last name begins with *A* or *B*: `WHERE au_lname< 'C%'`
<=	Less than or equal to. For example, the following shows all author ID numbers less than or equal to 300: `WHERE au_id <= 300`
>	Greater than. For example, the following shows all author ID numbers above 300: `WHERE au_id > 300`
>=	Greater than or equal to. For example, the following shows all author ID numbers above 299: `WHERE au_id >= 300`
=	Equal to. For example, the following shows `au_id` 300 only, if it exists: `WHERE au_id = 300`
<>	Not equal to. For example, the following shows all author ID numbers other than 300: `WHERE au_id <> 300`
BETWEEN	Within a range. For example, the following shows all authors whose name begins with *A*, *B*, or *C*: `WHERE au_lname BETWEEN 'A' AND 'D'`
LIKE	Matches a pattern. For example, the following shows all authors whose name begins with the characters *Adam*: `WHERE au_lname LIKE 'Adam%'`
IN	Matches items in a list. For example, the following shows all authors whose name is either Andrews or Brown: `WHERE au_lname IN ('Andrews', 'Brown')` This syntax does not permit pattern matching (where you use the %, *, _, or ? symbols). Notice that the term `IN` here is used to mean "in this list." It does not mean between.

BETWEEN: Specifying a Range

The BETWEEN operator enables you to specify a range, such as between two dates or two zip codes. This example shows how you use the BETWEEN operator:

```
SELECT      zip
FROM        dbo.authors
WHERE       (zip BETWEEN '20000' AND '40000')
```

Figure 19-1 shows the resulting DataSet when you run this example.

The zip code data is stored in a column that uses the Integer data type. If this column were a Date data type, you would have to surround the criteria with # symbols, like this:

```
BETWEEN #1993# AND #1995#
```

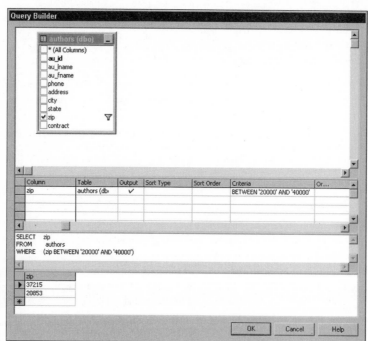

Figure 19-1:
This is your
DataSet.

LIKE: Using a Pattern Match

The LIKE operator enables you to use wildcards when asking for data. For example, if you want to see all the rows that begin with the letters *ab,* you use this operator in your SQL query:

```
WHERE (au_lname LIKE 'ab%')
```

The % means "plus anything else." In other words, all author names beginning with *ab* are returned.

You can also use an underscore character to represent a single character. For example, you can match any Author name that begins with *a* and ends in *c* by using WHERE (au_lname LIKE 'a_c'). To match any Author name that begins with *a* and has a *c* in the third character position, use LIKE 'a_c%'.

Alas, you specify wildcards in SQL in two ways. It's one of those oddities in computer languages that you just have to live with (like the fact that some kinds of lists start counting from 0, but others count from 1).

ANSI SQL (the version of SQL used by Query Builder) uses % to mean and "any number of other characters." For example, Ma% displays Max, Max Headroom, and Maximillian, among whatever other rows contain text that begins with the letters *ma*. On the other hand, Microsoft's Access SQL uses a * symbol rather than %.

Likewise, to specify a single character, ANSI uses _ (underline) but Jet uses ? (as in Ma?, which would match May but not Mayo). If one kind of pattern-matching symbol isn't working for you, try the other.

ORDER BY: Sorting the Results

The ORDER BY clause enables you to specify how you want data sorted: numerically or alphabetically, ascending (from *a* to *z*) or descending (from *z* to *a*). Here's an example:

```
SELECT      au_lname
FROM        dbo.authors
ORDER BY    au_lname
```

This example orders the Authors table, based on the contents of the Author column, alphabetically from *a* to *z* (ascending). To reverse the order (descending from *z* to *a*), use this clause:

```
ORDER BY    au_lname DESC
```

You can also order by multiple columns. If a table has separate LastName and FirstName columns, for example, you could alphabetize the names first by the last names and then, within any duplicate last names, by the first names, like this:

```
ORDER BY    LastName, FirstName
```

To create a descending order by last name, but ascending by first name, you would use this code:

```
ORDER BY    LastName DESC, FirstName
```

To sort both columns in descending order, use this code:

```
ORDER BY    LastName DESC, FirstName DESC
```

TOP: Limiting a Range

If you have a large database with thousands of rows, and someone wants to see only the 25 best-performing products, you can use the `ORDER BY DESC` clause to make a list of the products in order of total sales (from most to least sales, thanks to `DESC`). Then, instead of stuffing the DataSet with this list of all 2,000 products, you can lop off the top 25 by using the `TOP` keyword, like this:

```
SELECT TOP 25 *
FROM tblSales
ORDER BY TotalSales DESC
```

If any of these products sold the same number, you'll get more than 25 rows when you run this example. Ties count as a single result, thereby inflating the list.

At this time, the Query Builder has a problem dealing with the `TOP` keyword. The SQL code in this example, however, is correct.

You can also request a percentage of the total number of rows, rather than a specific number of rows (as in the preceding example). To see the top 5 percent of the TotalSales column, use this code:

```
SELECT TOP 5 PERCENT *
FROM tblSales
ORDER BY TotalSales DESC
```

Using a JOIN: Getting Data from More than One Table at a Time

To create a DataSet that includes data from more than a single table, you use the JOIN feature. (For a thorough description of this technique, see Chapter 18.)

To create a join, you use an equal sign to connect identical columns in two tables, as in the following example:

```
SELECT      dbo.authors.au_lname, dbo.titleauthor.royaltyper
FROM        dbo.authors INNER JOIN
            dbo.titleauthor ON dbo.authors.au_id =
            dbo.titleauthor.au_id
```

The INNER JOIN command specifies that the details in the third line represent the join. The third line specifies that the authors table is joined to the titleauthor table. (They both share a column named au_id, so they can join using that column.) The first line says, "Display the au_lname column (their names are in this column) from the Author table, and display the royaltyper column from the titleauthor table." Figure 19-2 shows the result of this query.

Figure 19-2:
If you want to display columns from different but related tables, try a JOIN.

au_lname	royaltyper
Bennet	60
Blotchet-Halls	100
Carson	100
DeFrance	75
del Castillo	100

AS: Renaming Columns (Aliasing)

In some cases, you want a column to have a different name. Perhaps the column's real name (its name in the database) is misleading or overly complicated, and it would confuse folks if displayed in a report.

Or perhaps you're building a calculated or aggregate column, and you must give the new column a name. (For an example showing how you use AS with an aggregate, see the "Calculating with the Aggregate Functions" section later in this chapter.)

You use the AS clause to name or rename a column. The following example shows how you use the AS clause when a database uses the unclear field name au_lname:

```
SELECT     au_lname AS [Authors' Last Names]
FROM       dbo.authors
```

This example renames the obscure au_lname column from the Authors table to Authors' Last Names. Figure 19-3 shows the result.

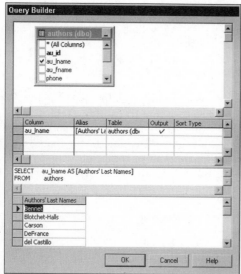

Figure 19-3:
With the AS clause, you can rename this database's confusing au_lname column.

DISTINCT: Eliminating Duplicates

Sometimes, you get extraneous information when you do a query. For example, if you ask for a DataSet that includes the City column in a Publishers' address table, you get lots of New York entries in the DataSet. To avoid duplicates, you can use the DISTINCT keyword, as in this example:

```
SELECT DISTINCT City
FROM Publishers
```

Using DISTINCT can hinder performance in a large database such as BIBLIO.MDB. When I ran this example in the Query Builder, my hard drive thrashed away for several minutes, I was notified that I was running low on virtual memory, and I finally reset the computer. You've been warned.

COUNT, SUM, AVG, MAX, and MIN: Calculating with Aggregate Functions

You can use the five aggregate functions to figure out the number of rows (COUNT), the sum total of numeric rows (SUM), the average value of numeric rows (AVG), and the highest (MAX) or lowest (MIN) numeric row. Only the COUNT function can be used with text rows.

To try constructing an aggregate function using Query Builder, you can create an SQL query that tells you how many author names the Authors table contains. To see how to construct an aggregate function, follow these steps:

1. **Open Query Builder, and then add the Authors table to it.**

   For details on how to add the table, see "Building an SQL Query" in Chapter 18.

2. **In the Authors window, click the check box next to au_lname.**

   The SQL statement changes to the following:

   ```
   SELECT      au_lname
   FROM        dbo.authors
   ```

3. **Right-click anywhere in the background of the Diagram pane (at the top of the Query Builder window) and choose Group By.**

   A Group By option appears in the Grid pane, as shown in Figure 19-4.

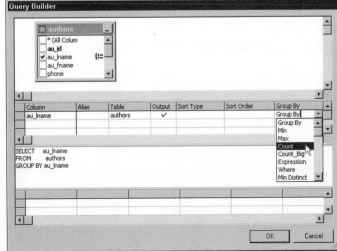

Figure 19-4: The Group By option enables you to specify the various aggregate functions.

4. **In the Group By drop-down list, select Count.**

   Now, the SQL statement looks like this:

   ```
   SELECT      COUNT(au_lname) AS Expr1
   FROM        dbo.authors
   ```

   The AS clause has created an alias named Expr1. That's not too descriptive of what you're doing.

5. **In the Grid Pane, change Expr1 to** Total Authors.

   Here's what the SQL statement looks like:

   ```
   SELECT      COUNT(au_lname) AS [Total Authors]
   FROM        dbo.authors
   ```

   Notice that because you're using two words for the alias, they've been enclosed in brackets.

6. **Right-click the gray Diagram pane and choose Run.**

   You see the total number of authors in the Author column, as shown in Figure 19-5.

Figure 19-5:
The result
of the
aggregate
function
count.

GROUP BY: Summarizing

Use the GROUP BY clause if you want to collapse more than one row into a single row. For example, you can ask for a count of the number of publishers in each city. The following SQL query lists each city and the total number of publishers in that city:

```
SELECT COUNT(City) AS Total, City
FROM Publishers
GROUP BY City
```

HAVING: Narrowing Criteria

The example in the preceding section shows how you can display all the cities stored in the table and, at the same time, list the number of times each city appears in the table.

If you want to narrow the number of cities, use the HAVING clause. (HAVING is similar to the WHERE clause, which I describe earlier in the chapter. However, you must use HAVING with the GROUP BY clause.) In the following example, you display only cities whose names begin with the letter *s*:

```
SELECT COUNT(City) AS Total, City
FROM Publishers
GROUP BY City
HAVING (City LIKE 'S%')
```

SQL Action Queries: Changing a Database

SQL returns a DataSet, but you can also use SQL to change the data in a database. You can even use SQL to append new rows with the INSERT clause or add new tables with the SELECT INTO clause.

Using SQL statements to modify databases or their data is called an action query — but surely the word *query* isn't quite right here because nothing is being questioned. Nonetheless, you can do a lot to a database with this technique. Using SQL this way can be a dangerous business because you can wipe out an entire database with very little SQL code. To see what I mean, take a look at the next section.

DELETE: Removing rows

The following SQL statement (don't do it!) would destroy the entire Authors table in the BIBLIO.MDB database:

```
DELETE * FROM   dbo.authors
```

If you didn't follow my advice and destroyed the Authors table, you can always restore the database by copying the pubs sample database from your VB CD.

You can substitute the DELETE clause for SELECT in any of the examples in this chapter. When you use DELETE, all the data that would have been returned by the SELECT clause vanishes — poof! You've been warned. Don't experiment with this clause unless you've backed up the database first.

You can use all the usual filters when defining what you want to delete. For example, the following code wipes out any author whose last name begins with *A*:

```
DELETE      au_lname
FROM        dbo.authors
WHERE       (au_lname LIKE 'A%')
```

Some versions of SQL leave out that first au_lname between the DELETE and FROM, but Microsoft Access SQL uses it.

A DELETE query removes entire rows from a table. If you want to delete data from individual columns, use an UPDATE query (described next).

Additional action queries

You can create the following additional types of queries in the Diagram and Grid panes of Query Builder:

- ✔ **Insert into query:** Adds a new row (record) and inserts its data into specified columns. This query creates an SQL INSERT INTO-VALUES statement.

- ✔ **Insert from query:** Copies existing rows from one table to another or within the same table; this process creates new rows. It uses an SQL INSERT-SELECT statement.

- ✔ **Update query**: Changes the data of individual columns (fields) in one or more existing rows in a table. It uses an SQL UPDATE statement.

- ✔ **Make table query:** Creates a new table. It uses the SQL SELECT...INTO statement.

In addition to the queries you can create using the Query Builder's Diagram and Grid panes, you can also type *any* SQL statement you want into the SQL pane. However, if you do type a query using SQL statements that the Query Builder can't illustrate in its Diagram or Grid panes (or simply can't understand), when you click the OK button to close Query Builder, it informs you that it can't parse (figure out) the query. Then you have the option of returning to Query Builder to correct the error or ignore the message and continue working.

Part VIII
The Part of Tens

The 5th Wave — By Rich Tennant

"Your database is beyond repair, but before I tell you our backup recommendation, let me ask you a question. How many index cards do you think will fit on the walls of your computer room?"

In this part . . .

This part is called The Part of Tens after a mystic ritual performed precisely once every 489 years on the island of Samnos and involving three large fish, green ribbons, and a goat. You really don't want to know.

Actually, Part VIII is The Part of Tens because both chapters in this part have ten items in them. Chapter 20 gives you what I consider some of the better tips and techniques that a VB .NET programmer needs to know. You find out how to create and destroy directories and files, customize your IDE layout, access the Registry, and more.

Chapter 21 is a catchall of items that I wanted to tell you about, but didn't find appropriate locations for in the rest of the book. Some of the topics are how to send documents to a printer in VB .NET (it's not as easy as it used to be!), how to use the new macros feature in the VB .NET editor, and how to use the Internet to get solutions to VB .NET database programming problems — in the unlikely case that you come up with a question not answered in this book.

Chapter 20

Ten Great VB .NET Tips

*V*B .NET represents a nearly complete break from previous versions of VB. For those who are relatively new to programming, VB .NET will likely demand of you a steeper learning curve than previous versions of VB. If you're already familiar with traditional VB, you must now unlearn some old techniques and figure out the new syntax, diction and punctuation that VB .NET employs. This chapter offers some hints and tips that should assist you in learning VB .NET.

Using the Upgrade Wizard as a Teaching Tool

If you are stumped and can't figure out how to do something in VB .NET that you know perfectly well how to accomplish in earlier versions of VB, try using the Upgrade Wizard, a migration utility built into VB .NET. Start VB 6 (you can run it simultaneously with VB .NET), write the problem programming in VB 6, and then save the VB 6 project to your hard drive.

Now, using Windows Explorer, locate the .VBP (Visual Basic Project) file you just saved and double-click it. Or start VB .NET, choose File⇨Open⇨Project, and select VB Project Files (*.VBP, *.VBPRO) in the Files of Type ListBox in the Open Project dialog box. Find the file you just saved and open it.

As soon as you open a VB 6 project in VB .NET, the Upgrade Wizard kicks into action. It does its best to translate VB 6 into VB .NET. When the Wizard is finished with its efforts, use the VB .NET code window to examine the source code that the Wizard wrote. Sometimes this will tell you how to translate classic VB to VB .NET.

Talking to the Clipboard

Sometimes it's useful to use the Windows Clipboard object in your programming. Here's how to bring text in from the Clipboard in VB .NET:

```
Dim txtdata As IDataObject = Clipboard.GetDataObject()
```

Or, if you need to check first to see whether the Clipboard holds text (as opposed to a graphic image or some other object):

```
If (txtdata.GetDataPresent(DataFormats.Text)) Then

    TextBox1.Text =
            txtdata.GetData(DataFormats.Text).ToString()

End If
```

And to save the contents of a TextBox to the Clipboard, use this code:

```
Clipboard.SetDataObject(TextBox1.Text)
```

Managing Directories

Here's how to create and destroy directories and subdirectories in VB .NET. First, at the top of your VB .NET code window, type this:

```
Imports System.IO
```

Then type the following code:

```
Private Sub Form1_Load(ByVal sender As System.Object, ByVal e
        As System.EventArgs) Handles MyBase.Load
    Try
        Dim s As Integer
        s = DestroyDirectory()
    Catch er As Exception
        MsgBox(er.ToString)
    End Try

End Sub

    Public Function DestroyDirectory()

        Dim objDir As New DirectoryInfo("C:\TestDir")
        Try
            objDir.Delete(True)
        Catch
            Throw New Exception("Failed to delete")
        End Try

    End Function

    Public Function CreateDirectory() As String

        Dim objDir As New DirectoryInfo("c:\TestDir")

        Try
            objDir.Create()

        Catch
            Throw New Exception("Failed to create new
            directory")
        End Try
    End Function

    Public Function CreateSubDirectory() As String

    Dim objDir As New DirectoryInfo("c:\TestDir") 'parent
        directory
        Try
    objDir.CreateSubdirectory("TestSubDir") 'name for new
            subdiretory

        Catch
            Throw New Exception("Failed to create new
            subdirectory")
        End Try
    End Function
```

Randomizing

Generating a series of random numbers has uses in games, encryption, and other programming tasks. In VB .NET, you the `System.Random` function to get random numbers. Type this code in a form's `Load` event:

```
Private Sub Form1_Load(ByVal sender As System.Object, ByVal e
        As System.EventArgs) Handles MyBase.Load
    Dim i As Integer
    For i = 1 To 100
        Debug.Write(rand(i) & " ")
    Next
End Sub
```

And elsewhere in that form's code window, type this function. It returns random numbers between 1 and 12:

```
Function rand(ByVal MySeed As Integer) As Integer
    Dim obj As New system.Random(MySeed)
    Return obj.next(1, 12)
End Function
```

When you press F5 to run this example, you'll see the `Debug.Write` results in the Output window in the IDE.

Although the arguments say `1, 12` in the `Return obj.next(1, 12)` line, you will not get a single 12 in your results. The numbers provided by the `System.Random` function in this case range only from 1 to 11. Everyone is hoping that this error will be corrected by the time VB .NET ships to customers.

Here's an example that illustrates how you can use the `NOW` command to seed your random generator. Type this code in the `Form_Load` event:

```
Private Sub Form1_Load(ByVal sender As System.Object, ByVal e
        As System.EventArgs) Handles MyBase.Load

    Dim sro As New coin()
    Dim x As Integer
    Dim i As Integer

    For i = 1 To 100
        sro.toss()

        Dim n As String

            x = sro.coinvalue
            If x = 1 Then
                n = "tails"
```

```
            Else
                n = "heads"
            End If

            n = n & " "

            debug.Write(n)
        Next i

    End Sub
```

Then, at the bottom of your code window, *below* the End Class line, type this new class, which tosses a coin and returns:

```
Class coin

    Private m_coinValue As Integer = 0

    Private Shared s_rndGenerator As New
            System.Random(Now.Millisecond)

    Public ReadOnly Property coinValue() As Integer
        Get
            Return m_coinValue
        End Get
    End Property

    Public Sub toss()
        m_coinValue = s_rndGenerator.next(1, 3)
    End Sub

End Class
```

CStr versus .ToString

It would seem that the .ToString method (which many objects in VB .NET have) and the CStr function do the same job: convert an object or numeric data type into a string data type. If you get an error message telling you that something cannot be converted to a string, you can usually correct the problem using .ToString or CStr.

Here's an example:

```
Private Sub Form1_Load(ByVal sender As System.Object, ByVal e
            As System.EventArgs) Handles MyBase.Load

    MsgBox(sender)

End Sub
```

Press F5 to test this code. VB .NET displays an error message saying, among other things, Argument prompt cannot be converted to type string. (Note that sender is an argument prompt.) To correct this, change the code to

```
MsgBox(sender.ToString)
```

CStr, however, will not work in this case. It can be used only with objects that can be formatted in more than one way. CStr checks to see what locale (such as USA or China) is in effect in the current system and then formats the string according to the needs of the local language. .ToString executes faster because it does not bother with locale formatting issues.

Making Quick Layout Changes

It's easy to quickly switch between alternative IDE layouts and behaviors. You can switch between layouts from the VB .NET Start Page. Here's how:

1. **To get to the VB .NET Start Page, choose View⇨Web Browser⇨Home.**

   If that doesn't work, restart VB .NET so you see the Start Page. If you still don't see a page named Start when you fire up VB .NET, choose Tools⇨Options. In the left pane of the Options dialog box, under Environment, select General. Locate the At Startup and choose Show Start Page.

2. **On the left side of the Start Page, select the My Profile option.**

   The Profile Editing options appear, as shown in Figure 20-1. The Visual Studio Default layout auto-hides the Toolbox and Server Explorer on the left side, with Solution Explorer and Class View tab-docked on the right. The Properties window and Dynamic Help are tab-docked below. The Visual Basic 6 layout is identical, except the Toolbox is docked (visible).

3. **Select the profile you like or save a custom profile.**

4. **Then click one of the tabs at the top of the design window (such as Form1.vb) to return to ordinary IDE editing mode.**

No matter which layout you choose, as you work with the IDE, you are likely to make further adjustments to auto-hiding (I recommend it for all windows other than the design window), position, and other elements. Visual Studio .NET is smart enough to retain your changes between sessions. So, the next time you start VB .NET, you should see the same arrangement that was in effect when you last shut it down. (Note that switching layouts does cause your previous layout customizations to be lost.)

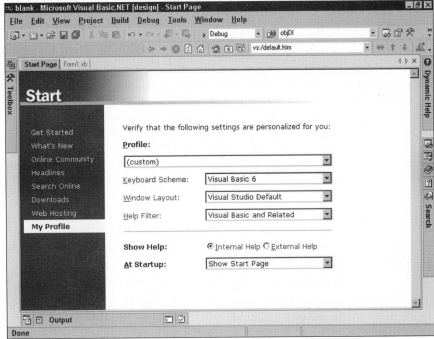

Figure 20-1:
You can
choose
different
editor
layouts.

Understanding How the Registry Works with VB .NET

The Windows Registry is downplayed in VS .NET programming languages. They avoid registration and the idea of a common repository of DLLs by putting any necessary code libraries (assemblies) and other dependencies in the same path (the same folder or a subfolder) as the application that needs them. The idea is that you can deploy (give someone else your VB .NET project or solution) by merely copying the folder and its subfolders where your VB .NET application resides.

You copy the folder to the other machine's hard drive. That's it. No need to register code libraries or worry about which version of those libraries is currently used by Windows. Instead, your VB .NET project relies only on the files it finds in its own folder and subfolders. Oh, well, yes . . . all VB .NET projects also need the massive common language runtime (CLR) library that all Visual Studio languages rely on. But the CLR is supposed to be embedded as part of future operating systems. At this point, though, your project will not work on a computer that doesn't have the CLR.

The Windows Registry, though currently in disgrace in some ways, is nonetheless unlikely to go away any time soon because too many applications and operating system features depend on the information held in the Registry. It holds everything from user preferences to user identities — and much more.

Reading from the Registry

A VB .NET programmer may well need to know how to read information from and write information to the Registry. In VB .NET, you can query the Registry using the RegistryKey object. Here's an example that shows you how to access the Registry with VB .NET code.

1. **Start a new VB .NET Windows-style project.**

2. **Double-click TextBox in the WinForms tab of the Toolbox to add it to your Form1.VB.**

3. **Double-click a Button to add it to the form as well.**

4. **Click the TextBox to select it, and then press F4 to display the Properties window.**

5. **Change the TextBox's MultiLine property to True.**

6. **Double-click the Button to get to its** Click **event in the code window.**

7. **Type this in the Button's** Click **event:**

```
Protected Sub Button1_Click(ByVal sender As Object, ByVal
      e As System.EventArgs)

    Dim objGotValue As Object
    Dim objMainKey As RegistryKey = Registry.CurrentUser
    Dim objOpenedKey As RegistryKey
    Dim strValue As String

    ' put this next on a single long line
    objOpenedKey =
        objMainKey.OpenSubKey("Software\\Microsoft\\Windo
        ws\\CurrentVersion\\Internet Settings")

    objGotValue = objOpenedKey.GetValue("User Agent")

    If (Not objGotValue Is Nothing) Then
        strValue = objGotValue.ToString()
    Else
        strValue = ""
    End If
```

```
      objMainKey.Close()

      TextBox1.Text = strValue

End Sub
```

8. **You must also type** `Imports Microsoft.Win32` **as the first line at the top of the code window.**

   The Microsoft.Win32 namespace contains the Registry-access functions such as the `OpenSubKey` method that you need in this example.

9. **Press F5 to run this example, and click the button.**

   If your Registry contains the same value for this key as my Registry, you should see a result similar to this:

   ```
   Mozilla/4.2 (compatible; MSIE 5.0; Win32)
   ```

Note that the complete name (path) of the entire Registry entry is divided into three different locations in the example code. First the primary key, `CurrentUser`, then the path of subkeys, and finally the actual specific name: `objOpenedKey.GetValue("User Agent")`.

Writing to the Registry

The RegistryKey class includes a group of methods you can use to manage and write to the Registry. These methods include `Close`, `CreateSubKey`, `DeleteSubKey`, `DeleteSubKeyTree`, `DeleteValue`, `GetSubKeyNames`, `GetType`, `GetValue`, `GetValueNames`, `OpenSubKey`, and `SetValue`.

The Wizard of Wizards

Microsoft uses wizards to walk users or programmers step-by-step through a relatively complex task. The Data Form Wizard, for example, takes a programmer through the complex job of creating a connection to a database, extracting a DataSet from it, and then showing the DataSet to users so that they can read or modify the database. The Wizard adds the necessary controls, such as TextBoxes, and even writes hundreds of lines of source code to support this application. You, the programmer, have to only answer a series of questions in several pages of a dialog box.

Wizards such as the Add-in Wizard are a type of application that leads a user step-by-step through a series of actions to accomplish a complex or difficult task and, once completed, go away. Wizards are created using the IDTWizard interface and have only one method, `Execute`, which contains the code you want the wizard to run. A wizard can be programmed to create either a fully working application for the user or a skeletal application to which the user must add code for it work correctly, such as with the Add-In Wizard.

You can also create your own wizards. This could be a useful tool if you are teaching others how to use VB .NET or if a sophisticated job needs to be performed more than one time. Think of wizards as advanced, interactive macros.

Building a wizard isn't a trivial job, but if you want to learn how to do it, use VB .NET's Help Index to find "Wizards, creating in Visual Studio." Visual Studio 6 had a Wizard of Wizards. It stepped you through the process of creating your own wizards. Perhaps by the time VB .NET is officially released, this handy tool will have been added to Visual Studio .NET.

Simplifying Source Code in Two Ways

Programmers usually welcome ways to reduce the noise (unnecessary typing and hard-to-read clutter) in source code. VB .NET introduces to the Visual Basic language two optional shortcuts that most programmers will quickly grow fond of.

Combining the declaration and the assignment

Instead of declaring a variable on one line and then assigning a value to it on a second line, like this:

```
Dim a As String
a = "Hello"
```

you can now combine declaration and assignment into a single statement, like this:

```
Dim a As String = "Hello"
```

Avoiding repetition

In previous versions of VB, you could modify the current contents of a variable in only one way: You had to repeat the variable name. For example, to increment variable a, you would write:

```
a = a + 1
```

That's not so bad with a simple, short variable name like a. But in VB .NET, qualification can make object and variable names huge, like this:

```
Textbox1.Text = Textbox1.Text & objFileRead.ReadLine()
```

Some programmers (users of the C language and its offspring) have been using a set of operators that combine two ideas into one. The fundamental difference is that the C-style moves the operator (+, -, *, or whatever) over next to the assignment (=) symbol. For example, you get

```
X += 1 'the new style
```

Instead of

```
X = X + 1
```

This comes in handy when you are working with longer variable or object names:

```
textbox1.Text += objFileRead.ReadLine()
```

If you want to try out the C syntax, here are the variations:

VB	VB .NET
`X = X + Y`	`X +=Y`
`X = X - 5`	`X -= 5`
`X = X * 4`	`X *= 4`
`X = X / 7`	`X /= 7`
`X = X ^ 2`	`X ^= 2`
`String1 = String1 & "ed"`	`String1 &= "ed"`

VB 6 used the & operator to concatenate strings. This helped VB understand when you wanted to concatenate as opposed to perform numeric addition. Sometimes your intentions were ambiguous because of the variant variable type, which freely mixed strings and numbers, sorting them out during runtime as best it could. Now that the variant type has been banished from VB .NET, the & operator is no longer needed. You can concatenate strings with the + operator without ambiguity: `"This" + "That"`. Even though it no longer serves a purpose, the & operator is nonetheless still supported in VB .NET.

Chapter 21

Ten Important Topics that Don't Fit Elsewhere

Don't take the title of this chapter as a confession of disorganization and confusion when I planned this book. It merely represents some ideas and resources I think you should know about, even though they don't fit comfortably in other chapters. Anyway, glance at the headings in this chapter and see whether any of these subjects interest you. I think you'll find a few topics here worthy of your inspection.

Reading the Latest News

Microsoft maintains Web sites devoted to the latest database topics. You may want to visit the Web site at the following address:

```
http://www.microsoft.com/data/ado/
```

And also look here for information on ASP.NET:

```
http://www.asp.net/
```

Getting Answers to VB .NET Questions

Try these newsgroups to ask questions and get (usually) good answers:

- ✔ `msnews.microsoft.com:`
  `microsoft.public.dotnet.framework.adonet`
- ✔ `msnews.microsoft.com:`
  `microsoft.public.dotnet.framework.odbcnet`
- ✔ `msnews.microsoft.com: microsoft.public.dotnet.xml`
- ✔ `msnews.microsoft.com: microsoft.public.vsnet.ide`
- ✔ `msnews.microsoft.com: microsoft.public.vsnet.debugging`
- ✔ `microsoft.public.data.ado`
- ✔ `microsoft.public.data.ado.rds`
- ✔ `microsoft.public.it.dotnet.beta.ado`
- ✔ `microsoft.public.vb.database.ado`

Keeping Visual Basic Healthy

Microsoft's Visual Basic support sites contain information and, in particular, occasional updates (service packs) that correct bugs. Check these sites on a regular basis:

- ✔ `http://www.microsoft.com/data/download.htm`: The page that offers updates and downloads related to database programming
- ✔ `msdn.microsoft.com/vbasic`: The main Microsoft VB home page
- ✔ `msdn.microsoft.com/vstudio/downloads/updates.asp`: Updates and bug fixes for VB and other Visual Studio components
- ✔ `msdn.microsoft.com/vstudio/downloads/addon.asp`: Third-party add-ons you might find useful
- ✔ `msdn.microsoft.com/vbasic/downloads/samples.asp`: Sample source code
- ✔ `http://msdn.microsoft.com/vbasic/downloads/controls.asp`: Control freebies

Discovering Microsoft's Plans for the Future of Database Technology

If you want to find out the latest information about ADO.NET, OLE DB, and UDA (Microsoft's initiatives for universal data access), take a look at these sites:

- ✔ www.microsoft.com/data/oledb/default.htm
- ✔ www.microsoft.com/data/ado/default.htm
- ✔ www.microsoft.com/data/odbc/default.htm

Visiting Other Web Sites of Interest

The leading site for information on Visual Studio .NET and related programming is, as you might expect, hosted by Microsoft: msdn.microsoft.com/default.asp. One of the more active sources of useful VB information is Fawcette Technical Publications, publisher of Visual Basic, Visual Studio, and .NET Magazines. Find Fawcette's latest news at www.fawcette.com.

Also, be sure to visit the following sites:

- ✔ www.devx.com: Considerable information of value to Visual Basic programmers
- ✔ www.elementkjournals.com/ivb: *Inside Visual Basic,* from Ziff-Davis
- ✔ www.pinpub.com/home.htm: *Visual Basic, SQL Server, .NET Developer,* and other publications from Pinnacle

You can find quite a few good links to sites involving VB programming also at dmoz.org/Computers/Programming/Languages/Visual_Basic.

Creating Macros

Perhaps you've created macros (little programs) in an application such as Word. Macros can be a real timesaver, automating tasks that you perform frequently.

Now, Visual Studio .NET proudly presents editor macros! Finally, with macros available for years in every other major Microsoft application, Visual Basic .NET and the VS .NET IDE now have a macro facility. You can automate the IDE is several ways: assigning layout configurations to tabs, adding built-in shortcut keys, making custom add-ins, creating your own wizards, modifying toolbars, and even extending the existing Tools⇨Options menu with your own options.

For those of us who love to program, macros are among the most pleasant of tools — easy, little utilities that can be quite simple to create but also powerful and useful.

The VS .NET IDE macro facility permits you to record macros. For example, suppose that you frequently display the index for the help system. Instead of pressing F1, which by default displays the dynamic help feature (information about the currently selected control or code), you want the index immediately. You could choose Help⇨Index menu or press Ctrl+Alt+F2, but these are cumbersome. You want to be a fancy macro user and press a single key to make the Index pop right up, right there, right now. You decide to redirect F12 to your macro because F12 defaults to Edit GoTo, which you never use. Follow these steps:

1. **Load a project or create a new Windows project.**

   Choose File⇨New⇨Project, and then double-click the Windows application icon.

2. **Click the Design tab at the top of the main VB .NET window.**

   Make sure the current solution is displayed in Solution Explorer.

3. **Choose Tools⇨Macros⇨Record Temporary Macro.**

   One of those cool new XP-style ghostly, opaque toolbars appears. It starts out around 90% opacity and after a few seconds fades to around 40%. Great effect. You can see that the toolbar is active, but it doesn't cover up what's underneath it.

4. **Choose Help⇨Index.**

5. **Stop the recording by clicking the middle icon on the ghost toolbar.**

6. **Choose Tools⇨Macros⇨Save Temporary Macro and name the macro** ShowIndex.

Now for another interesting trick:

1. **Choose Tools⇨Macros⇨Macros IDE.**

   A new IDE appears, devoted to the art and science of macros. You see the following code:

```
Option Strict Off
Imports EnvDTE
Public Module RecordingModule
Sub ShowIndex()
        DTE.ExecuteCommand ("Help.Index")
End Sub
End Module
```

2. **Go back to the VS IDE and choose View⇨Other Windows⇨Macro Explorer.**

3. **Right-click ShowIndex (your new macro) and choose Run.**

   The Macro Explorer window is replaced by the Help Index window, just as you'd hoped.

Now assign the ShowIndex macro to F12 as follows:

1. **Choose Tools⇨Customize.**

2. **Click the Keyboard button at the bottom of the Customize dialog box.**

   An Options dialog box appears.

3. **In the Show Commands Containing field, type** ShowIndex.

   You see a list of commands, one of which is your new macro: `Macros.MyMacros.RecordingModule.ShowIndex`.

4. **Click your new macro to select it, click the Press Shortcut Keys field, and then press F12.**

5. **Click the Assign button to formally assign F12 to your macro.**

   You see a message warning you that cannot modify one of the default keyboard mapping schemes.

6. **When asked whether you want to make a copy of the scheme, click the Yes button and name it** MyScheme.

7. **Click the Close button.**

8. **Click the Solution Explorer tab at the bottom of the upper-right window.**

9. **Press F12.**

   The upper-right window instantly displays the Help Index.

Printing Will Never Be the Same Again

Programmers are often called upon to print reports or other documents from within their applications. VB .NET offers you much more control over the fonts, graphics, and other elements of printing, but you pay a price for this freedom.

As always, the more options you get, the more options you must deal with in your source code. I want to thank my friend and sometime co-author Evangelos Petroutsos for giving me permission to include his solution to the printer margins problem in VB .NET in the following example. As you will see, printing is far from a straightforward, simple job in VB .NET. The primary problems are letting the printer know when to enforce the right margin to move down to the next line (word wrap) and when to enforce the bottom margin to move to the next page (eject page).

An in-depth explanation of the source code in this next example can be found in the appendix at this book's Web site, which is located at http://www.dummies.com/extras/VBNetDataProg/.

To see how printing works in VB .NET — and to discover the magic formulas that prevent your text from being cut off at the bottom or right margins — follow these steps:

1. **Start a new Windows-style VB .NET project by choosing File⇨New⇨Project and then double-clicking the Windows Application icon.**

2. **Double-click the form in the design window.**

   You now see the code window.

3. **Drag your mouse to select *all* the default source code in the code window. Then press the Del key to delete all this source code.**

4. **Copy the following source code and paste it in the code window.**

   The following source code can be downloaded from this book's Web site at http://www.dummies.com/extras/VBNetDataProg/.

```
Public Class Form1
    Inherits System.Windows.Forms.Form

#Region " Windows Form Designer generated code "

    Public Sub New()
        MyBase.New()

        'This call is required by the Windows Form
        Designer.
        InitializeComponent()

        'Add any initialization after the
        InitializeComponent() call

    End Sub

    'Form overrides dispose to clean up the component
        list.

    Private WithEvents TextBox1 As
        System.Windows.Forms.TextBox
    Private WithEvents Button1 As
        System.Windows.Forms.Button
    Private WithEvents PrintDocument1 As
        System.Drawing.Printing.PrintDocument
```

```
Private WithEvents PrintPreviewDialog1 As
        System.Windows.Forms.PrintPreviewDialog

    Friend WithEvents PageSetupDialog1 As
        System.Windows.Forms.PageSetupDialog

    'Required by the Windows Form Designer
    Private components As System.ComponentModel.Container

    'NOTE: The following procedure is required by the
        Windows Form Designer
    'It can be modified using the Windows Form Designer.
    'Do not modify it using the code editor.
    Private Sub InitializeComponent()
        Me.TextBox1 = New System.Windows.Forms.TextBox()
        Me.PrintPreviewDialog1 = New
         System.Windows.Forms.PrintPreviewDialog()
        Me.PrintDocument1 = New
         System.Drawing.Printing.PrintDocument()
        Me.PageSetupDialog1 = New
         System.Windows.Forms.PageSetupDialog()
        Me.Button1 = New System.Windows.Forms.Button()
        Me.SuspendLayout()
        '
        'TextBox1
        '
    Me.TextBox1.Font = New
        System.Drawing.Font("Verdana", 9!,
        System.Drawing.FontStyle.Regular,
        System.Drawing.GraphicsUnit.Point, CType(0,
        Byte))
        Me.TextBox1.MaxLength = 0
        Me.TextBox1.Multiline = True
        Me.TextBox1.Name = "TextBox1"
        Me.TextBox1.ScrollBars =
        System.Windows.Forms.ScrollBars.Vertical
        Me.TextBox1.Size = New System.Drawing.Size(728,
        408)
        Me.TextBox1.TabIndex = 0
        Me.TextBox1.Text = "TextBox1"
        '
        'PrintPreviewDialog1
        '
        Me.PrintPreviewDialog1.AutoScrollMargin = New
        System.Drawing.Size(0, 0)
        Me.PrintPreviewDialog1.AutoScrollMinSize = New
        System.Drawing.Size(0, 0)
        Me.PrintPreviewDialog1.ClientSize = New
        System.Drawing.Size(400, 300)
        Me.PrintPreviewDialog1.Enabled = True
        Me.PrintPreviewDialog1.Icon = Nothing
        Me.PrintPreviewDialog1.Location = New
        System.Drawing.Point(88, 88)
```

```
            Me.PrintPreviewDialog1.MaximumSize = New
              System.Drawing.Size(0, 0)
            Me.PrintPreviewDialog1.Name =
              "PrintPreviewDialog1"
            Me.PrintPreviewDialog1.Opacity = 1
            Me.PrintPreviewDialog1.TransparencyKey =
              System.Drawing.Color.Empty
            Me.PrintPreviewDialog1.Visible = False
            '
            'PrintDocument1
            '
            '
            'Button1
            '
            Me.Button1.Font = New System.Drawing.Font("Times
              New Roman", 11!,
              System.Drawing.FontStyle.Regular,
              System.Drawing.GraphicsUnit.Point, CType(0,
              Byte))
            Me.Button1.Location = New
              System.Drawing.Point(584, 416)
            Me.Button1.Name = "Button1"
            Me.Button1.Size = New System.Drawing.Size(136,
              32)
            Me.Button1.TabIndex = 1
            Me.Button1.Text = "Preview && Print "
            '
            'PrintTextForm
            '
            Me.AutoScaleBaseSize = New System.Drawing.Size(5,
              13)
            Me.ClientSize = New System.Drawing.Size(728, 453)
            Me.Controls.AddRange(New
              System.Windows.Forms.Control() {Me.Button1,
              Me.TextBox1})
            Me.Name = "PrintTextForm"
            Me.Text = "Printing Text Demo"
            Me.ResumeLayout(False)

        End Sub

#End Region

    Private Sub PrintDocument1_PrintPage(ByVal sender As
        Object, ByVal e As
        System.Drawing.Printing.PrintPageEventArgs)
        Handles PrintDocument1.PrintPage
        Static currentChar As Integer
        Dim txtFont As New Font("Arial", 10)
        Dim txtH As Integer =
        PrintDocument1.DefaultPageSettings.PaperSize.Heig
        ht - _
```

```
PrintDocument1.DefaultPageSettings.Margins.Top -
        PrintDocument1.DefaultPageSettings.Margins.Bottom
    Dim LMargin As Integer =
        PrintDocument1.DefaultPageSettings.Margins.Left
    Dim TMargin As Integer =
        PrintDocument1.DefaultPageSettings.Margins.Top
    Dim txtW As Integer =
        PrintDocument1.DefaultPageSettings.PaperSize.Widt
        h - _

        PrintDocument1.DefaultPageSettings.Margins.Left -
        PrintDocument1.DefaultPageSettings.Margins.Right
    Dim linesperpage As Integer = txtH /
        txtFont.Height
    Dim R As New RectangleF(LMargin, TMargin, txtW,
        txtH)
    Static line As String
    Dim word As String
    Dim lines, chars As Integer
    Dim fmt As New
        StringFormat(StringFormatFlags.LineLimit)
    e.Graphics.MeasureString(Mid(textToPrint,
        currentChar + 1), txtFont, New SizeF(txtW, txtH),
        fmt, chars, lines)
    e.Graphics.DrawString(Mid(textToPrint,
        currentChar + 1), txtFont, Brushes.Black, R, fmt)
    currentChar = currentChar + chars
    If currentChar < textToPrint.Length Then
        e.HasMorePages = True
    Else
        e.HasMorePages = False
        currentChar = 0
    End If

End Sub

Function GetNextWord(Optional ByVal reset As Boolean
        = False) As String
    Static currPos As Integer
    Dim word As String

    If reset Then currPos = 0
    If currPos >= TextBox1.Text.Length Then Return ""
    While Not
        System.Char.IsLetterOrDigit(TextBox1.Text.Chars(c
        urrPos))
        word = word & TextBox1.Text.Chars(currPos)
        currPos = currPos + 1
        If currPos >= TextBox1.Text.Length Then
    Return word
    End While
    While Not
        (System.Char.IsWhiteSpace(TextBox1.Text.Chars(cur
```

```
rPos)))
                word = word & TextBox1.Text.Chars(currPos)
                currPos = currPos + 1
                If currPos >= TextBox1.Text.Length Then
        Return word
        End While
        Return word
    End Function


    Dim textToPrint As String

    Private Sub Button1_Click(ByVal sender As
        System.Object, ByVal e As System.EventArgs)
        Handles Button1.Click
        textToPrint = TextBox1.Text

        PageSetupDialog1.PageSettings =
        PrintDocument1.DefaultPageSettings
        If PageSetupDialog1.ShowDialog() =
        DialogResult.OK Then
            PrintDocument1.DefaultPageSettings =
        PageSetupDialog1.PageSettings
        End If
        Try
            PrintPreviewDialog1.Document = PrintDocument1
            PrintPreviewDialog1.ShowDialog()
        Catch exc As Exception
            MsgBox("Print operation failed " & vbCrLf &
        exc.Message)
        End Try
    End Sub

End Class
```

5. **Press F5 to run this utility.**

6. **Copy a large amount of text into the TextBox so that you can see that the right and bottom margins are being correctly calculated.**

7. **Then click the Preview and Print button.**

   The Page Setup dialog box appears.

8. **Click OK in the Page Setup dialog box.**

9. **Click the printer icon at the top left of the Print Preview dialog box to begin the printing.**

This codes has some very long lines, and each must be preserved as a *single long line* in the code window. When you press F5 to test this, if you see all kinds of error messages in the Task List (such as Expected an expression), you have some broken lines. It's hard to correct these in the code window and get everything right. Instead, try going back and copying the source code from the Web site (at http://www.dummies.com/extras/ VBNetDataProg/).

This time, run Windows Notepad and use Notepad's Edit⇨Word Wrap feature to *turn off* word wrap. Paste the source code in Notepad. Then select all the source code in Notepad and copy it. Finally, paste this code into the empty VB .NET code window.

As you can see, contacting peripherals using VB .NET is less simple and less direct than in previous versions of VB. There's more code to write, and it's the kind of code in which you have to use properties and methods in ways that are sometimes not intuitive. Nonetheless, you can just use a monkey-see, monkey-do approach to the filestream (for loading and saving disk files) and the PrintDocument object (for printing). It's not *that* complex. Just copy the code you see in this book and it will work.

When you print in VB .NET, you use the PrintDocument control to hold the actual text or graphics that will be printed. You can read and in many cases change the following properties in `PrintDocument1.Printersettings`: CanDuplex, Collate, Copies, DefaultPageSettings, Duplex, FromPage, IsDefaultPrinter, IsPlotter, IsValid, LandscapeAngle, MaximumCopies, MaximumPage, MinimumPage, PaperSizes, PaperSources, PrinterName, PrinterResolutions, PrintRange, PrintToFile, SupportsColor, and ToPage. The PrintDocument PageSettings collection has these properties: Bounds, Color, Landscape, Margins, PaperSize, PaperSource, PrinterResolution, and PrinterSettings.

Using the PrintPreview Control

The preceding example included an illustration of how to use the PrintPreview control, but it's worthwhile to also isolate a simple example of its use. You can display to users how their output will appear when printed (so that they don't waste paper printing pages that are not yet formatted to their liking). They can then click a Print button in the PrintPreviewDialog to initiate printing. Use the following code to show the user a sample of their output:

```
PrintPreviewDialog1.Document = PrintDocument1
PrintPreviewDialog1.ShowDialog()
```

If you use PrintPreviewDialog, however, make sure that you do *not* include this line elsewhere in your program:

```
PrintDocument1.Print()
```

The reason you avoid this line is that the PrintPreview dialog box shows the user a Print button and a Close button. If the user clicks the Print button, document printing is initiated from there. Otherwise, if the user clicks the Close button without printing, it means the user doesn't want to print. So you would permit the user to modify the PrintDialog and PageSetupDialog controls again and then see the PrintPreview again.

Attending Technical Conferences

Microsoft's Professional Developers Conference (PDC) and TechEd are excellent conferences if you want to learn how to build the latest applications using the latest tools and technologies. Find out about these annual events at microsoft.com/events.

Check out www.windx.com for information on VBITS, the Visual Basic Insiders' Technical Summit. The conference sponsors describe it as "the leading international conference for professional Windows programmers. You'll join the core of the Visual Basic development community as we discover new and better ways to use VB and related technologies."

No More Null or IsNull

The traditional VB Variant data type could hold some special kinds of values: Null (not known), Empty (no value was ever assigned to this variable), and Missing (this variable was not sent, for example, as part of a procedure's parameters).

Null was sometimes used to identify fields in databases that are not available or unknown. The Empty command could be used to represent something that doesn't exist — as opposed to simply not being currently available.

Some programmers used the IsMissing command to see whether an optional parameter had been passed to a procedure:

```
Sub SomeSub(Optional SomeParam As Variant)
        If IsMissing(SomeParam) Then
```

The VB .NET object data type does not use Missing, Empty, or Null. You can use an IsDBNull function with databases instead of the now-missing IsNull command. Similarly, an IsReference command replaces the IsObject command.

You can still use optional parameters with procedures, but you must declare them As Type and supply a default value for them. You can't write code in a procedure that will tell you whether or not a particular parameter has been passed.

If you need to test whether an optional parameter has been passed, you can "overload" a procedure. *Overloading* is a technique in which a function (or a method or a property) can be made to behave differently based on what is passed to it. My advice is that you forget about overloading until you feel confident about your programming skills, and even then you might want to avoid it. For an in-depth discussion of the pros and cons of overloading, see the entry titled "Overloaded Functions, Properties, and Methods" in the appendix at this book's Web site, which is at http://www.dummies.com/extras/VBNetDataProg/.

Index

Notes

Notes

Notes

Notes

Notes